MAY   1979

EUROPE'S WONDERFUL LITTLE HOTELS AND INNS

EUROPE'S WONDERFUL LITTLE HOTELS AND INNS

edited by

HILARY RUBINSTEIN

Thomas Congdon Books
E. P. Dutton   New York

For information contact: E. P. Dutton, 2 Park Avenue,
New York, N.Y. 10016

Library of Congress Catalog Card Number: 78-50960

ISBN: 0-525-10060-1

10 9 8 7 6 5 4 3 2

Contents

Acknowledgments

Many scores of people, through their help and encouragement, have made this enterprise possible. To start chronologically, I should like to thank first my British publisher, Tom Maschler of Jonathan Cape Ltd., who, when I tried out on him the notion of such a book, reacted to it with the instant high-octane enthusiasm which makes him the exceptional publisher that he is. (One day somebody will compile a guide to good publishers, and he will have a warm write-up.) The second person I approached was Edward Mace, the Travel Editor of the London *Observer*, and he, too, kindled to the idea and gave me a truly invaluable launch-pad by allowing me his 'Time Off' column to announce the project and appeal for contributions. That single article, which appeared on October 17, 1976, produced within a fortnight well over 100 letters, and many more continued to dribble in over the next few months.

All the other newspaper travel editors whom I approached were warmly responsive and offered assistance of the most welcome kind—namely, a piece about the guide in their columns. My most grateful thanks to the following: Adrienne Keith-Cohen of the *Guardian*, Elizabeth De Stroumillo of the *Daily Telegraph*, Nigel Buxton of the *Sunday Telegraph*, John Higgins of *The Times*, Jean Robertson of the *Sunday Times* and Tom Pocock of the *Evening Standard*. I would also thank Anthony Howard of the *New Statesman*, the editors of *Harper & Queen* and of *Vogue* and Claire Rayner of LBC for their support.

Throughout the nine-month gestation period of the work, from the October article to June 1977, when the typescript was delivered to the publishers, I have been blessed in having Diana Petry, for many years the *Observer*'s Travel Correspondent, as my assistant. It sounds a familiar line, but I could not have produced this work without her. The book owes an incalculable debt to her editorial skills, her prodigious energy and her unwavering confidence that all the multifarious problems of a new kind of guide could be overcome. Through Diana's friends in the Guild of Travel Writers came practical support in the way of nominations from many professional hotel-watchers, and an especial acknowledgment must be given to Roger Smithells, a doyen among British hotel writers, who has contributed almost a score of blue-chip entries. I would also mention here the contribution of Susan Grossman, formerly of *Holiday Which*, who not only gave us valuable entries, but also technical expertise.

A number of national tourist offices, also Michelin, have generously helped in the checking of detailed information.

The final vote of thanks must be given to all those hundreds of people who responded to the appeal for an unknown venture and sent in contributions. Most of them had no more than a brief printed postcard by way of acknowledgment. The names of many of these supporters are printed in italics after their entries, but there were many more who nominated hotels which, for one reason or another, we decided against including. My grateful thanks to them all.

Introduction

The perfect hotel may be an idyllic fantasy, but many of us go on looking for it year in and year out. This guide is to help those engaged on the
quest. The hotels we have listed are amazingly diverse, and no one will
warm to them all. But they have a single element in common: each has
endeared itself so strongly to at least one of its guests that he or she has
taken the trouble to write—often at considerable length—to share that
satisfaction with others. Only an exceptional hotel can evoke such a
tangible expression of appreciation.

How do people find their good hotels? Brochures are an aid, but are
often deceptive. It's not the fault of the copywriters that most of their
products sound alike: they mostly *are* alike. Travel agents can sometimes be helpful if they specialise in particular localities, but they often
only know at recent first-hand a fraction of the hotels on their books.
Michelin is an invaluable touring companion, especially to the gourmet,
but, for the majority, the agreeableness or otherwise of the lodging is
every bit as important as the excellence of the board; and all those conventional signs, useful though they are, can tell us almost nothing about
the feel of a place. By far the most reliable way to choose a hotel is by
word-of-mouth recommendation. This guide, if it achieves its purpose,
is — word-of-mouth made print.

Of course, the idea of inviting members of the public to contribute
their experiences for the common weal is not a new one. We all owe an
immeasurable debt of gratitude to Raymond Postgate, whose *Good
Food Guide* has been an institution now for over a quarter of a century,
and has helped to bring about a beneficent revolution in the standards
of British catering. If this hotel guide can do a fraction as much for
the welfare of the discriminating traveller, it will have amply justified its
existence. But the present enterprise is, in one critical respect, more
hazardous: we all want such different things from our hotels.

To illustrate the point, here are impressions of two very different
Irish hotels. The first is Currarevagh House at Oughterard in County
Galway, a mid-Victorian country house which has been run by suc-
cessive generations of Hodgsons:

> There are no keys to the bedrooms—not that one would be likely
> to take one's diamonds to this remote spot. The decor hasn't changed
> much since 1900: the beds are marvellously capacious, with heavy
> linen sheets; splendid bathroom fittings, lots of Edwardian furniture.

There are huge baskets of turf and large open fires in the two reception rooms—and the public rooms and hall are so spacious that it is easy enough to be on one's own. The food is good plain home cooking, such as one would get if one were lucky as a weekend guest in the country. Excellent home-made brown bread for breakfast, for instance, and first-rate coffee, kept hot over individual spirit lamps. Trout from the lough for dinner, simply cooked with melted butter.

In contrast here is how another correspondent described her discovery of a dream hotel: 'Spent two weeks in Eire in the summer of 1976. Stayed at half-a-dozen hotels in the South—all vile. Dirty, school-dinner food. Don't want even to think about them,' she wrote, before telling of the happy end of her Irish travels in the Hotel Europe, a 175-roomed purpose-built, German-run hotel overlooking Lough Leane in Killarney: 'After what we had been to over the past few days, we couldn't believe our eyes. Beautiful furniture in the public rooms. Expensive Persian carpets. Marble floors.' The Europe is a de luxe establishment with most of the trimmings—heated indoor pool, sauna, health centre, nightclub, hairdressing, as well as conference and banqueting facilities—and, in marked contrast to what had gone before —*clean*: 'Spotless eating areas and spotless rooms. Always someone cleaning bedrooms or corridors, but never the noisy sound of Hoovers or anything to disturb one.'

It sounds like the immaculate conception translated into hotel terms. One person's idea of bliss? Certainly not everyone's. And, as the previous example shows, the true Irish experience, from which visitors to the Hotel Europe are effectively insulated, need not be vile.

No computer could possibly catalogue the multiplicity of tastes and prejudices. Some crave swank from their favourite hotels, others prefer informal service. Fleshpots will seek *haute cuisine*; ascetics, simple fare. There are those who demand night spots, and others who regard discos, cabarets and casinos as so many forms of night pollution. We all enjoy congenial company, but many will sympathise with the misanthropist who wrote: 'The worst thing about hotels is the people who insist on staying there at the same time as yourself. You run such appalling risks.'

But taste is by no means the only differentiating factor. Income is equally crucial. Age, too, comes into it: we make special demands on a hotel if we are travelling with children; we care more about our creature comforts as we grow older. How on earth can a guide hope to reconcile such a plethora of conflicting requirements?

The short answer is that it can't. And this highlights a vital difference between this guide and *The Good Food Guide*. There is general agreement about what constitutes *haute cuisine*. Not all of us can recognise a classic *crêpe suzette* when we are served one, but we acknowledge the existence of trained palates capable of spotting weakness in ingredients or preparation. There are no equivalent ways of distinguishing good hotels from second-rate ones. They can, of course, be graded according to objective criteria: number of rooms equipped with television sets, telephones and private bathrooms; the presence of a night porter; availability of meals at all hours and similar minutiae. These are the data that determine the number of stars awarded by the AA and RAC, or the number of gables in Michelin's classification. But they are peripheral to what ultimately makes us feel that one hotel is delightful and another a morgue.

Does this central anomaly invalidate the whole notion of a guide to good hotels and inns? I do not think so, and the huge number of letters we have received in response to the press appeal for nominations upholds me in that conviction. Some of the letters of commendation were perfunctory, but the best succeeded in conveying clearly the specific quality in a hotel which, for that individual, had made it something special. These letters were, in a sense, self-validating. The crucial test of the guide will be whether its entries enable the reader to say instantly, on reading a description, 'that's my sort of place', or 'that may be somebody's idea of a good hotel, but it certainly isn't mine'.

Moreover, though there is no ultimate criterion for a good hotel, there is a striking consensus among our correspondents about the things that matter. If we were to put all the entries we have received through a computer, the results would show the frequency with which certain words and phrases recur—words like relaxed, unstuffy, personal; phrases like country house atmosphere, made to feel welcome, treated as an individual. The commendations which appealed to us most had another feature in common: almost all mentioned by name the proprietor or the couple running a hotel who had significantly contributed to the success of a visit. The *patron* is like a director of music and orchestral conductor all in one: he chooses the music, rehearses the players, and sets the tempo. A good hotel reflects the personality of its owner as surely as a good magazine or newspaper is a self-portrait of its editor. Bad hotels can be personally bad or impersonally bad. Good hotels can never be faceless.

Another preference was for small hotels: there were few nominations for hotels with more than fifty bedrooms, and many were for houses—often inns—with a dozen rooms or less. Our first inclination was to preclude any place with fewer than ten rooms, but we soon realised that we should then be leaving out some of the most distinctive and colourful entries in the book. So we stopped making any rules—at either end of the scale. Nevertheless, we have exercised our editorial privilege in selection. We have aimed to provide for a wide spectrum of ages, incomes, needs and tastes, but have been much more cautious in accepting nominations for the larger, grander kind of establishment as we believe that catering for substantial numbers is generally inimical to individuality.

The Hotel Europe, referred to on p. x, despite the pleasure and relief which it plainly gave our correspondent, does not appear among the entries in the Irish section. This is partly because we felt, perhaps unfairly, that Killarney is the kind of tourist trap which those in search of a good hotel would instinctively avoid. But there was a stronger, though equally subjective reason: the Europe and its like provide a homogenised aseptic experience far removed from the notion of a good hotel we want this guide to represent. The view from the balconies may be uniquely Lough Leane, but the inside could be a posh hotel in London, Tokyo, Frankfurt or Miami.

We accept that big modern hotels, providing dependably excellent service with maximum privacy, meet a genuine demand. Business people mostly want hotels of this sort, which explains the success of Hiltons, Holiday Inns, Berni and similar chains. If you book at one of these hotels, you know what's in store for you: no nasty surprises after a hard day's bargaining. And such hotels have other advantages: conference facilities, for instance, and bargain packages. They are the natural partners of the charter jet and block bookings. The package-deal operators offer value for money, often staggering value in the off-season.

The hotels that have been built to cope with the new age of travel feed plenty of human needs, but they are not what many of us want in a holiday hotel. Since this is essentially a guide to the out-of-the-ordinary hotel, whether for a night-stop or a protracted visit, we have tended (though inconsistently) to keep them out of this book.

The pitfalls of the large establishment catering for group bookings were underlined for us by a letter from someone who had previously recommended a famous hotel in Umbria:

> We got there early in the evening, a marvellous immense moon was lighting the ancient abbey, we stood there bewitched by this sublime atmosphere, when suddenly we heard a fantastic roar as if a hundred Chieftain tanks were approaching. The roar was produced by twenty enormous coaches carrying 900 tourists of the most appalling sort stopping on their way back from a Rome-Florence-Rome day trip. Dinner was indescribable and made utterly unpalatable by the shortage of toilets (four toilets could not cope with 900 people shut in coaches for the last four hours) which compelled the brave new world-men to use every corner, plant or tree available (believe me, whatever happens I shall not use that swimming pool!). When the coaches left after a long and distasteful argument about hotel properties stolen (how can you search 900 tired, boozy, quarrelsome tourists?), everybody else left. The moon—wonderful earlier on—now looked livid above us, the silence lugubrious, the ruins no longer sublime—quite sinister—hiding beheaded ghosts, and triumphant and all-pervading, the incredible stench left by the untoileted tourists.

Coach parties need not be as gruesome as the plague of incontinent locusts that descended on the Umbrian plain, but all large groups create a turbulence not just in the restaurant, or when checking out *en masse* in the foyer. Their vibrations are felt throughout the public rooms. The single individual or couple cannot avoid feeling crushed; there seems to be less air about for the rest when a big party is on the move through a hotel.

Although we have done our best, through questionnaires we have sent out to hotels, and by other means, to weed out those which rely substantially on trade of this kind, there remain a number of hotels in this book which from time to time entertain large groups. One example is a hotel in the extreme north of Scotland that takes periodic bookings from parties of bird-watchers; another is a Mediterranean hotel that will occasionally provide lunch for a visiting cruise. There are relatively few grand hotels that can resolutely turn away block bookings for conferences, particularly in the off-season. Like much else, it's a matter of degree.

There is one category of hotel where size has seemed to us less important: the city hotel. People make different demands when they stay in a city. Large numbers matter less. If you are out all day sightseeing, plumbing and insulation may have a higher priority than character. If the city has plenty of fine restaurants, you don't have to worry whether your own hotel services good food or not. For all these reasons we have included, among city hotels, some which are large, spanking modern, essentially convenience establishments.

We are naturally eager that readers, including hoteliers, who welcome this kind of guide, will be outspoken in their views as to the kind of information they would like to see included in future editions, and will also let us know of any blatant omissions in specific cases. Of course we are equally keen to hear—indeed, it is absolutely vital that we do hear— from readers both about their experiences, confirmatory or contradictory, when staying at hotels named in the guide, and when staying at some other hotel they would like to see mentioned in the next edition. You will find nomination forms at the back of the book. But please don't expect to be paid for your contribution(s). There are no payments in this guide: neither to contributors nor from hotels listed.

Many of us hesitate to divulge our favourite places for fear that popularity will spoil them, or at least put up their prices. We respect the scruples, but they should be resisted. If a single hotel is written up in a newspaper, it will certainly attract undue attention; but the greater the number of good hotels that are recommended, the more the demand can be spread. Moreover, while the mass-market hotel, living off its block-bookings, can prosper year after year, irrespective of praise or complaint, the hotel with character needs all the encouragement it can get: it thrives on recommendation, it dies from neglect.

There is a further reason why those who care about excellence in a hotel should respond. When *The Good Food Guide* started in 1951, it had only about 200 entries; today it has 1,000. This increase has come about not through a fall in standards—quite the contrary—but at least in part through a transformation in the quality of restaurant cooking in response to the demand for better food. And the improvement has not, of course, been confined to restaurants listed in the Guide, but has rubbed off on innumerable other establishments that are aspiring to make the grade. This hotel guide, once established, could have a similarly beneficial effect on the whole hotel industry. If people are seen to care about a particular kind of hotel, and it prospers from a mention in the guide, you may be sure that other hotels will seek to emulate its example.

This guide, the first of its kind, is necessarily an imperfect thing. Some European countries get no mention at all or are grossly underrepresented. Many hotels all over Europe deserve to be included in the guide, but do not appear in these pages. I make no apologies for omissions. We made a rule—no representation without nomination— and have stuck by it, except that we have made a few editorial suggestions in the case of London. Naturally our hope is that in future editions the Continental section of the book will become stronger, and more and more of the special hotels—the ones to write home about—will be recommended by readers and qualify for inclusion.

We worry more about errors in the text. We have done our utmost to check factual details, but inevitably some descriptions will be misleading. It is all very well to print a disclaimer—the management takes no responsibility for any false pretences—but of course we shall feel bruised if and when we hear of an unpleasant experience that results from an entry in this guide being woefully inaccurate. Nevertheless, we shall mind more if we are not told, and are not therefore given the chance to put matters right. Subsequent editions should, of course, steadily diminish the degree of unreliability—too many of the present listings represent one person's views only. But there will always be entries which readers will challenge. However, the enterprise will succeed if enough readers find that this sort of discursive guide is to their taste and useful.

Let me end on a personal note. If I had to offer a single reason why I have embarked on this arduous and risky undertaking, it is in the hope that the guide can help the dedicated individual hotelier to survive and flourish against the formidable opposition of the big battalions with all the resources and economies of scale which they are able to deploy. As will already be clear from the foregoing, I loathe the safe, boring, homogenised hotel that insulates its guests from their environment. I treasure the personal and idiosyncratic establishment that is waging a fight against entropy. I am hopeful that, from the response so far, and from some of the eloquent entries in this book, many others share these tastes and prejudices.

January 1978   HILARY RUBINSTEIN

How to read the entries

As with any initial effort, we have been feeling our way over many different aspects of this guide, not least the essential information to be given. We have not lacked advice! We have been urged to include a great many routine details as well as a few more esoteric requests: a well-known concert pianist wanted our guide to tell her whether a piano could be hired and whether she would be allowed to play it in her room.

Rightly or wrongly, we have erred on the side of giving too little information rather than too much. This decision is in part a reaction to the dehumanising effect of a great block of hieroglyphics, usually conveying fairly obvious information. They are justified in Michelin which aims, by using a minimum of words, to be multi-lingual, but seem to us to be out of place in a wordy, single-language guide such as this one. We have aimed to provide the more crucial facts about number of rooms, with or without baths, and terms, but have omitted reference, *inter alia*, to access for the disabled, credit cards, central heating, parking facilities—and much else besides. If there is clearly a demand for more detailed information, we shall hope to remedy some of these omissions next time. For the moment, if you want specific assurances on such matters, you will need to write direct to the hotel.

After some deliberation, we have resisted the impulse to employ any system of grading. Stars and their like have their uses, but they seem more appropriate to the kind of guide which has a list of objective criteria to distinguish one sort of hotel from another. Good hotels, in our sense, reveal their good features in such a multiciplity of different ways that any formal classification, on a scale of one to five or whatever, would be hopelessly arbitrary and misleading. By the same token, we have eschewed any suggestion that we should award accolades for special merit.

We have been much exercised as to how to deal with prices. Our task would have been a lot easier a decade ago, before inflation and when exchange rates were reasonably stable. As it is, the terms given need to be treated with circumspection. For a start, they are 1977 prices. At the time this book is going to press, it would be rash even for the International Monetary Fund to speculate how far prices will have risen in all these different countries by the spring of 1978. Then hotels everywhere have a bewildering assortment of tariffs, sometimes including and sometimes excluding local taxes and service. (How welcome it would be if British hoteliers could regularly quote prices 'service and tax inclusive' as do most of their Continental counterparts.) Some hotels will refuse to serve just bed and breakfast, or will do so only at certain times of the year. It would be fruitless to attempt to summarise all the possible permutations, and in our view a mistake to go for absolute consistency in the information provided. In some cases, weekly rates seemed more worth mentioning; in other cases, individual meal prices or special bargains for minibreaks. Almost always, whatever else we have included or left out, we have quoted for bed, or bed and breakfast. Where hotels have different rates for different seasons, the figures quoted are for high season rates. If a hotel has baths *en suite*, then the figure given is for the room with bath. If a single room costs more than half the double, we have given the price per person for sharing a double room. Terms are inclusive of service and taxes, unless otherwise stated.

We have also thought it sensible to quote the tariffs of foreign hotels in the local currency, inconvenient though it may be if you don't happen to know how the peseta is doing *vis-à-vis* the dollar this month; but dollar equivalents of a currency at the date of going to press are given in a section at the back of the book, and exchange rates are quoted daily in the papers. In general they should be useful in indicating the comparative prices of different hotels, and a very rough guide only as to the size of the bill to be expected at the end of your stay.

The descriptions themselves fall into two categories. First, there are those which, even if the hotel has more than one nominator, appear as an extended quote from a single contributor. The spontaneous tone of voice of an enthusiast will often help the reader to judge whether a hotel is his or her sort of place or not. When we have not had a single entry that can stand on its own, we have synthesized contributions, quoting when appropriate. In all cases we have done our utmost to confirm from independent sources that a hotel earns its mention. Names of nominators appear at the end of entries. Where the entry has an extended quote and there are several nominators, the quoted matter has been contributed by the first name listed.

If the hotel is in a city or in familiar terrain, we have said little about the setting. The more out-of-the-way the locale, the more space we have devoted to describe its attractions as well as those of the hotel itself. If a hotel is celebrated for its cuisine, we have dwelt on that subject. The length of the entries vary enormously, but this should not be taken as an indication of comparative merit as much as of the relative attractiveness of an individual contribution. Details of facilities also vary, depending on what information was available to us. Not all our questionnaires were returned or fully answered, especially in the case of hotels abroad.

Readers may choose to use the guide in various ways. I would like to think that some of the entries in the present guide, and even more in future editions, will be sufficiently entertaining in themselves to make good reading for the armchair traveller. But of course I hope it will be useful as well as fun: that it will help people who are planning a holiday to find the more dependably rewarding hotels, and perhaps to direct them to a particular region which they might not otherwise have thought of visiting.

Part One
Great Britain and Ireland

ENGLAND
WALES
SCOTLAND
CHANNEL ISLANDS
IRELAND

The Plough Hotel, Clanfield, Oxfordshire

England

ABBERLEY, Nr Worcester, Worcestershire

The Elms Hotel *Telephone:* Great Witley (029 921) 666

This exceptionally beautiful and grand Queen Anne house (though with two modern wings) is set well back from the road in a small village not far from the Abberley Hills. *The Elms* has been on any hotel connoisseur's short list of the best of England's country house hotels for more than twenty years. 'The ground floor rooms have been left exactly as they were, and therefore the proportions are beautiful. They are furnished with antique though comfortable furniture of the sort found in any well-kept country house of that period, the decorations are superb and the colour schemes just right; one feels at peace with the world, that always comes with good proportions and appropriate decorations. The food is excellent, varied, well served, and most of it fresh grown and local. The wine list is first-rate. The bedrooms are comfortable and warm. One's early morning tea is still brought up by a maid, and at the time it is asked for. The staff are friendly, kind and efficient. On your second visit you are remembered, and your likes, dislikes and infirmities respected. You are greeted by the owner and staff as an old friend. Another good point: there was no TV downstairs. I have never felt so at home and so at peace in any hotel I have stayed in anywhere else, at home or abroad.' (*Mrs P. Leeming*)

Open: all year.
Rooms: 15 double, 4 single, all with bath; colour TV, radio and telephone.
Drawing room, gallery room, lounge hall, library, bar. Grounds consist-

ing of 12 acres, with 7 acres of formal garden; croquet lawn, putting green, tennis court; golf, fishing and riding near by.

Terms: B & B: £10.20; lunch: £3.20; dinner: from £5.00.
        Reduced rates for 2 or more days in winter, 3 or more in summer.

AMBLESIDE, Cumbria

Rothay Manor Hotel   *Telephone:* Ambleside (096 63) 3605

There are hotels which offer a particularly friendly ambience, others which are in an exhilarating location, and others again which concentrate on *haute cuisine*. Hotels which combine all three virtues are comparatively rare, but the Rothay Manor belongs to this class. The Nixons, who run this handsome Georgian house close to the head of Lake Windermere and within a few minutes' walk of Ambleside, have managed to preserve the atmosphere of a private house. 'The cooking is imaginative (though a bit on the rich side if you are staying a long time) and the service excellent. Naturally it makes a good centre for exploring the Lake District; but because of the friendly relaxed atmosphere, it is also a good place for just doing nothing.' (*Dr P. J. Glenny*)

Open: March–December.
Rooms: 10 double, 2 single—9 with bath or shower; all with electric
        blankets and telephone.
Two lounges (1 with bar), small library. Half-acre garden with croquet lawn; steamer services, sailing and water-skiing on Lake Windermere ($\frac{1}{4}$ mile); riding and golf near by.
Terms (exclusive of service): bed, early morning tea and newspapers,
        Cumberland breakfast and afternoon tea, £11.00 (minimum
        stay of 2 nights at weekend).
        Restaurant much used by non-residents. Dinner (5 courses
        and coffee): £6.25; informal bar lunches.
        Mini-breaks (2 or 3 days) in March, November and December;
        special Gourmet weekends in November and December.

ARNCLIFFE, Nr Skipton, North Yorkshire

Amerdale House Hotel   *Telephone:* Arncliffe (075 677) 250

A newly opened hotel in a spectacularly beautiful part of the North Yorkshire Dales. The house itself is a large grey-stone building in its own grounds, and the village is small and attractive, with fine views in all directions. You will certainly need a car as Arncliffe is an isolated spot; but this is superb walking country, and there's good fishing in the Skirfare which runs by the village. The hotel itself has been beautifully furnished. The bedrooms are modern, with duvets, and there are radios in all rooms. Run in country-house style, the gong goes at 8p.m. for a four-course dinner—no choice of menu, but excellent home cooking. Breakfast, also, is at a set time. There is no television. 'Although I had my eight-year-old daughter with me, I would not recommend this as a hotel for children, as the house is so beautiful that even a well-behaved child can be a worry.' (*J. Greengrass*)

Open: March–October, and December.
Rooms: 8 double, 2 single, 1 family room—none with bath; all have radio.
Lounge; garden; fishing near by, good walking all around.
Terms (excluding service): B & B: £7.50.

ASTON CLINTON, Buckinghamshire

The Bell Inn   *Telephone:* Aylesbury (0296) 630252

'The Bell has long been famous for its good food. But although the dining room may be familiar, with its leather chairs, mahogany tables, glass, silver, and log fires, the hotel bedrooms are less well-known. They lie across a narrow lane around the cobbled courtyard of an old brew-house which is planted with geraniums and hollyhocks. Outside steps lead to the first-floor bedrooms. Umbrellas are provided for damp days. Our suite consisted of a comfortable bedroom, a warm and well-appointed bathroom, and a sitting space overlooking a cottage lawn at the back. The small fridge contained spirits and a half-bottle of excellent champagne. In the morning breakfast was brought punctually at an early hour with the newspapers. The illusion of having crossed the Channel during the night was enhanced by the good coffee, the croissants, and the fact that the waiter not only wore a short white coat, but spoke with a French accent.' (*Adrian House*)

Open: all year.
Rooms: 20 double and single, some with sitting room, all with bath, radio, TV, telephone, mini-bar. 'Flat 16' is a luxury suite.
Drawing room, bar, writing room (can be used for private lunch or dinner parties, or small business meetings); dancing in the Pavilion (a separate building) on Saturdays, with buffet supper if required. Two-acre garden.
Terms (excluding VAT):   B & B: £10.50–£12.00; most meals *à la carte*; Saturday buffet supper & dancing: £4.50; special Saturday dinner (restaurant): £8.50.

BARBON, Nr Kirkby Lonsdale, Cumbria

Barbon Inn   *Telephone:* Barbon (046 836) 233

'A 17th-century inn nestling in a delightful village at the foot of Barbon Fell in the Lune valley, just off the Kirkby Lonsdale to Sedbergh road.

It is undoubtedly one of the most welcoming hotels I know, perhaps at its best on a dry, frosty day, when the fells are tipped with snow and one can enjoy an excellent afternoon tea (a rarity these days) by a roaring fire in the comfort of deep, chintz-covered armchairs, surrounded by gleaming copper and delightful flower arrangements. Whatever the season, however, the meals are excellent and, more important, consistently so. The bar is friendly, the cellar well-stocked, and the food expertly—nay, lovingly—prepared and cheerfully served. We have been often over a long period of time, and have never been disappointed.' (*Joyce Hargreaves*)

Open: all year.
Rooms: 7 double, 1 single.
Over ½-acre of garden.
Terms: B & B: £6.60; half board (weekly): £68.60; full board (weekly): £74.20. Meals: from £3.00.

BASLOW, Nr Bakewell, Derbyshire

Cavendish Hotel   *Telephone:* Baslow (024 688) 2311

'Derbyshire, one of the finest counties in Britain, has been notoriously short in hotels. It has now got a beauty in what used to be the old Peacock Inn, renamed the *Cavendish*, on the Chatsworth Estate and on the foothills of the Peak District. It is a very old house, modernised and enlarged with impressive skill. I shouldn't think it has ever been so attractive. Eric Marsh, the young manager, combines conventional training with great enthusiasm. Enthusiasm being, fortunately, every bit as catching as surliness, his staff is also excellent. What the dining-room waitresses lack in finicky finesse they make up in cheerfulness which, in my opinion, is the right way round. What has disappeared, along with the rising damp, is the awful old snobbishness. It's only to be expected that the interior is a delight: the bedrooms have a head-start in overlooking Chatsworth Park. You can't see the great house, which lies behind a mole, but its presence is felt. Some of the furniture came from Chatsworth because of the Duchess of Devonshire's involvement in setting up the hotel. I dare say that the easy-going country house atmosphere, hard to achieve and indefinable when you have, has something to do with her.' (*Edward Mace; also Mary Links*)

Open: all year.
Rooms: 13 double—all with bath, telephone, colour TV, mini-bar (chargeable) and tea-making facilities (complimentary), and all overlooking Chatsworth.
Sitting room, cocktail bar, public bar; 3 acres of gardens; fishing on the Derwent and Wye.
Dogs at the management's discretion.
Terms (exclusive of VAT): B & B: £8.20; meals: from £3.50.
        Special weekend rates 8 October–28 March.

BATH, Avon

Francis Hotel *Telephone:* Bath (0225) 24257
Queen Square *Telex:* 449162

The hotel graces most of the south side of the elegant Queen Square, between Royal Crescent and the Abbey, combining six 18th-century residences built by John Wood the Elder. Rebuilt after war damage in the original style and furnished in the period, it is a distinguished and highly popular hotel on one of Bath's most beautiful squares. 'Above average, with excellent service, cuisine and room attendance.' (*W. R. Peel*)

Open: all year.
Rooms: 50 double, 15 single, some suites—all have private bath, telephone, radio and TV; tea and coffee making facilities; baby-listening services.
Lift, lounge, two bars; some double-glazing.
Dogs admitted but not in public rooms.
Terms: B & B: £10.30.
        Reduced rates for winter weekends.

The Priory Hotel   *Telephone:* Bath (0225) 21887/26015/21331
Weston Road

'The hotel matches the grace of the city, being converted from a large Gothic-style Georgian house built of mellow Bath stone. Only a mile from the centre, it still has the air of a country house furnished with antiques and decorated in rich, glowing colours. The hotel is run with lively intelligence and taste. John Dupays is the chef-*patron* and something of a gastronomic magician. His wife, Thea, is a welcoming hostess and a talented painter whose works adorn the hotel walls. Lounges are spacious, bedrooms individual and very pretty (pine lotion *ad lib* and other agreeable trimmings). A hotel of great quality and spirit.' (*Roger Smithells*)

Open: all year except 23 December–6 January.
Rooms: 15 double—all with bath/shower.
Spacious sitting rooms, conference rooms. Two acres of lawns and gardens where (weather permitting) you can take tea under gigantic cedar trees; heated swimming pool which lurks discreetly behind flower beds.
Terms (excluding VAT):   B & B: £13.25.

Prices quoted, unless otherwise specified, are for bed and breakfast for a person sharing a double room with bath or shower in the high season. We have also given half and full board prices per person in high season when available.

7

Highbury Hotel   *Telephone:* Bembridge (098 387) 2838
Lane End

'My family has been going to Bembridge for thirty-three years. As a
child I loved it and now, as a parent, I see my children loving it. It is as
unspoiled and uncommercialised today as it was all those years ago.
When I first discovered *Highbury*, it was a small Edwardian guesthouse.
Today, however, it is a superior family hotel. Extensive additions have
provided more spacious and well-furnished bedrooms; at the same time
the kitchens have been redesigned and the dining room enlarged, and
the excellent restaurant now attracts many non-residents. The owners,
Tony and Frances Cobb, have created a special atmosphere which sets
it apart from the normal British holiday hotel.' (*M. J. Hollyer; also
David and Marian Oare*)

Open: all year, except Christmas.
Rooms: 8 double, 1 single—5 with bath or shower, all with telephone
            and baby-listening services.
Lounge (with colour TV), bar; sauna, solarium. The garden has a
heated outdoor swimming pool. Four minutes' walk to the nearest beach
with safe bathing; sailing, fishing, water-skiing, underwater swimming;
several riding stables in the village.
No dogs in public rooms.
Terms (excluding service and VAT):   B & B: £8.25; lunch: £1.75;
            dinner: from £2.95–£3.95.

Yeoldon House Hotel   *Telephone:* Bideford (023 72) 4400
Northam

'Where the rivers Taw and Torridge enter the Atlantic by a joint
estuary there is a big, deep bay on the North Devon coast. The head-
lands are Baggy Point to the north-east and Hartland Point in the west,
with magnificent cliffs leading to both. On each side of the estuary are
long stretches of good, hard, golden sands, excellent for surfing and
bucket-and-spade holidays. *Yeoldon House Hotel*, in the village of
Northam, is little more than a mile down river (the Torridge) from the
old port of Bideford, and has a charming garden overlooking the
estuary. The special quality of the place is due to the owner-managers,
Chris and Judi Fulford, who give a personal friendly welcome to their
guests and are always ready to help with local information, and yet never
force themselves on visitors. Judi Fulford is a cordon bleu cook and
personally supervises the cuisine, which has won an outstanding local
reputation. They provide dinner, bed and good English breakfast. No
lunches, though snacks can be had to order. I spent three weeks here
three years running. Each time I paid full rates, and as a working travel

writer I can hardly give better evidence of how highly I rate the place
for a restful holiday than that!' (*Penelope Turing*)

Open: all year.
Rooms: 9 double, 1 single—9 with bath or shower, all with radio, some
with TV.
Sitting room, bar; 2 acres of grounds surrounded by fields and river; at
near-by Westward Ho! there are 2 miles of sandy beach with safe bathing and malibu surfing, golf at the championship Westward Ho! course,
and at Saunton; sailing on the estuary, sea, river and reservoir fishing,
riding and pony-trekking.
Terms (excluding VAT):   B & B: £7.40; half board: £9.80; half board
(weekly): £61.00.
Weekend breaks, winter breaks, special Gourmet weekends
in winter.

BLOCKLEY, Nr Moreton-in-Marsh, Gloucestershire

Lower Brook House   *Telephone:* Blockley (038 676) 286

'Blockley is a tiny, quiet Cotswold village which rambles up a hill and
makes a good base for exploring the surrounding countryside. I was
there in autumn when there wasn't another visitor around, even though
the near-by town of Broadway was still thronged with tourists.

'*Lower Brook House* is a small house, next to similarly small houses,
with a tiny garden with a little brook and views of open countryside. The
house itself was cosy and comfortable. When we arrived, we were shown
to a room at the top. Now we are small, but bigger people might have
been unhappy about the size of the room. It was lovingly decorated and
furnished and full of character—like the old oak beams—but I did have
to stand on tiptoe to look out of the window. The bathroom was nice
enough to look at—so we kept the door open which made the whole
room feel more spacious. There seemed to be only two bedrooms on this
floor though the wall dividing them was so thin that we could hear the
couple next door turning over the pages of their newspapers. Downstairs
the lounge fitted snugly round the fireplace, and there were just enough
seats for residents—though not enough for nightly diners who crowded
into the tiny bar and forced us to bed after dinner as there was nowhere
to sit. The food was home-cooked in an English tea-shop type dining
room. For all its Lilliputian aspects, it was a charming house and very
comfortable.' (*Susan Grossman*)

Open: all year except one month from 25 December.
Rooms: 5 double, 1 single—4 with bath; TV available.
Lounge and bar; ⅓-acre garden, through which the Lower Brook flows.
No children under 5. No dogs.
Terms (excluding service):   B & B: £8.00; lunch: from £2.00; dinner:
from £2.75.
Mid-week and weekend breaks in winter.

Royal Norfolk Hotel   *Telephone:* Bognor Regis (024 33) 26222
The Esplanade

We have had nominations for a number of traditional grand hotels along the South coast from *The Cavendish* and *The Lansdowne* at Eastbourne, past *The Belmont* at Sidmouth, and *The Devoncourt* at Exmouth, all the way to *The Imperial* 'palace' at Torquay. It may seem eccentric that we should include *The Royal Norfolk* and omit the rest. It is a handsome iron-balconied three-storeyed Regency building standing four-square on the Esplanade, with good sea views; the same might be said, with minor variations in period or siting, of all the others. The rooms at *The Royal Norfolk* are elegant, the conveniences modern, the management efficient, the service friendly; so are they all, all honourable hotels. *The Royal Norfolk*, uniquely, has royal associations: Queen Victoria slept or took tea here, so (maybe) did Edward VII and Napoleon III. But that would hardly be a reason, in a Guide of this kind, for special treatment. Our general policy (see the Introduction) has been to exclude grand hotels, at home and abroad, because their virtues are usually predictable, and we wish the Guide to concentrate on hotels of special or unusual merit. Our excuse for making an exception of *The Royal Norfolk* is simply that we were beguiled by the eloquence of Roland Newman's panegyric on his Bognor mini-break:

'A number of hotels these days operate a mini-holiday scheme. The idea is that you can go to a hotel, anytime in the year, for a specified number of days, usually about four or five, and have a short holiday at very advantageous rates. Recently we took a holiday of this kind at *The Royal Norfolk*. The all-in cost was about £44 per person for a five day, four nights, visit. It was a very pleasant and surprising holiday. As we expected from a luxury hotel, the accommodation was excellent, with a private bathroom and colour TV in the bedroom, and the staff were most helpful; but above all, the food was superlative. So good and so plentiful was the cuisine that, to a large extent, our holiday soon only revolved around the meals.

'It was on the first day—and you want to try and get there as early as possible and leave as late as possible, for the tariff includes all meals for the whole five days—that we began to realise what we had let ourselves in for. The menus presented at each meal offered such a variety of specialist dishes that to choose was almost impossible. For example, try choosing between Fillet of Bream D'Antin (poached with white wine sauce, tomato, parsley and croutons), Roast Sussex Turkey Boston (almond stuffed, with sugared apple and cranberries), and Lamb Cutlets Maréchale (cooked in butter, asparagus tips, Parisienne potatoes)—all this supplemented by as much as you could eat of Haricots Verts au Beurre, Chouxfleur Polonaise and Macaire, and new potatoes. To make matters worse one had already got through a choice of six Hors d'Oeuvres Variés, then either Crème de Champignon or Iced Vichyssoise, and still had to be prepared to make a choice of sweets from a huge sweet and cakes trolley, and all of these beautifully cooked and served in pleasant and luxurious surroundings.

'The results of such gargantuan and delicious meals were twofold. First, it was no longer a question of allocating half an hour for lunch, as was our normal custom. If one was to eat one's way through these superb meals one had to get into the restaurant early and give at least one and a half hours' attention to digesting the food—allowing frequent pauses between courses (and sometimes during one course) to aid the digestion. Secondly, it became necessary to organise a daily routine that would incorporate sufficiently long walks and exercise in the bracing sea air of Bognor Regis to digest the previous meal and prepare for the next one. Well, we managed it. By the third day, with brisk early walks before breakfast and a dip in the hotel swimming pool, by longer walks in the morning and by even lengthier treks in the afternoon and evening, we were able to face each meal not only with appetite and confidence, but were even able to manage some crisps and peanuts in the bar before dinner. By the fourth day it was no longer a struggle and what was undoubtedly a unique and gastronomically interesting holiday was ending.

'Though the newspapers today are often full of the horrors of the standard of service and food in many hotels in this country—the *Royal Norfolk Hotel* gave to us, on our mini-holiday, a standard of luxury to which we would both always like to be accustomed.' (*Roland Newman*)

Open: all year.
Rooms: 37 double, 12 single—41 with bath, all with radio, TV and
        telephone.
Lift, 3 lounges, cocktail bar; dancing on Saturday; 1 acre grounds with heated swimming pool.
Terms (excluding VAT):   B & B: £11.00; meals: £2.85–£4.55; full
        board: £10.50–£19.50.
        Mini-holidays (5 days, 4 nights), and special weekend rates.

BONCHURCH, Nr Ventnor, Isle of Wight

Peacock Vane   *Telephone:* Ventnor (0983) 852019

When you consider the affluence of the sailing community on the Isle of Wight and on the marinas across the Solent, it is surprising how wretchedly the island has catered for gourmets. *The Peacock* has long been an exception to the mediocre rule; the food is dependably excellent and the wine list equally exhilarating. But unlike many hotels with renowned restaurants, the *Peacock Vane* is likely to leave its residents as well-satisfied with the accommodation as with the board. The hotel is very much a family affair of the Wolfendens, who have been running their house as a hotel for nearly a quarter of a century. We put it this way because, as with all the best small hotels, the owners make you feel a welcome guest in their civilised Regency home, full of family pictures and antiques. The bedrooms in the main house and in the flats of the two neighbouring cottages are furnished (some with four-posters) in the same personal and un-hotel-like way as the public rooms. (*C. N. Maplethorpe*)

Open: all year except mid January to mid February.
Rooms: 9 double, 2 single—8 with bath, all with TV.
Large drawing-room; 4 acres of lawns and gardens with heated outdoor swimming pool; ¼-mile from the sea, with sand and good bathing at low tide; 18-hole golf course at Sandown, 7 miles.
No children under 7.
Terms (excluding VAT): B & B: £9.50; lunch: £3.00; dinner: £5.00; half-board: £13.75.

BOURTON-ON-THE-WATER, Gloucestershire

The Old Manse   *Telephone:* Bourton-on-the-Water (0451) 20642

'Bourton is a place to avoid during the summer season. It is a beautiful village, with the river Windrush flowing alongside the main street, and spanned by Venetian-style miniature bridges, but you can't see it for people! However, out of season there is the opportunity to enjoy all this, free of the crowds. It is an excellent centre for exploring the Cotswolds. *The Old Manse,* an 18th-century Cotswold-stone house with a modern wing, stands on the banks of the Windrush. Don Knight, formerly manager of the International Hotel, Persia, cooks imaginatively and to perfection. His wife manages, including training her young waitresses (partly local and partly Antipodean during my stay) to standards of service beyond expectation in a small country establishment. Oriental themes in the decoration and furnishings.' (*Gordon Smith*)

Open: all year except January.
Rooms: 9 double—8 with bath, all with telephone and radio.
Cocktail bar, lounge bar, coffee lounge, TV lounge.
Children: not recommended for under 12s.
Terms: B & B: from £9.10; meals: £5.50.
      Winter weekend breaks.

BRADWORTHY, North Devon

Lake Villa   *Telephone:* Bradworthy (040 924) 342

'Bradworthy, Anglo-Saxon in origin, is a drowsy village seven miles south of Bideford Bay in the peaceful Devon farmlands between the rivers Tamar and Torridge. Neat houses and spruce shops are ranged round a vast market square. No tourist trappings here. Tamar Lake bird sanctuary is three miles away. When peace palls, you can be off to the nearby coast—Bideford, picture-postcard Clovelly, the wild cliffscapes of Hartland Point or the five-mile stretch of faultless sands north of rather boring Bude. Dartmoor, Exmoor and Bodmin Moor are within day-excursion range. *Lake Villa,* a centuries-old farmhouse with Victorian additions, is the home of James and Anne Robertson, which is how they like you to feel about their country house hotel when you stay there. The old buildings have been impeccably adapted and decorated to receive guests with a taste for good food, wine, and home comforts enlivened with witty and beautiful trimmings. There is a cosy bar. Bedrooms are gay, cottagey and individual. The Robertsons have children and welcome others. Family suites have separate children's bedrooms. An early children's supper is served. Barbecues are an occasional happening. This is a peach of a place, gently sophisticated, totally relaxed.' (*Roger Smithells*)

Open: all year, except December.
Rooms: 7 double, 3 single—5 with bath or shower, all with tea-making facilities.
Lounge, bar, colour TV, solarium, games room, baby-listening. One acre of garden with badminton; fishing and sailing on Tamar Lake; 8 miles to surfing coast; riding and shooting near by.
No dogs.
Terms (excluding service):   daily half board: £11.00; weekly half board: £67.50.
         Special rates for 2/3-day breaks and for off-season.

BUDE, Cornwall

The Falcon Hotel   *Telephone:* Bude (0288) 2005

'Bude as a tourist town lives pleasantly up to John Betjeman's description of it as Britain's "least rowdy resort". It has a faded air, which is attractive and uncommercialised, rather than failed in character. Even in high summer it is never overcrowded and there are ample parking facilities in the centre, with near-by access to two superb beaches: Crooklets is considered one of the best surfing beaches in Britain and is often nicknamed "Britain's Bondi". It also has a canal for boating and fishing, and a downland golf course. The town has done a lot to pioneer beach safety and employs teams of life-savers.

'*The Falcon Hotel* is on the canal side, raised on a bank with a garden alongside bedecked with old carriages which recalls its foundation in 1798 as the headquarters of the coastal transport system. It is a small family hotel run by the Brendon family. The present owner, George, an ex-copywriter, is seen around in fisherman's jerseys, jeans and thongs, helps to promote Bude on the tourist scene, and creates an informal, friendly atmosphere. His ancestors would take lady guests they fancied hunting or entertain them to more intimate indoor sports. The house retains an old-fashioned flavour, but is warm and cosy, with hot-water bottles supplied when it's cold, though there is room heating and an increasing number of the rooms have private bathrooms. The rooms are kept exceptionally clean. Some have a flamboyant Victorian line in exotic furniture pieces such as an inlaid wardrobe for a *poule de luxe*. Some of the corridors are lined with a unique collection of samplers and postcards of the First World War era. Food in the main dining room has a traditional local bias and is very good; there is a French-style *à la carte* bistro called La Bicyclette, and a cocktail bar. Adjacent is the Falcon pub where the lifeboat crew tend to gather beneath too evocative pictures of local wrecks, and it's a good place to get to know some of the North Cornish characters.' (*Carol Wright*)

Open: 3 May–8 October.
Rooms: 28 double, 19 single—13 with bath, 15 with shower, all with telephone.
Large residents' lounge, small sun lounge, cocktail bar; 1½ acres of garden with putting green; boating and fishing on canal, golf and surfing beaches near.
Terms (excluding VAT):   B & B: £10.65; half board: £13.95; full board: £15.35.
Special weekend rates usually available. Some coach parties.

BURFORD, Oxfordshire

The Bay Tree   *Telephone:* Burford (099 382) 3137

Some people would claim that Burford is the most beautiful village in England. Even those who would hesitate to go that far would acknowledge the exceptional charm of its steep High Street, lined with magnificent Cotswold buildings, recalling the days when Burford was a prominent wool town, sloping down to the fine old bridge crossing the Windrush. Burford-lovers, while agreeing about its beauty, fall out as to whether *The Bay Tree* or *The Lamb* (see opposite) is the better place to stay. Both are in Sheep Street, just off the High Street. *The Bay Tree*, a mellow 16th-century mansion, is the classier of the two, its tone being set by the attractive young staff, most of whom are hotel trainees who have come to work for and learn from Miss Gray, who has run the hotel for many years. The house offers an old-fashioned standard of comfort. It is full of polished oak and chintz, with a fine formal garden for the summer and crackling fires for the winter. 'I've had to spend time in dozens of English hotels,' writes one enthusiast, recommending in particular the exceptional value of the hotel's out-of-season weekend rates. '*The Bay Tree* is the only one I know which is more of a pleasure than a penance to stay in.' Another has special praise for the cooking: 'the most interesting and varied menu in the region'. (*Jonathan Raban, Gillian Vincent, Doris Dudley, Mary Cunynghame, Carolyn Wilson*)

Open: all year.
Rooms: 15 double, 9 single—17 with bath.
Four lounges, cocktail bar; 1-acre garden with sun loggia, stone terraces and lily ponds; Burford golf course near by.
Dogs not admitted in public rooms.
Terms: B & B: from £7.00; dinner: £3.25; full board: £10.25.
Budget weekends (November to March): £24.

If you consider any entry inadequate or misleading, please let us know <u>now</u>.

The Lamb   *Telephone:* Burford (099 382) 3155

'To enter *The Lamb* is an experience, almost an emotion, as if one's worries gently fall away with the quiet, courteous welcome of this hotel. The beautiful old place, built originally in 1430 for monks visiting the Priory, is a perfect setting for the china, glass, copper, brass, old pictures, maps, and bowls and bowls of flowers arranged with loving care along the Gallery as you go towards the spacious dining room. And the food! Small whitebait cooked to perfection, crisp and light, and served with thinly cut brown bread and butter. Fresh salmon, poached exactly right. Gammon grilled to succulence with peaches and pineapple, etc., etc. Breakfast, lunch, tea and dinner—traditional and all of the best. Coffee—the richest and "cleanest" I have tasted—may be taken out into the lovely old garden, colourful, sheltered, a delight to all. Bedrooms, furnished in the old style, but with comfort and modern amenities. *The Lamb* is the epitome of all that is best in small hotels. Most of all, one experiences a generosity of nature, concern and kindness extended by Mrs North Lewis, her family and staff.' (*Nora Bagshaw; also E. M. Haynes*)

Open: all year.
Rooms: 9 double, 5 single—4 with bath.
Two lounges, bar; golf, fishing, tennis, hacking and hunting near by.
Children: not encouraged under 12.
Terms: B & B: £7.00; half board (for stay of 3 days): £9.50.
            Winter weekend breaks: 12 November–14 March.

BURY ST EDMUNDS, Suffolk

The Angel   *Telephone:* Bury St Edmunds (0284) 3926
Angel Hill

'The small town of Bury, with its many fine Georgian buildings, its little squares and old shop fronts, is a pleasure to visit in its own right as well as being a good touring centre for Cambridge, Newmarket and the many unspoilt villages of East Anglia. *The Angel*, patronised by Dickens (who immortalised it as the place where Sam Weller first encounters Job Trotter), is an ivy-covered series of linked buildings on the main square opposite the great abbey gate, one of the glories of the town. If you are allergic to noise, you should avoid the front, especially on market days. The hotel, run by a friendly young couple, has a number of four-poster beds, and runs inclusive "four-poster weekends", with a free bottle of sherry by the bedside. The restaurant is in a cellar-like basement, with tables set under arches—part of tunnels that once joined the hotel to the abbey opposite. The menu is a little on the pretentious side, but the portions are generous, there's a good cold table, and the service is motherly and pleasant.' (*Carol Wright*)

Open: all year.
Rooms: 28 double, 16 single—28 with bath and colour TV, all with

15

radio and telephone; baby-listening services.
Two lounges, Charles Dickens Bar, Pickwick Bar (for men only till
7.30p.m.), TV lounge.
Terms: B & B: £8.25. Meals: from £3.10.
'Old English Weekends': October to end April. A few coach
parties.

CAMBRIDGE, Cambridgeshire

Garden House Hotel   *Telephone:* Cambridge (0223) 63421
Granta Place

Grown from a small riverside residence into a luxurious modernised
hotel on a dead-end road with no passing traffic to disturb light sleepers.
In fact, 'a soothing lullaby' (says the brochure) is provided by the fall of
the waters of the Granta over the weir to join the Cam. Seven ground-
floor rooms open on to paved private terraces, fine for non-stair-
climbers. 'Bedrooms are well-designed, decorative and comfortable,
though the clock can be disturbing at night. Modern, agreeable furnishings with attractive old prints of Cambridge. Service friendly and helpful, atmosphere congenial, food very good.' Try for a room with a river
view. (*E. H. Hibbert;* also *Chloe Green*)

Open: 1 January–24 December.
Rooms: 55 double (some are suites)—all with bath, telephone, radio
and colour TV, double glazing, drinks cabinet, baby-listening
service; most have balconies overlooking river and gardens.
Large lounge–cum–cocktail bar, banqueting suites; 3 acres of lawns and
gardens reaching to the river, where tea and drinks can be taken; boating
and fishing.
No dogs.
Terms (excluding service):   B & B: £11.50; lunch: from £3.50; dinner:
from £3.70.

CAMELFORD, Cornwall

Lanteglos Farmhouse Hotel   *Telephone:* Camelford (084 02) 3551

Most entries in this book have a single nominator; very few have more
than two or three. But within a fortnight of the first public announce-
ment of the Guide, no less than a dozen commendations had been
received for *Lanteglos*—from many different parts of England and all
having in common a lyrical enthusiasm for the place. A clear case of
collusion? It would be ridiculous not to think so. But the care which so
many satisfied guests of this exclusively family hotel had taken to
describe in exhaustive detail the pleasure of their stays (almost all had
been to *Lanteglos* for several years running) was in itself significant.
Fortunate and rare are the hotels which can evoke such eloquence and

loyalty from their customers. We have chosen one letter of recommendation to stand for all:

'Locale: North Cornwall, a few miles inland from commercialised Tintagel. Car advisable if one is to enjoy the surrounding beaches and countryside. Everything within a few minutes' drive along good quiet main roads or deserted country lanes. Two large safe sandy beaches, two or three excellent surfing beaches, innumerable rocky coves for sunbathing, swimming, snorkelling, canoeing or fishing. A different beach every day if needed—the furthest being thirty minutes' drive. The moors are within walking distance. Riding and golf, old quarries and mines, museums, historic houses, and day courses in pottery, painting or woodwork, are all at hand.

'The hotel, which lies in a tiny hamlet, complete with rustic stream, bridge and old church, is a beautiful old converted vicarage built by Pugin in 1847 and still retaining an air of tranquillity and security. The decor is pleasant and comfortable rather than luxurious. So are the bedrooms. The residents' lounge/television room is a little small, but then it's rarely used. No one wants it!

'During the day *Lanteglos* is geared to children. Breakfast is homely and casual—every type of cereal is at hand at a central table, with a full English breakfast to follow. Lunch—again pleasant traditional plain fare—though most families prefer to take advantage of the excellent packed lunches and remain outdoors. Many guests stay in the hotel grounds, which are ample and informal. There are innumerable play areas for the children—slides, climbing frames, etc., tennis and badminton courts, a large games room and a superb heated swimming pool. One can safely and happily lose one's children for hours.

'Tucked out of sight behind trees is a small holiday village of self-catering bungalows. These, like the rooms in the hotel itself, are wired to a central two-way call system and baby-sitting intercom.

'It is in the evening that the grown-ups realise that the charisma of *Lanteglos* is something special and that the two couples who run the place, Mike and Bridget Power and Mike and Janet Collins, really do create the holiday that all parents long for. The dining room changes in atmosphere, and one feels that one is out for dinner rather than just having a meal. There's a five-course menu, with a wide choice for each course; delicacies such as quail's eggs, fried squid and other exotica are commonplace. If you want to order something special—chateaubriand steak or lobster—the price is very reasonable. After dinner there is usually some sort of entertainment in one or both of the bars: there's a disco and dance once a week, a traditional Jazz Band, folk singing and spontaneous party nights with competitions, zany games and songs.

'*Lanteglos* is a place which, when one thinks of it, one smiles. It is so full of friendship. Within twenty-four hours of your arrival you know people and you relax. It is Christmas and Bonfire night, homecoming and reunions and heart-warming laughter. PS: Do not expect your children to be fussed over after 9p.m. They are all tucked away for the night—a law which suits everyone!' (*Valerie Neill; also A. D. Atkins, J. M. V. Barrett, M. W. Curtin, P. F. Holland, Therese Howard, M. J. C. Hughes, David Penrice, B. L. Pagett, M. E. Saggers, T. D. Walsh and I. H. Alterman*)

Open: Easter–October.
Rooms: 10 double or family rooms, 2 single, plus 6 family suites in grounds, each sleeping up to 6; double rooms have showers, suites have baths; all rooms have radio and intercom; suites have TV.

One lounge (with TV), 2 bars, games room, baby-listening services. Fifteen acres of grounds with heated floodlit swimming and paddling pools, hard tennis and badminton courts, children's fort, swings, slides, etc. Within twenty minutes by car: river, lake and sea fishing (including for sharks); sailing, surfing and safe bathing; pony-trekking, cliff walks. No dogs.

Terms (excluding service and VAT): weekly bookings only accepted from end May to 10 September; full board weekly in high season: £74; B & B (off season): £5.65.

CARBIS BAY, Nr St Ives, Cornwall

St Uny Hotel   *Telephone:* St Ives (073 670) 5011

The bay of St Ives is ringed with hotels, big and small, but Carbis Bay, two miles to the east of the teeming and frenetic town of St Ives itself and set well away from the busy Penzance-St Ives road, is a comparative haven of tranquillity even in the high season. And *St Uny*, an impressive castellated house after the fashion of the grander sort of domestic building in this part of Cornwall, set in two acres of semi-tropical garden sloping down towards a good safe sandy beach and the sea, scores high marks for its relaxed peaceful atmosphere. Formerly a private residence, it still retains the feel of a family home. The dining room is closed at lunch, but hot and cold snacks are served in the bar and cheerfully carried by the young staff to guests in the sun lounge or grounds. The cooking is praised, particularly the local fish. The proprietor, we are told, has refrained from installing a swimming-pool as not everyone appreciates wet screaming children running around ... (*Mrs D. H. Baker*)

Open: 14 May–1 October.
Rooms: 30 double, 3 single—17 with bath or shower, most overlooking St Ives and the bay.

Lounge, hall lounge, bar lounge, verandah; 2 acres of lawns, with many sheltered corners, and 9-hole putting green; 250 yards to the 'safest beach in Cornwall'; within a few miles of West Cornwall Golf Club; riding; surfing at Porthmeor Beach, St Ives.

Dogs: not allowed in public rooms.

Terms (excluding service and VAT): half board: from £8.00.

Details of amenities vary according to the information—or lack of it—supplied by hotels in response to our questionnaires. The fact that lounges or bars or gardens are not mentioned must not be taken to mean that a hotel lacks them.

CARTMEL, Cumbria

Aynsome Manor Hotel   *Telephone:* Cartmel (044 854) 276
Nr Grange-over-Sands

'The seemly village of Cartmel lies in a valley on the gentle fringes of the Lake District, two miles from the coast at Grange-over-Sands, four from the foot of Lake Windermere; well clear of desperate holiday traffic jams. The village has a huge Priory Church, pretty cottages, good painting and craft galleries, some genial pubs—an excellent base for exploring lovely, less-frequented Lakeland byways. *Aynsome Manor*, a country house hotel, lies outside the village, below the green fells. Its sober exterior gives no hint of the endearing mixture of grandeur and cosiness within. There is grandeur in the splendid proportions of the dining room and lounge; a gracious sweep of Georgian staircase; fine antiques. The cosiness lies in blazing log fires, an amplitude of downy chairs, a relaxed houseparty-ish atmosphere. A five-person family team runs the place with total devotion to the welfare of their guests and a united passion for good living. Alan Williams, the cheerful extrovert who heads the family team, confides the details of the menu to you in terms of pure gastronomic poetry. His wife cooks superbly. Her sister's sweets trolley glides to your table—a galleon loaded with goodies. Bedrooms are cheerful, sometimes stylish, many with fine sweeping views. A happy sybaritic place which puts on no airs.' (*Roger Smithells*)

Open: all year.
Rooms: 14 double, 2 single—9 with bath. Part of the accommodation
         is in the Cottage, across a cobblestone courtyard, where rooms
         can be taken separately or by a family or group of friends.
Two lounges (one in the Cottage, with own TV), bar; ½-acre of garden with lawns surrounded by trees. Sea and sands at Grange-over-Sands, 2 miles; boating, water-skiing, etc., on Lake Windermere, 4 miles. Dogs tolerated, but not in public rooms.
Terms (excluding service):   B & B: £6.50; half board (weekly): £59.50;
         full board (weekly): £63.00.
         Mid-week and weekend off-season breaks (2 nights): £15.50–
         £21.00. Some winter conference facilities.

CASTLE CARY, Somerset

George Hotel & Restaurant   *Telephone:* Castle Cary (096 35) 215
Market Place

'There is no particular reason for going to Castle Cary—which itself makes it a good choice for an overnight stop in Somerset when more obvious places are thronged. This pleasant little market town lies in a no-man's-land between Shepton Mallet on the A37 and Wincanton on the A303. It has few distinguished buildings. Its Market Hall tries valiantly to look medieval but is, in fact, Victorian. *The George Hotel* faces the Market Hall. Two-storeyed, stone-built and thatched, this hostelry is one of the most attractive old buildings in the town. As a hotel it is a good deal more sophisticated than its cottagey exterior would suggest. And it is rapidly going up in the world under the enthusiastic management of two generations of the Pushman family. The large comfortable bars are the rendezvous of local residents. Good bar snacks are served. There is a wing of spruce modern bedrooms with private bathrooms in converted stables entered from the courtyard. Older bedrooms in the main building are attractive, but there is a shortage of bathrooms (more are planned). There is a rather poky little residents' lounge; but the great triumph of *The George* is its welcoming, candle-lit restaurant where food, wine and service are beyond reproach. Roast Somerset duckling with black cherry sauce is a speciality of the house. The menu is changed daily and wisely restricted to a few dishes very well prepared and cooked to order. The fact that the menu is in French (with translations) is a bit of gastronomic snobbery faintly comic in a very olde English *auberge*.' (*Roger Smithells;* also *Norma Jenkinson*)

Open: all year.
Rooms: 12 double, 2 single—4 with bath.
Lounge, bars. Riding and golf near by.
Terms: B & B: £7.50; meals: £3.50–£5.00.

CASTLE COMBE, Wiltshire

The Manor House Hotel   *Telephone:* Castle Combe (0249) 782206

The village of Castle Combe, a few miles from Chippenham, is a jigsaw puzzle artist's Olde England dream: stone-built cottages, tall church tower amid old trees, and an arched bridge spanning the Bybrook stream. *The Manor House* is a minor Stately Home of a building and fits perfectly into the general picture: The gardens are Gardens: steps lead down to grassy Italianate walks lined with rose arbours, statuary, rare plants and quiet tree-shaded corners. The house is mostly 16th and 17th century, but contemporary creature comforts have been skilfully grafted into the sleeping quarters; some of the bedrooms have four-posters or testers. The new Garden Wing, rebuilt from a line of old cottages, also combines modern luxury with original features such as oak beams and huge fireplaces. The main rooms are spacious and elegant; the dining room, chandeliered and candle-lit, serves ambitious and sophisticated dishes, with wines to match. (*Robert and Eunice Edmunds*)

Open: all year.
Rooms: 29 double, 5 single—32 with bath or shower, all with radio, TV, telephone and baby-listening services.
Three sitting rooms, 1 bar. Twenty-six acres of gardens and parkland with lawns stretching down to the river Bybrook. Trout fishing by arrangement (a swimming pool is in course of construction); championship golf course within 15 minutes' drive.
Terms (excluding service and VAT):   B & B: £10.00; meals: from £4.80.

CASTLETON, Nr Sheffield, Derbyshire

Ye Olde Nag's Head   *Telephone:* Hope Valley (0433) 20248

Ye olde elements are visible, but not obtrusively so, in this 17th-century coaching inn in the heart of the Peak District at the western end of the Hope Valley. It would make a good centre for a walking holiday or for touring the many-splendoured stately homes round about—Chatsworth, Haddon Hall, *et al.* The hotel is in the centre of the village, with a certain amount of village traffic; the public bar is popular locally. 'I'm not usually given to casting superlatives, especially about hotels, but I confess that the *Nag's Head* is one establishment I consider to be worth a lengthy detour. The place was wonderfully maintained, clean, charming and utterly comfortable. The kitchens proved to be capable, the waiters amenable and the products of both enjoyable. The only criticism: Muzak in the dining room.' (*P. L. Woodward*)

Open: all year.
Rooms: 8 double, 3 single.
Residents' lounge (with TV), bar lounge. Pot-holing, pony-trekking and golf near by.
Terms: B & B: £8.50; half board: £11.50; meals: from £3.25.

CAWSAND BAY, Cornwall

The Criterion Hotel   *Telephone:* Plymouth (0752) 822244

'Forget the metropolitan aura of Criterion: this one is small, informal, friendly, free and easy. The hotel is literally two-faced: the street frontage is squeezed into a narrow village street (you could almost shake hands from your bedroom with someone in the pub across the way) and has three storeys; while at the back, because the building tumbles down the rocks, the three storeys become five and the outlook is a vast sweep of Cawsand Bay out to Plymouth Sound beyond, with balconies abutting from the two lower floors and a stairway down to the rocks and beach below. The dining room occupies the ground floor; bedrooms are on the two floors above; the sitting room is one floor down from the dining room, the bar one floor down from that. Rooms are small, but ingeniously equipped and furnished to make the most of the space, so that you have ample wardrobing, dressing table mirrored and lit and stooled, handy bedside table with lamp; each room has its own thoughtful colour scheme.

'The hotel is run by Mr and Mrs Shimell, with a handful of village girls as waitresses and village women as domestics, all friendly and helpful. Mrs Shimell is so absorbed in the kitchen that you rarely see her; she produces excellent meals, a limited but genuine and contrasted choice each evening, specialising in local crab, lobster, strawberries and such. There's early morning tea and, if you're not out and about, mid-morning coffee, salady lunch (in the lounge, in the bar, on the balcony, as you like), afternoon tea with delicious gateau from the kitchen. In the evening guests gather as a family in the cellar bar before dinner, and over drinks Mr Shimell describes the evening's dishes in mock-heroic detail before one of the girls takes orders.

'While there is charming coastline and pleasant country all round, one can enjoy just staying at the hotel (as we discovered because my wife fell ill), since the two balconies provide a splendid panorama of endless activity and infinite variety, with yachts skimming, packets steaming, kayaks bobbing, speedboats bumping, water-skiers bouncing, bathers splashing, smacks returning—and with the girls always at hand to take orders or run errands.' (*W. L. Prentice*)

Open: 6 May–24 September.
Rooms: 7 double, 1 single—2 with bath or shower.
Lounge (with TV), cellar bar, balcony bar. Direct access to the sea from the hotel; sandy beach and rocks, with safe bathing; boating, sailing, fishing, etc.
Babies welcome, otherwise no children under 12. No dogs.
Terms (excluding VAT):   B & B: from £5.00; half board (minimum 3 days): from £8.00 daily or from £55 weekly.

CHARMOUTH, Dorset

Sea Horse Hotel   *Telephone:* Charmouth (029 76) 414
Higher Sea Lane

'A modernised 18th-century house stands in an acre of walled garden overlooking the sea and cliffs, well away from any main road. Mr Elliott, the owner, supervises all the cooking and has devised a selection of fabulous "afters"—i.e. hazelnut meringue with layers of meringue, cream and raspberries. The hotel is warm, cosy, friendly, and children are made very welcome (charged two-thirds adult price). Fantastic value! Comfortable lounge with colour TV in a special TV annex, a child-listening service, laundry and ironing facilities. Four minutes' walk across a field and you're on the beach, which is smooth, safe and smothered with fossils. My kids thought it was SMASHING.' (*Val Hennessy*)

Open: 1 April–31 October.
Rooms: 11 double, 3 single, 2 family—all with radio and baby-listening service.
Two lounges, one with TV, bar. An acre of lawns and shrubs. Four minutes' easy walk to the sea with sand and shingle and safe bathing; Lyme Regis golf course, 1½ miles.
Terms (exclusive of VAT):   B & B: from £5.50; half board (weekly): £49.

Most hotels have reduced rates out of season and for children. For details, you will need to write to the hotel direct.

CHIPPING CAMPDEN, Gloucestershire

King's Arms Hotel   *Telephone:* Evesham (0386) 840256

Even by Cotswold standards, Chipping Campden is exceptional—and a lot less touristy than Broadway and Burford. Its main street is a parade of spectacularly beautiful houses, all in delectable honey-coloured Cotswold stone. The *King's Arms* is in the centre of things, beside the old Market Square. It is made up of two adjoining buildings—one Georgian, the other 17th-century, both stone-built, with a pleasant garden at the rear. The hotel is owned by Hugh Corbett, who previously owned as well the near-by Dormy House at Willersey Hill (*q.v.*), and similar attention to much above average cooking (with good use of local produce) combined with friendly informal service, is apparent at both establishments. The hotel serves late suppers for theatre-goers to Stratford, only twelve miles to the north, and will also apply for tickets, though advance booking is prudent. (*Diana Petry*)

Open: all year.
Rooms: 9 double, 5 single—2 with bath or shower.
Reception room, sitting room, saddle room; an acre of garden.
Dogs admitted, but not in public rooms.
Terms: B & B (excluding service and VAT): £7.50; snack lunches; dinner: from £3.75.
Weekend breaks in winter.

CHITTLEHAMHOLT, Nr Umberleigh, North Devon

Highbullen Hotel   *Telephone:* Chittlehamholt (076 94) 248

'The food, the views, the comfort and the house itself are the best things about this lovely hotel, isolated near the North coast of Devon. It's a typical English country hotel in all respects and better at it than many others. The house is a dramatic red-brick mansion with turrets, surrounded by rolling green hills and deserted country lanes for walking off the excellent meals. The bedroom we had was huge and overlooked trees and countryside, and the furniture was solid and comfortable. The lounge was more formal with picture windows and remarkable views, a blazing log fire and magazine racks with copies of *Country Life*. It was the sort of room you felt you oughtn't to talk too loudly in—and there were some chairs that looked as if they shouldn't be sat on. The cellar dining room is what has given *Highbullen* its reputation. I certainly haven't been able to fault the food. Can you remember a bowl of soup you drank eighteen months ago? More recently, Mrs Neil's chicken Mère Michel left me wondering if I dare ask for more, and her Mushrooms Arménienne with garlic mayonnaise, veal dishes, meringues and almond cream, are as vivid as if I'd eaten them yesterday. One feels obliged to dress fairly formally for dinner, but is quite at home in jeans for breakfast. A venerable institution.' (*Susan Grossman*)

23

Open :   all year.
Rooms :   25 double—all with bath, some with TV and tea-making facilities.

Drawing room, library (with TV), bar, billiards room, small dance floor off bar; sauna. Forty acres of grounds with gardens and parkland in which are tennis court, squash court, 9-hole golf course, croquet lawn; outdoor and indoor heated swimming pool. Safe sea bathing, 40 minutes by car.

No children under 13. No dogs.

Terms :   half board : £12.00.

CIRENCESTER, Gloucestershire

The King's Head Hotel   *Telephone :* Cirencester (0285) 3322
                                         Telex : 43470

'Unofficially designated "the capital of the Cotswolds", Cirencester is the oldest of all the Cotswold towns and villages, founded by the Romans. It is a lively market town with the wide curve of Market Place dominated by a parish church of exceptional Gothic splendour. In a maze of small streets and alleys are interesting old buildings of all periods from the 16th century onwards. Public parklands spread into the centre of the town. This is a thoroughly genuine place, not dolled up for tourists. It is convenient as a Cotswold touring centre with the Wye Valley, the Forest of Dean, Gloucester, Cheltenham, Stratford and the Malverns within a day's range.

'From its Market Place façade, *The King's Head Hotel* might be any traditional coaching inn. It is, in fact, much larger than it looks since it has gradually incorporated several adjoining buildings. Bedrooms thus added are linked by a rabbit warren of up-and-down passages in which it is quite easy and normal to get lost. The bedrooms are modern, convenient, fairly impersonal. There is a rather opulent dining room and the food is good. What distinguishes *The King's Head* from other provincial hostelries is a standard of service rare enough in a top five-star hotel. The staff are consistently cheerful, friendly and genuinely concerned for your welfare. Tea, coffee, cocoa and other beverages and light refreshments can be served at any hour of the day or night. Books left in every room can be exchanged for others of your choice. Shoes left outside your door will be polished within an inch of their lives. And a note in your room says: "Our staff receive realistic wages. Please co-operate by NOT TIPPING".' (*Roger Smithells*)

Open :   all year.
Rooms :   51 double, 20 single—61 with bath or shower, all with colour TV and telephone.

Lift, residents' lounge, cocktail bar, skittle alley.

Terms :   B & B : £8.95. Lunch : from £2.90; dinner : from £3.60. Various weekend breaks including Brass Rubbing and Hot Air Ballooning weekends. Occasional conference and other block bookings.

CLANFIELD, Oxfordshire

The Plough Hotel
& Restaurants

Telephone: Clanfield (036 781) 222

The name Harry Norton has given his beautiful small Elizabethan manor house in Cotswold stone, tells you one important feature of his establishment—that he cares most specially for the quality of his cooking. Much rosetted and starred, his ambitious menus and his wine list (500 bins) attract a lot of non-resident visitors to his three inter-connected restaurants. But those who stay at *The Plough* are also appreciative: 'The pleasure of staying there includes (apart from the excellent food and wines), the *care* Mr and Mrs Norton give their guests, and a feeling of staying with friends with lots of highly trained servants! The dining room is shining—with silver, glass and flowers—and has interesting seating arrangements so that every table is a wall table. Bedrooms are simple, but have a country charm—and the local girls who wait and look after you all seem to be charming too.' (*Kay Plater;* also *Derek Cooper*)

Open: all year.
Rooms: 5 double, 1 single—1 with bath and TV.
Large lounge bar, residents' lounge with TV; small walled garden (lunches served outside in fine weather). $1\frac{1}{2}$ miles from the Thames, 5 miles from Lechlade (boating).
No children under 5. Small dogs only.
Terms (excluding VAT): B & B: from £11.20; lunch (3 courses): from £2.55; dinner (*à la carte* only): minimum charge £3.80.

COMBE MARTIN, North Devon

Higher Leigh Hotel

Telephone: Combe Martin (027 188) 2486

A white, elegant country house hotel attractively sited on a hill overlooking Combe Martin. There are substantial grounds: the lawns and flower-beds are well-kept without being manicured, and there are also woods with small streams and waterfalls. The house itself is surprisingly spacious for a hotel with less than a dozen bedrooms. Food is plentiful and imaginative. Home-baked bread appears every day; home-made éclairs, meringues and gâteaux are also regulars on the menu. Beneath the house are labyrinthine cellars, dry and attractively lit, and dinner is served in the cellars one night a week, with candles and special cutlery. 'Disco lovers might feel the cellars are under-used, but lovers of peace welcome things as they are.' Bedrooms are large, airy and well-appointed. 'From the day you arrive you feel as though you are one of several country house guests almost personally invited, and cared for with solicitous but never obtrusive vigilance.' (*Mary E. Sherratt*)

Open: 1 April–30 September.

Rooms: 9 double, 2 single—1 with bath/shower, all with radio.
Lounge (with TV), billiard room, games room, ballroom, sauna, solarium; baby-listening. Fourteen acres of grounds with lawns and gardens and putting green. Three miles from the sea; fishing, riding and golf near by.
Terms (exclusive of service): B & B: £6.00; half board: £8.00; light lunches.

CRANBROOK, Kent

Kennel Holt Hotel   *Telephone:* Cranbrook (058 04) 2032

Hotel connoisseurs on both sides of the Channel have long known and appreciated the hospitality of this fine Elizabethan manor house, lovingly modernised and furnished by its present owners, Mr and Mrs Fletcher. The house itself is in five acres of beautifully tended gardens, with the orchards and hopfields of the Weald of Kent all round. There are plenty of good walks in the vicinity; for those with cars, Sissinghurst, Hever Castle, and Tunbridge Wells are all close at hand, and the Kent coast not far away. The cooking is 'traditional English', with an 'either/or' menu, but well-prepared and making good use of home-grown vegetables and fruit. No nightlife. It's the sort of relaxed country house hotel run on personal lines, where people can depend on being cosseted for a week or a weekend break. (*Gillian Vincent; J. Freeman*)

Open: all year.
Rooms: 5 double, 2 single—4 with bath, all with radio.
Two lounges (1 with colour TV), log fires. Five acres of grounds with garden chairs and tea on the lawn. Two riding schools within 5 miles, golf courses at Lamberhurst, 5 miles, and Hawkhurst, 6 miles; sea bathing, 30 minutes by car; coarse fishing and some dry-fly trout reservoirs near by.
Terms (exclusive of VAT): B & B: £7.50–£9.00; half board (3 days minimum): £10.70–£12.20. Lunches not served.

CRANTOCK, Nr Newquay, Cornwall

Crantock Bay Hotel   *Telephone:* Crantock (063 77) 229

The address is Crantock, but the hotel is, in fact, a mile beyond the village and in a beautiful and absolutely quiet situation on the West Pentire headland. It faces four-square on to the Atlantic, with sandy and rocky beaches, caves and pools, easily accessible on either side. Good surfing. The hotel is unostentatiously agreeable, and puts itself out for families with small children. It's the kind of place that tends to be habit-forming; some visitors have been regulars for over 25 years. 'It is quite the nicest hotel of its standard that we have stayed at; we go there again as often as we can.' (*Captain A. D. Lenox-Conyngham*)

Open:　　Easter–early October.

Rooms:　　20 double, 11 single—9 with bath or shower, all with radio, tea-making equipment, baby-listening service; most have sea views.

Lounge, bar, TV room, games room; dancing and competitions in the evening. Four acres of grounds with putting green, croquet, children's play area, and donkeys. Sea with sandy beach and safe bathing (life-guard service) 200 yards from the hotel, reached through the grounds. Tennis courts, riding and golf near by.

Terms:　　half board: £8.95; lunch: £1.50.
　　　　　　Spring Holiday rates.

DEDHAM, Nr Colchester, Essex

Maison Talbooth　　　　　*Telephone:* Colchester (0206) 322367

The Vale of Dedham is the heart of Constable country, and Constable himself painted Le Talbooth, the fine old building rich in gables and exposed beams on the banks of the Stour—though you will have to go to the National Gallery of Scotland to see it. Le Talbooth was the hotel *and* the restaurant when Gerald Milsom bought it in 1952, but for many years now the two have been separated. The original building is now pure restaurant, one of the best in this part of the country, and attracting plenty of outside custom. The residents stay half a mile away in a luxuriously modernised Victorian house, *Maison Talbooth*.

'*Maison Talbooth* relishes in excellence of a special kind. It is a simple quiet house. Immediately you enter the large, elegantly furnished double drawing room, you imagine that you have arrived at home—but with the difference that the running of it is none of your concern, and that you are here for the precise purpose of being cosseted. A charming young girl arrives to conduct you to your suite. These vary widely, but all are impeccably decorated with an eye to comfort. There is a thought-out largesse: sofas, chaises, a small bar, flowers and fresh plants, magazines, and pretty tables, colour TV and radio. A lovely place to hibernate should you so wish it. And if you care—as I do—that your bathroom should be a place of comfort and serenity, then these bathrooms are for you. Deeply carpeted, gorgeous curtains, great big towels, bath oils, and a number of other items, help to make it feel your own. In this atmo-sphere of home, you don't have to follow any routine. No need to dress up unless you want to. But there are beautiful walks, easy or arduous as the mood takes you. Near-by Dedham village nestles prosperously round its ancient church. It is a pleasure after such walks to return to the house and know that you are, as it were, at home!

'You may have supper in your room, and one of the delightful girls on duty will bring it up. But if you decide to go to the restaurant, then a treat awaits you. *Le Talbooth*, with its lawns, gardens and weeping willows over the Stour, is a perfect setting to the eye in all seasons. On a summer evening it is pure enchantment. The quality of the food and service is again one of striving for excellence—a wish to create a harmonious environment for every guest; it is a characteristic emanating from the owner, Mr Milsom, who supervises personally with obvious pleasure.' (*Mariana Duncan; also Edward Bostock, Adrienne Keith-Cohen, Mrs B. A. Wyatt, H. G. R. Erben*)

Open: all year.
Rooms: 9 double, 1 single—9 with bath, 1 with shower; all with TV, radio and telephone.
Drawing room with open fire, large hall with French windows on to the garden. The hotel stands in 3 acres of grounds, the restaurant in 2 acres by the river. Boating; seaside with sand beaches within half an hour by car.
No children under 7, except babies. No dogs.
Terms (excluding service): B & B (breakfast served in rooms): £12.50; meals: from £5.00.

DORCHESTER-ON-THAMES, Oxfordshire

The White Hart Hotel   *Telephone:* Oxford (0865) 340074

Formerly a Roman station, then an important Saxon town, later the cathedral city first of Wessex then of Mercia, Dorchester-on-Thames has seen plenty of history, though it's now little more than a winding old village street, full of tea-rooms and antique shops with, as the surviving monument to former greatness, a glorious Abbey, richly endowed with fine windows and brasses. *The White Hart*, in a central position, is a picture-postcard 17th-century coaching inn, with plenty of exposed beams, flowers and plants in copper pans, and old prints on the walls. The service is reported friendly and efficient, the food delicious and good value, and the furnishings comfortable. Since the M40 was opened, Dorchester no longer gets the full burden of the Oxford-London traffic, but front rooms would still be noisy. (*N. L. Maunsell*)

Open: all year.
Rooms: 11 double, 6 single—1 with bath, all with radio, 4 with telephone, all with tea-making facilities.
Lounge (with TV), 4 bars, coffee shop; live jazz once a week. The river Thames, 1 mile; Oxford, 9 miles.
Terms: B & B: £7.25; lunch: £2.75; dinner: £3.00.
Summer package: half board: £21.50 per couple per night.
Autumn packages from October.

EAST PORTLEMOUTH, Nr Salcombe, Devon

Gara Rock Hotel   *Telephone:* Salcombe (054 884) 2342

'An ideal hotel for a family holiday, situated in the middle of National Trust land on cliffs overlooking the sea. Even at the height of the tourist season, when neighbouring Salcombe and Kingsbridge are crowded, it is quiet here because of the winding roads which lead to Gara Rock and the steep cliffs down to the beach, which is a lovely combination of sand and rocks. Apart from going to the beach, you can take wonderful cliff walks or explore charming villages in the hinterland. You can go sailing or visit Dartington, walk on the moors, or ride on the Dart Valley Steam Railway.

'The hotel itself has a heated swimming pool and hard tennis courts. There is a large garden in front which is completely safe for children. Accommodation is flexible. There are flats which are self-catering at some times of the year, though not in the high season. There are suites as well as double and single rooms. Bunk-beds and cots are brought in if required. Many of the rooms have beautiful views of the sea and cliffs. They are kept spotlessly clean. Service is friendly but unobtrusive. The food on the whole is good. (The hotel has its own vegetable garden.) Terms are half-board, but buffet lunch or snacks are available, also cream teas. There is a special supper for the younger children at 5.45p.m., with fish fingers, sausages, chips and so on, and a baby-alarm system so that parents can enjoy their dinner in peace later on. As evening outings are not easy, due to the remoteness of the hotel, entertainments are laid on—a ping-pong match, "The Brain of Gara Rock" contest, and so on—but no one minds if you opt out and watch TV instead. The hotel offers good value for money. The standards are kept consistently high by close supervision by the owner and manager.' (*Adam and Caroline Raphael*)

Open: April–October.
Rooms: 53 double, 9 single—21 with bath or shower, some with TV; baby-listening services.
Three lounges (separate TV lounge); weekly dance and regular entertainments in summer. Five acres of grounds, with heated swimming pool, tennis court, garden games, 2 acres of vegetable garden. Two large private sandy beaches with safe bathing, boating and fishing immediately below the hotel and 5 minutes away.
Terms (excluding service and VAT):   B & B (until mid-July): £7.50; half board: £11.25; snack lunches.

GITTISHAM, Nr Honiton, Devon

Combe House Hotel   *Telephone:* Honiton (0404) 2756

A grand and beautiful Elizabethan mansion standing in its own grounds at the head of a steep and typical Devonshire combe (marvellous walking country) with lovely views to the west, and beautiful gardens with some exceptional trees, especially cedars. A pond in the garden is an additional attraction, as you can look into the water and choose your trout for dinner. Gittisham village now belongs in its entirety to the National Trust and is full of historical associations. *Combe House* has its own associations, but they are Scottish. The hotel is owned and run by John Boswell, a direct descendant of James Boswell, who has restored *Combe* with great fidelity to its present elegant incarnation, and has filled it with furniture, books and pictures from the ancestral home of the Boswells, Auchinleck House in Ayrshire. There are large open log fires (sometimes smoky) in the public rooms, and big chintzy armchairs and sofas to match the handsome tall proportions. The bedrooms, too, are spacious, with glorious views, and with little personal touches—homemade biscuits by the bedside—that reveal the attentive management. The quality of the food is an important feature of the hotel. Therese Boswell, a Cordon Bleu cook, is in charge of the kitchens, and the restaurant attracts a lot of outside visitors. Fresh lobster, salmon, trout and game are always on the menu if in season. (*Edward Booth*)

Open: all year except January and February.
Rooms: 13 double—5 with bath, 1 with shower.
Large reception room, panelled log-fired drawing room (with TV), cocktail bar, games room. Eight acres of gardens in the 2,000-acre estate, with croquet and putting green. Fishing rights (dry fly only) on the river Otter. Nearest beach: Sidmouth, 11 miles; sandy beach, Exmouth, 16 miles; golf and riding near by.
Children under 10 not allowed in the dining room at night; dogs admitted, but not in public rooms.
Terms (exclusive of service and VAT):   B & B: £9.50; bar lunches; dinner: from £5.00.

GOATHLAND, Nr Whitby, North Yorkshire

The Goathland Hydro   *Telephone:* Goathland (094 786) 296

An unpretentiously pleasant country house in a small village well sited in the heart of the North Yorkshire moors. Whitby, Robin Hood's Bay, Rievaulx Abbey, are all within easy motoring distance.

'An old, quite big hotel, with a croquet lawn outside. It was built in the 1920s, and all the doors are solid oak and so is a lot of the furniture. The beds are reasonably comfy. The reason I prefer *The Hydro* to other hotels is that you can always get lost in it. Also, one of the most important things—food! The food at *The Hydro* is marvellous, stupendous and not "fancy", and the afternoon teas are unspeakably good. I must warn you that unless you miss out some of the meals you will most certainly put on weight. Children are welcomed (or else I would not have gone there) and the atmosphere is very friendly, though some (one) of the waiters, well … you don't feel they are the "servants". Altogether, *The Hydro* is much to be desired.' (*Catherine Wainwright*, aged 11; also *Winifred Ebsworth*)

Open: Easter–mid October.
Rooms: 20 double, 13 single—9 with bath or shower, all with radio.
Main lounge, coffee lounge, TV room, apéritif bar; garden and 1 acre
of lawns with croquet. Sand beach, 9 miles; boating at Ruswarp on
river Esk, 6 miles.
No dogs.
Terms: B & B: £8.60; lunch: £1.95; dinner: £2.40; full board:
£9.40–£9.75.
Mini-weekends and Special Offers between Easter and Spring
Holiday.

Mallyan Spout Hotel   *Telephone:* Goathland (094 786) 206

Stone-built and draped with creepers, the *Mallyan Spout Hotel*, with
fine moorland views, takes its name from the fairylike waterfall dropping
through trees behind it. The public rooms are comfortably furnished,
with big open fires in the lounges; the dining room looks across the
woodland gardens; the food is first class. Home-grown vegetables are
used, and guests are often served with Yorkshire specialities such as
Goathland Broth and local game, though Continental dishes turn up,
too; also 'something late at night' if you want it. The restaurant is closed
at lunchtime but there is a good variety of hot and cold snacks in the bar/
lounge. For the active, walking the moorland paths is the thing, but
there is also fishing on the river Esk, shooting on the moors, or golf at
Whitby or near-by Ganton; for the less energetic, a ride on the steam
trains running through Newtondale Valley. A car would be an advantage for exploring further afield. (*Barbara Wolstenholme*)

Open: all year except 4–28 January.
Rooms: 18 double, 4 single—13 with bath or shower, all with TV.
Three lounges; cocktail bars and public bar. Half-acre of garden; sauna
and Health Club with plunge bath, solarium; fishing in near-by lake.
Terms: B & B: from £4.50; dinner: from £3.75.
November–May (excluding Bank Holidays) bargain rates;
also special mid-week rates during June.

GRASMERE, Cumbria

Beck Allans Hotel   *Telephone:* Grasmere (096 65) 329

A friendly, unpretentious private hotel in the centre of Grasmere, but
set in a large attractive garden at the bottom of which flows Words-
worth's favourite river, the Rothay. Beverley and Kay Yates have been
running *Beck Allans* for the past seven years, but it has had a faithful
following of Lakeland addicts dating back many years before their
arrival. Some use it as a centre for touring the district, others come back
from a wet day on the fells soaked to the skin and make good use of hot

baths and drying facilities. When the hotel is full, as it is for much of the season, both the lounge and the dining room tend to be a bit crowded. No television, but one correspondent said she regarded this as an asset in a small hotel as it makes for a more sociable and friendly atmosphere in the evenings. Substantial packed lunches (8op.) only, available midday. The variety and quality of the evening meal is praised, also the very generous helpings. (*Eunice Banks, D. C. Saunders, J. Attwood, F. W. Tonge*)

Open: end March–early November.
Rooms: 9 double, 2 single—3 with bath.
Lounge, bar; an acre of gardens bordered by the river Rothay.
No dogs.
Terms: half board: £11.40; meals: £3.20.

White Moss House   *Telephone:* Grasmere (096 65) 295
Rydal Water

Two stone cottages overlooking Rydal Water have been converted into an exceptionally agreeable small hotel. The restaurant, which has received accolades from other Guides, is very popular with the gourmets of the district, but *White Moss* pleases as a hotel in its own right, not simply as a lodging after a five-course culinary experience.

'My favourite hotel is this home of Jean and Arthur Butterworth, who epitomise English old-fashioned hospitality at its best. The house has so many personal touches: literature to read, maps of the area to assist, sewing kits, plenty of well-placed lights, bric-à-brac, etc., and extremely comfortable beds. The wood panelling shines, the floors sparkle, the linen is crisp and the brass and silver reflecting. Plenty of hot water to hand at all times of the day, and warm rooms. But it is the fare that is so appealing—served, more often than not, with items freshly picked that afternoon out of the garden. Good food, cooked with love, care and attention.' (*Doris Raby*)

Open: April–October.
Rooms: 5—2 with bath.
Lounge; garden with views.
Terms (exclusive of VAT):   B & B: £12.00.

GRETA BRIDGE, Rokeby, Nr Barnard Castle, North Yorkshire

The Morritt Arms Hotel   *Telephone:* Whorlton (083 37) 232

'First, the associations: the hotel stands almost on the site of a Roman encampment; the graceful single-arched bridge spanning the river Greta close by, was made famous by Cotman and Turner; Rokeby Hall, loved by Sir Walter Scott, lies between the Greta and the Tees, and the hotel overlooks Rokeby Park; Dickens arrived at Greta Bridge in 1838. But *The Morritt Arms* deserves commendation for more than setting and name-dropping. It is a handsome Georgian building fronting on to the main road near the bridge, with fine river views. Private fishing can be arranged for guests. The large lounge-cum-hall is cheerful with flowers and good furnishings; a separate TV room ensures that not everybody need look at it. The Dickens Bar is decorated with paintings by Gilroy of Dickensian characters. The proprietors have worked enthusiastically and hard to bring it to its present high standard. They serve food that is a long way beyond merely acceptable, and put themselves out to make something memorable of a visit.' (*Diana Petry;* also *Meg Edenborough*)

Open: all year.
Rooms: 19 double, 5 single—14 with bath or shower, and tea-making facilities.
Lounge, TV room, Dickens Bar; 2 acres of grounds, including a play area for children, with swings etc.; fishing in the river Greta, 100 yds from the hotel.
Terms: B & B: £8.50; dinner: from £3.75.
Mini-weekends, October to end April.

GULVAL, Nr Penzance, Cornwall

Trevaylor   *Telephone:* Penzance (0736) 2882

The location of this 18th-century granite-built house is attractive: out-side and above the Penzance scrum, with fine views across to Mount's Bay. A former manor house, it keeps something of the atmosphere: rooms are large, some furnished with antiques; the dining room is panelled; open fires brighten chilly evenings; there is a liberal use of fresh flowers. You would need a car here to get farther afield, but walkers will enjoy the Cornish cliff path, exploring remote sea coves, bird-watching, riding, fishing, golf, and the little Minack Theatre—all are reasonably handy. Good food (half board only) is served, using fresh produce from the vegetable and fruit gardens and greenhouse; the packed lunches, we are told, are splendid. As one guest puts it: 'gracious surroundings, good food, and above all, peace and quiet in an area usually a bedlam of tourist "tat" and traffic jams'. (*D. G. M. Jones, David W. Langley*)

Open: Easter–October.
Rooms: 5 double, 3 single—4 with bath or shower.
Two lounges (1 with TV), bar. Ten acres of lawns and beech woods. The sea, 2 miles away.
Dogs by prior arrangement.
Terms (exclusive of service):   B & B: £5.60; dinner: from £3.25.

Details of amenities vary according to the information—or lack of it—supplied by hotels in response to our questionnaires. The fact that lounges or bars or gardens are not mentioned must not be taken to mean that a hotel lacks them.

HATHERLEIGH, Devon

The George Hotel *Telephone:* Hatherleigh (083 781) 454

'A charming old thatched coaching inn, well placed in the central square of this small market town in lovely unspoiled countryside between Dartmoor and the north coast of Devon. The building dates from 1450, when it started life as a monks' retreat house. The atmosphere of an old hostelry has been retained, with a cobbled courtyard, plenty of oak panelling and venerable furniture. The bedrooms, on the other hand, are well equipped with modern facilities, and the hotel also has its own private swimming pool. Mary and Martin Giles are mine hosts, and cheerfully meet the needs of guests with good meals—at odd hours if necessary.' (*Penelope Turing*)

Open: all year.
Rooms: 10 double, 3 single—2 with bath or shower.
Two lounges (1 with TV), 2 bars; ½-acre of grounds with swimming pool. Riding, golf, tennis, shooting and fishing available near by. North Devon coast, 20 miles; Dartmoor, 7 miles; Exmoor, 20 miles.
Terms (excluding VAT):   B & B: £6.50; lunch: £1.80; dinner: £3.00.

HAWKRIDGE, Nr Dulverton, Somerset

Tarr Steps Hotel *Telephone:* Winsford (064 385) 293

Very much a hotel for country pursuits, the *Tarr Steps*, formerly the Georgian rectory of Hawkridge, lies beside the river Barle, on which it has 3½ miles of trout and salmon fishing, limited to six rods daily to prevent overcrowding. Guests' horses and dogs are accommodated, and pony-trekking and hacks are available near by. The Tarr Steps, from which the hotel takes its name, is a rough stone clapper bridge, owned by the National Trust and possibly of Bronze Age origin, which crosses the river opposite the hotel drive. Above the Steps is a wide ford giving safe paddling for children in normal low water. Wild life is prolific: deer occasionally come right down to the hotel, woodpeckers nest in the garden, buzzards hover overhead.

'The atmosphere is that of a leisurely and beautifully organised country house. There is a blessed absence of television. Nobody shouts, nothing is strident. The staff are friendly without being too familiar. Paul Hulme and his wife have made many changes since they took over in 1974. Rooms have been redesigned and redecorated, and more single rooms provided; further improvements are planned. Mrs Hulme is a Cordon Bleu cook, and the food is *superb*. Breakfast is immense, and early morning tea is a huge pot containing at least nine cups. Lunch is bar snacks —well, they call it bar snacks, but it is all one wants to eat. Dinner is a gourmet experience served impeccably by candlelight. A typical menu might start with a choice of home-made soup with wine, home-made

34

pâté, mushroom gratinée en scallop, or whitebait; main course: boeuf bourguignon, trout with kümmel, baby chicken in wine, veal chops with mushrooms; the sweet trolley is loaded with syllabub, soufflés, vacherin, hazelnut meringue, etc. The wine list runs to *cru classé* claret and vintage port by the bottle or by the glass. And excellent coffee.' (*J. H. Keen*)

Open: all year; but fully from March to November; in winter, at weekends only.

Rooms: 11 double, 3 single—5 with bath.

Sitting room, bar (no TV); 8 acres of grounds and gardens. Fishing (fly fishing only—salmon and trout) on the river Barle; shooting over 500 acres of privately-owned land; hunting—stags, foxes, otters; riding and trekking (the hotel has its own stables); river bathing, 100 yards; sea bathing, $\frac{1}{2}$-hour by car.

Dogs not allowed in hotel, but kennels available.

Terms: B & B: £7.20; light lunches from the bar, except Sunday; lunch: £2.90; dinner: from £3.75.

HOPTON CASTLE, Nr Craven Arms, Shropshire

Lower House Country Lodge   *Telephone:* Bucknell (054 74) 352

'*The Lodge* is in an area of great natural beauty on the edge of the Chu Forest in Welsh border country: splendid for walking, and an excellent area for birds. The proprietors are John and Sally Dann who, having had enough of London (John was an executive with British Steel and Sally was a nurse) bought *The Lodge* in a state of total disrepair, rebuilding it as faithfully as they could, and with great success, to the original style of the black-and-white Tudor houses of that region, but with the modern requirements of a small hotel.

'We have now stayed at *The Lodge* on four occasions. The particular attraction for my wife and me is the way the Danns run the hotel as their home, with the guests staying with them as friends. The standard of cooking, done by Sally Dann, is very high, of good quality and quite enormous helpings. At our last stay, for example, we were given one day pissaladière, fillet steak with mushrooms, braised leeks, creamed artichokes and anna potatoes, and walnut torte with fresh pears and cream; and on another day, sale, salmon in cream, tournedos, asparagus tips, dolmas and parisienne potatoes, and pavlova with fresh fruit and cream. There is no choice, which we have found, both here and elsewhere, to be far more satisfactory than over-extending in trying to provide a variety. The general atmosphere of *The Lodge* is one of quiet and complete relaxation. In our experience, the place is a gem.' (*Mr and Mrs E. J. H. Lloyd; also Molly and Ann Childs, Anthony Clatworthy, Roger Smithells*)

Open: all year except January.

Rooms: 4 double.

Two lounges (1 with TV); 2 acres of garden.

Terms (excluding VAT): B & B: £6.50; dinner: £3.00
Weekend breaks: 1 November–31 March.

HORTON-CUM-STUDLEY, Oxfordshire

Studley Priory   *Telephone:* Stanton St John (086 735) 203

Some people use *Studley Priory* as a convenient, comfortable and very peaceful base from which to explore Oxford. Others—nature lovers in particular—are drawn by Boarstall Duck Decoy and Nature Reserve, Bernwood Forest, and Shabbington Wood, all within walking distance of the hotel, and offering exceptional rewards to bird-watchers. The manager, Jeremy Parke, is himself an enthusiastic naturalist, and keen to offer his guests advice and suggestions as to walks and viewing platforms. The hotel started life in 1184 as a Benedictine priory, but its present incarnation is that of a Cotswold-stone Elizabethan manor, dating from the 16th century, with some Victorian additions. It stands in its own secluded grounds, with fine views towards Blenheim Palace and the Chilterns. Its public rooms have a distinctly manorial air, with coats-of-arms, Jacobean panelling, huge open log fires, and some fine antique furnishing. Guests tend to be middle-aged, and children might feel slightly awed by the atmosphere. The restaurant offers decent *table d'hôte* (generous helpings) or a wide and ambitious choice on the *à la carte*; extensive wine list. You can make tea or coffee in your own rooms —mostly very spacious and some with four-posters—but a full English breakfast (no Continental nonsense!) is served downstairs. Friendly and obliging staff. (*Evelyn Davis*)

Open: all year.
Rooms: 12 double, 8 single—15 with bath or shower; all with telephone and tea-making facilities.
Residents' lounge, bar, conference room; 13 acres of lawns and woodland; tennis, clay-pigeon shooting.
Terms (excluding VAT): B & B: £9.10; dinner: £3.50.
Winter breaks, October to March.

HOVINGHAM, Yorkshire

Worsley Arms Hotel   *Telephone:* Hovingham (065 382) 234

A pleasant small family-run hotel, formerly a Georgian coaching inn, in a peaceful village in good touring country: York, the North Yorkshire moors, Ampleforth and Castle Howard are all within easy reach. Hovingham is famous for its cricket, and the Cricket Room is full of nostalgic photographs of great Yorkshire cricketers who have played locally. The owners and staff offer the kind of personal service that is becoming rarer—cleaning shoes left outside bedrooms, for instance. The cooking is well above the regional standard. (*Emily White*)

Open: all year.
Rooms: 11 double, 3 single—all with bath.
Large residents' lounge, public lounge, Cricket Room (with TV); ½-acre garden with croquet lawn; river fishing near by.
Terms: B & B: £6.75; lunch: £2.30; dinner: from £4.00.
Winter breaks, November to March. Occasional coach parties.

KINGHAM, Nr Chipping Norton, Oxfordshire

The Mill Hotel
Telephone: Kingham (060 871) 255

If you want to get right off the beaten track in the heart of the Cotswolds, *The Mill* should be the answer. Formerly a mill and bakehouse, this wholly traditional village inn, mainly of the 17th century, is truly rural, a mile off the B4450 between Chipping Norton and Stow-on-the-Wold. Downstairs is full of beams and generous open fireplaces. Upstairs, there are small but thoroughly comfortable bedrooms with lovely views. (*J. M. Cullington*)

Open: all year.
Rooms: 10 double, 1 single—2 with bath.
Lounge bar, residents' lounge (with TV), coffee lounge; 7 acres of grounds and gardens with stream.
Terms (excluding service): B & B: £5.75; Chef's Bar Lunch: £1.00; half board: £8.50.
Winter breaks (2 days minimum), 1 November–end February): half board: £8.20.

KING HARRY FERRY, Nr Truro, Cornwall

King Harry Hotel
Telephone: Devoran (0872) 862202

'An enlarged farmhouse, all in style, with low ceilings. The dining room has wooden tables, high-backed, wooden, rush-bottomed chairs, flowers on every table, and china I want to pinch and take home. It looks over sycamore and oak tree-dotted fields sloping down to the end of an estuary which meets the sea on the horizon ten miles away. The only sounds are from the birds and a herd of cows. At night I heard owls. During the three days I was there I walked in the woods packed with rhododendrons. I met three persons. The day I arrived, so did two doctors, grey-faced with overwork, with nervous hands. After three days of absolute quiet—no bedroom telephones—we were calm and human again with colour in our cheeks. I illegally peeped into the kitchen one evening. It was shining and modern like a *House & Gardens* private house spread.'

So writes a civil servant, who has asked to remain anonymous 'as there is a rule about these things'. (Can that be true? How monstrous.) Other visitors, named below, are equally enthusiastic about the idyllic features of this hotel recently taken over (it was previously called The Trelissick Home Farm Hotel) by Ted Kirkham and his Swedish wife, Margaretha, who have undertaken major improvements. The location is outstanding: on the tip of one of the little inlets of the Falmouth estuary, within National Trust park and farmlands and bordering on the National Trust Trelissick Gardens. The interior aspects of the hotel also receive warm tributes: the flair shown in the bedroom furnishings and in the design of a delightful bar leading out to a walled cobbled courtyard. The quality of the food is also praised; in summer Margaretha Kirkham serves reasonably-priced Swedish Smorgasbord in the courtyard. Overseas visitors are especially welcome: French, German and Swedish are spoken fluently. (*Graham Fulkes, Mr and Mrs R. P. McDougall, Mrs B. Osberg*)

Open: all year except January.
Rooms: 14 double, 1 single—7 with bath or shower, all with tea-making facilities.
Lounge (colour TV), bar, games room. 360 acres of National Trust parkland. The hotel adjoins Trelissick Gardens (open to the public March–October); overlooks the estuary of the river Fal with access to small rocky tidal beach with safe bathing; facilities for boating, fishing (river and sea), golf, surfing, etc. all within easy reach.
No dogs.
Terms (excluding service):   B & B: £9.00; light lunches and bar snacks; dinner: £2.50.
    Reduced rates for 3 nights or more, for children, for weekend or mid-week breaks, in spring, autumn and winter.

KINTBURY, Nr Newbury, Berkshire

Dundas Arms   *Telephone:* Kintbury (048 85) 263

'One of the good things about Kintbury is that you can get to it down the M4 in about 1½ hours from the centre of London, even on a Friday evening. And when you get there, you're as far removed from the big city as though you'd been travelling for days. Kintbury is a peaceful village, near Hungerford and Newbury. There are quiet country lanes, a few local shops, the church and the river. *The Dundas Arms* is a pub—flanked by the banks of the Kennet and Avon canal and an undisturbing railway line, level crossing and bridge. You can walk for miles along the banks of the canal, past magnificent old houses, lonely fishermen, and accompanied all the way—if you take enough bread with you—by the mallard population of the town (which probably outnumbers the residents). The pub (you can't really call it a hotel) has a low modern extension at the back with bedrooms and attached bathrooms. When we arrived, we were dubious from the outside as to what to expect of the standard—but throw open those bedroom doors and a little scene of rural bliss awaits. The far walls are all glass, with doors that open on to a narrow concrete patio that slopes down to a quiet backwater with woods on the opposite bank. The ducks made sure we were looked after, morning, noon and night. There is a tiny lounge on the other side of the public bar, but no one seemed to use it, and each bedroom has a kettle and tea things as well as room to move around, and the comfort of a boudoir. You have to walk through the pub—or out of the side door and in at the front to get to the dining room—a velvety, formal room with the same approach towards the food. We ate splendidly of home-made bread, dark green spinach soup with a sudden splash of cream in the centre, superior rack of lamb and difficult-to-choose sweets from the trolley. You can't hear the pub noise from the bedrooms and you can ask for a television in your room. A good idea for Londoners who want a short weekend without driving too far.' (*Susan Grossman*)

Open: all year.
Rooms: 6 double—all with bath; tea-making facilities; TV available. Small lounge, pub/bar. The hotel adjoins the Kennet and Avon canal; tow-path walks, fishing.
Terms: B & B: £8.40; dinner only: £4.60–£6.50 (closed Sunday and Monday).

LACOCK, Nr Chippenham, Wiltshire

The Sign of the Angel   *Telephone:* Lacock (024 973) 230
6 Church St

'Lacock was a flourishing wool town in the middle ages. It is now a captivating village of small, dignified houses and cottages, mainly of the 17th and 18th century. The village, praise be, is now in the care of the National Trust. Lacock Abbey (open to view) is still inhabited by the family which acquired it as a private dwelling in the reign of Henry VIII. William Henry Fox Talbot, inventor of photography in the 1830s, lived here. A splendid 16th-century barn at the Abbey gates houses a fascinating museum of early photography—a memorial to his work. *The Sign of the Angel* is not a pub but a licensed restaurant with bedroom accommodation, housed in a 14th-century half-timbered building with a pleasant garden running down to a rivulet. Mr and Mrs Levis, their son John, and his wife, Lorna, are the cheerful family team who run the place—Mrs Levis and Lorna in charge of the kitchen; Mr Levis and John in the two-room restaurant. The food is home cooking at its superb best and beautifully served. Vegetables are fresh and varied; sauces and gravies encouraging. Enough panelling, stout oak beams, sloping floors, bewildering stairways to satisfy any romantic's dream of Tudor England. An admirable overnight stopping place to or from the far West Country, and a good base for a longer stay to explore the unsung beauties of Wiltshire.' (*Roger Smithells*)

Open: all year.
Rooms: 6 double, 1 single.
Lounge; garden.
Terms (excluding service):   B & B: £7.00; half board (weekly): £60.00; meals: £4.50–£6.00.

LAMORNA COVE, Nr Penzance, Cornwall

Lamorna Cove Hotel   *Telephone:* Mousehole (073 673) 411/564

'Lamorna Cove lies at the foot of a long, leafy valley on the sheltered southern coast of the Penwith peninsula—the rugged toe of Cornwall running from Penzance to Land's End. Here Cornish magic is at its most primitive and powerful. On moorland heights loom huge, wind-carved boulders and ruined tin mine towers. On the north coast, savage seas batter formidable cliffs. Lamorna Cove itself is peaceful—a deep, rocky inlet with a little sand at low tide. The famous open-air theatre on the cliffs is at neighbouring Porthcurno. Penzance and St Ives are the big centres. The fishing villages of Newlyn and Mousehole, the white sands of Sennen Cove, the cliffscapes of Gurnard's Head and Zennor are delights near by. You can forget Land's End.

'*The Lamorna Cove Hotel* is a small luxury hideout created by the Bolton family from old buildings—originally part chapel, part quarry owner's home. It stands back, above the cove, in five acres of natural garden, with glorious seaward views from the picture windows of the large, split-level lounge and from cosy bedrooms. There are many facilities of a good modern hotel; but the character of the old buildings has been preserved. Each day's menu is sensibly limited to a few dishes very well cooked. Venison steak in the chef's secret sauce is a traditional speciality. The seafood is good; Cornish crab soup and grilled red mullet with parsley butter are particularly recommended. Peace, privacy and good living in a wildly beautiful setting.' (*Roger Smithells*)

Open: all year.
Rooms: 19 double, 2 single, 2 family—12 with bath, 4 with shower.
Lounge, sun-terrace, bar, colour TV, sauna; 5 acres of gardens; heated outdoor swimming pool.
Terms (excluding VAT):   B & B: £9.50; half board (weekly): £105.00;
          lunch: £2.75–£3.25; dinner: £4.00–£5.25.
          Cheaper rates for off-season weekends.

LASTINGHAM, North Yorkshire

Lastingham Grange Country House Hotel
          Telephone: Lastingham (075 15) 345

'My husband and I have stayed here many times over the last eleven years, at first with our three children (the youngest six when we first went), and have never failed to enjoy it. It is a true English country house hotel, dating back to the 17th century, run by a family, and situated in a charming village within yards of superb walking country— the road peters out at *The Grange* and becomes a bridle path stretching across the moors to Rosedale. It is very quiet—a blessing, we think— with a residential licence, but no bar and no TV. The menus are limited but usually excellent. Lunches and dinners are served at set times. Most of the double rooms are very pleasant; the single rooms can be rather hot in warm weather as they are over the kitchen quarters. Although the average age of the guests is middle to elderly, children are always welcome and great kindness was always shown to ours.' (*Margaret Fell*)

Open: Easter–mid November.
Rooms: 11 double, 4 single—4 with bath.
Large L-shaped lounge; 10 acres of grounds, with 2 acres of ornamental gardens. Fishing, riding and golf near by; sea (Scarborough), 20 miles. No dogs.
Terms (excluding service):   B & B: £7.50; half board (minimum 3 days): £11.50.

LONDON

Bailey's Hotel
140 Gloucester Rd, SW7

Telephone: (01) 373 8131

'Purpose-built towards the end of the last century, this building is now "preserved" and cannot be demolished. It has undergone careful modernisation and where possible, existing panelling, furniture and decorations are being restored rather than replaced with modern equivalents of the ersatz-plastic type. Courteous, attentive service.' (*John Duerden*)

Open: all year.
Rooms: 75 double, 75 single, some with bath/shower, telephone and radio.
Lounge, TV lounge, 3 bars.
Terms (excluding VAT):   B & B: £11.50.

Cordova House Hotel
14–16 Craven Hill, Lancaster Gate, W2

Telephone: (01) 723 1065/6; 262 0111

'Quietly situated just off the Bayswater Road, near Hyde Park and within short walking distance of Paddington Station. Family owned, it has the atmosphere and friendliness of a country hotel, even possessing a small garden. Well tended and, reassuringly, they seem to keep the same staff. The restaurant serves a good 3-course evening meal at a reasonable price; good value.' (*R. Tucker*)

Open: all year.
Rooms: 57 double, 3 single—with bath or shower, telephone, radio, TV on request; baby-listening service.
Lift; sitting room, TV room, Victorian-style cocktail bar; garden at the back for light refreshments and drinks.
Terms (excluding service and VAT):   B & B: £7.25.

Eden Plaza Hotel   *Telephone:* (01) 370 6111
68-9 Queens Gate, SW7

Modern hotel built in 1972 behind preserved outer walls, a few minutes from Hyde Park and Kensington Gardens, and West London Air Terminal. Noise suppressed by double glazing. Well spoken of for its general air of comfort, warm welcome, excellent service, decent food and moderate prices. '*The Eden Plaza* has become our home in London.' (*J. L. Iles*)

Open: all year.
Rooms: 35 double, 27 single—all with bath, telephone, radio and automatic message system; TV on request; double glazing.
Lift; lounge, coffee lounge, cocktail bar/lounge. Sauna, massage and solarium rooms with qualified staff.
Terms: B & B: £9.00.

Portobello Hotel   *Telephone:* (01) 727 2777
22 Stanley Gardens, W11   *Telex:* 21879/25247

The nearest thing to a Bohemian hotel in London, unconventionally friendly, a stone's throw from the weekend Portobello Road Flea Market. Rooms at the back overlook an agreeable public garden, though 'not for the use of guests'. The decor is Victorian with modern touches.

'When we lived in W10 we spent our wedding anniversaries in W11 at the *Portobello*. The attraction was the *round*, really round, bed in the round room; all-white, the ideal Honeymoon Suite. Now they have a new novelty, a romantic four-poster—and an exotic, multi-mirrored, adjoining bath and shower room. We give our unhesitating and rapturous seal of approval. The four-poster has the finest working surface in London! The sense of having embarked on an erotic adventure at the *Portobello* is aided by the lack of an intrusive Room Service. Although a full English breakfast, meals and drinks, are served in the Restaurant Bar downstairs, each room is equipped with a small fridge full of goodies. The *Portobello* understands the importance of privacy—and of catering to the needs of love.' (*Patrick Hughes and Molly Parkin*)

Open: all year.
Rooms: 26—all with bath/shower, telephone, radio and colour TV, fridge, coffee-making facilities.
Lift; lounge, restaurant bar.
Terms (excluding service and VAT):   B & B: £10.00.

All entries in this book are unsolicited testimonials from members of the public. But we received many fewer nominations for city hotels than for those elsewhere, and decided to make an exception in the one case of London, and offer in fairly brief form some editorial suggestions, given below, to supplement the contributions above. If there is a demand for similar sug-

gestions for other tourist cities—say for Madrid or Athens or Bruges—we shall enlarge this service next time. But we would prefer not to, and hope that readers will be as forthcoming in recommending good hotels in cities as in country areas or in coastal resorts.

Brown's Hotel
21-4 Dover St, W1

Telephone: (01) 493 6020
Telex: 28686

127 rooms and suites.
A decidedly traditional hotel, as central as you could wish, but retaining the air of Henry Jamesian good taste. Country folk still use it as their town base. Discreet comfort, elegant furnishings, expert service. There are quiet rooms on the inner court.
Terms: B & B: £20.50.

The Connaught Hotel
Carlos Place, W1

Telephone: (01) 499 7070

105 rooms and suites.
At the top of the price scale, but with one of the great restaurants of London, intimate and welcoming public rooms, and simply lovely bedrooms. The platonic idea of a city hotel.
Terms: Room only (excluding service): from £19.00; all meals à la carte.

Dukes Hotel
St James's Place, SW1

Telephone: (01) 491 4840
Telex: 28283

50 rooms.
In a tiny courtyard, tucked between St James's and Green Park. Opened in the Edwardian era and has preserved that atmosphere. Guest rooms are named for historic dukes and decorated appropriately.
Terms: B & B (excluding service and VAT): £18.50.

Durrant's Hotel
26-32 George St, W1

Telephone: (01) 935 8131

85 rooms.
Immediately behind the Wallace Collection and fifty yards from Maryle-bone High Street, one of the pleasantest village streets in central London, this family-owned Regency-fronted hotel maintains a reputation for traditional service. Not quite as central as Brown's, but considerably cheaper; it has the latter's air of quiet good breeding.
Terms: B & B (excluding VAT): £9.50.

Most hotels have reduced rates out of season and for children. For details, you will need to write to the hotel direct.

Ebury Court   *Telephone:* (01) 730 8147
26 Ebury St, SW1

38 rooms.
A small, highly personal hotel, within a few minutes' walk of Victoria
Station, but the furthest remove from a station doss-house. Privately
owned, and it shows in many welcoming touches alike in the intimate base-
ment restaurant, the friendly lounges on the ground floor, and in the smallish
bedrooms upstairs.
Terms: B & B: £12.00.

The Fielding Hotel   *Telephone:* (01) 836 8305/6/7/8
4 Broad Court, Bow St, WC2

26 rooms.
A tiny little private hotel in a pedestrian alley between Drury Lane and
Bow Street, with the Royal Opera House just across the road. Not on any
tourist map, but rumoured to be where the Foreign Office puts up diplomats
visiting incognito.
Terms: B & B: £8.25.

The Ritz   *Telephone:* (01) 493 8181
Piccadilly, W1   *Telex:* 267200

100 rooms and suites.
Hyper-elegant in all respects. Special features include the most beautiful
restaurant in London overlooking Green Park, and the fountained Palm
Court for afternoon teas. Wonderfully spacious, both on the ground floors
and in the bedrooms and suites above. Superbly unobtrusive service. Double
glazing defeats Piccadilly traffic.
Terms: B & B: £20.00.

LONG MELFORD, Suffolk

The Bull Hotel   *Telephone:* Long Melford (078 725) 494

The Bull has long been a showplace inn in one of Suffolk's more celebrated showplace villages—with other equally ravishing villages such as
Dedham, Lavenham, Clare and East Bergholt within easy motoring
distance. A handsome half-timbered house dating back to the mid 15th
century, it stands foursquare on the village green opposite the magnificent church of the same period. The decor is wholly traditional—
masses of great old beams, huge open fireplaces, and period furniture—
but the conveniences are modern. The chef, surprisingly in such an olde
English hostelry, is Italian, and the restaurant is strong on Italian dishes.
The hotel receives special praise for the exceptional welcome and help-
fulness of its staff. (*Joan Rix*)

Open: all year.

Rooms: 25—all with bath, telephone, radio and TV, and tea-making facilities.

Three sitting rooms and bars.

Dogs at the Manager's discretion.

Terms: B & B: £9.00; meals: from £3.65.
Winter breaks from November to March. Occasional block bookings.

LONG SUTTON, Langport, Somerset

Devonshire Arms Hotel   *Telephone:* Long Sutton (045 824) 271

'Touring Norfolk, Essex, Hertfordshire and Somerset on holiday, we stayed at many three-starred hotels. *The Devonshire Arms* had only two stars, but was the most comfortable and had the best service, food and hospitality of all we visited. None of the rooms had bathrooms *en suite*, but with two bathrooms and seven bedrooms, there was no problem. It is an 18th-century inn in a small village, set on the green in lovely countryside, and central for visiting many places of interest—Longleat, Stourhead, Bath, Wells, etc.' (*T. R. and B. E. Price*)

Open: all year (except Christmas Day).

Rooms: 6 double, 2 single—all with radio and tea-making facilities.

Residents' lounge, cocktail bar, Sutton Bar; baby-listening; weekly dances. One-acre gardens; coarse fishing, riding and golf near by; 5 miles from Fleet Air Arm Museum at Yeovilton.

Dogs at the management's discretion.

Terms: B & B: £6.75; half board: £9.10; Concorde Dinner (the menu served on Concorde's inaugural flight to Bahrein): £3.50 (pre-booked).
Weekend or mid-week breaks: £12.50–£15.00 for 2 days, half board.

LOWESWATER, Cumbria

Scale Hill Hotel   *Telephone:* Lorton (090 085) 232

Formerly a 17th-century coaching inn, and before that a farmhouse, this secluded hotel between Crummock and Loweswater, is in one of the least trippery parts of the Lake District and has spectacular views of lakes and fells. For those who don't fancy walking, there is swimming, rowing, or fishing (for trout, perch and pike) on the lakes. A pony-trekking centre is a mile away, and there are two golf courses within eight miles. The hotel is run with personal diligence by its resident owners, Mr and Mrs Thompson. Salmon and duck are often on the menu, and Mrs Thompson's range of salads and her sweets come in for particular praise. Bedrooms are centrally heated, but also have electric fires and electric blankets. There is no nightlife, not even TV or radio—

a feature much appreciated by two of the enthusiastic nominators who had derived special pleasure from after-dinner conversations. (*Rosemary Rigg, Dr B. Sandler, A. Sennett*)

Open: end March to early November.
Rooms: 15 double, 5 single—7 with bath or shower.
Four lounges, small bar counter; ½-acre gardens. Fishing, swimming, boating, pony-trekking, golf near by.
Dogs not allowed in public rooms.
Terms: half board: from £12; meals: £2.50–£4.50.

LUDLOW, Shropshire

The Feathers   *Telephone:* Ludlow (0584) 2919

'*The Feathers*, with its splendid half-timbered and pargeted façade is, of course, a showpiece of Tudor architecture, and would probably survive as a hotel by being simply an ancient monument and photographers' delight in a town rich in interest and historical associations. But the management have sensibly sought to fill their marvellous old frame with everything a guest could require by way of modern convenience. My wife and I had a room with bath, and she was delighted to find a reproduction four-poster in which to sleep. The hotel stands at the centre of Ludlow on a main road with risk of traffic noise, though Ludlow bypass should be open in 1978, and double-glazing of the front rooms helps a good deal. The sense of pride which the management has in the hotel runs through: there was a varied menu supported by good English cooking, and a comfortable bar which brings in discerning locals. The whole thing reminded me of a Spanish *parador*—an ancient monument with guests.' (*R. H. Stockton; also Major John Meade*)

Open: all year.
Rooms: 24 double, 5 single—26 with bath and TV, all with telephone, tea-making facilities and baby-listening service.
Three lounges, 2 bars.
Dogs not allowed in bedrooms.
Terms: B & B: £9.50.
Two-day breaks throughout the year, £26 per person. One coach booking a month.

LYNDHURST, Hampshire

The Crown Hotel   *Telephone:* Lyndhurst (042 128) 2722

'The capital of the New Forest', as Lyndhurst likes to be called, is an admirable centre for visitors. And *The Crown*, though the present gabled building in the main street is only a century old, has had a long tradition of welcoming travellers—there has been an inn on the site for at least

400 years. The present owners maintain the tradition of service. There is an attractive restaurant overlooking a small garden which is reckoned by local gourmets to serve the best food in this part of the Forest; the cooking has also won the hotel several national and international awards. But the quality of the hotel is not confined to its cuisine: 'On our first visit, we had Room 35 with bathroom. On our departure, we were asked how we liked the room, which was quiet and overlooked the garden. We said it was excellent. Each time since, without asking, we have had Room 35. There is an atmosphere of friendliness about the place which is hard to define, but which makes a stay very congenial.' (*C. N. Maplethorpe*)

Open: all year.
Rooms: 34 double, 14 single—all with bath, telephone, colour TV and radio.
Lift; residents' lounge, coffee lounge, bar; small garden. Golf (free at local golf course), riding, hunting, tennis near by; sea, 8 miles. Dogs not allowed in the restaurant.
Terms: B & B: £7.75; dinner: £3.50; dinner dance on Saturday nights.

MALVERN WELLS, Worcestershire

The Cottage in the Wood
Holywell Rd

Telephone: Malvern (068 45) 3487

'The whaleback range of the Malvern Hills soars out of the flat Severn plain, a dramatic eastern outpost of the Welsh mountains and rightly designated an area of outstanding beauty. From its high point at the Worcester Beacon there are incredible views over countless counties. The Malverns make a fine touring base for exploring the gentle beauties of Herefordshire, Worcestershire and the lush Welsh borderlands. There are enchanting black-and-white villages and mellow market towns. Hereford, Tewkesbury, Ross-on-Wye, Gloucester, Stratford-upon-Avon, Ledbury and Cheltenham are local centres for sightseeing, shopping, or leisurely ambling.
   '*The Cottage in the Wood* is an eyrie perched high on wooded slopes at Malvern Wells with an eagle's eye view over the vast Severn Valley and distant Cotswolds. It is a fairly grand cottage being, in fact, a cosily elegant Georgian dower house, with additional bedrooms in the recently converted Coach House, 200 yards from the main building. The hotel has the air of a private home with fine period furniture and flowers abounding. Bedrooms in the Cottage are pretty, stylishly individual; those in the Coach House are modern with huge picture windows and terraces or balconies. The food is good and imaginative, the proprietor, Michael Ross, being himself a distinguished chef and an expert on traditional English fare. The hotel stands in seven acres of natural wood and shrubland. On razor-trimmed lawns in front you can loll in a deck chair and contemplate the infinities of the view until your mind becomes a delicious blank. A soothing hideout of singular charm.' (*Roger Smithells; also Anne Edwards*)

Open: all year, except Christmas.
Rooms: 20 double—17 with bath, all with telephone, radio and colour TV; baby-listening service.
Lounge (no TV), bar; 7 acres of grounds.
No dogs.
Terms (excluding VAT): B & B: £7.50; set meals: £3.70.
Reduced rates for 2-night stays between 7 October and 31 March.

MAWNAN SMITH, Nr Falmouth, Cornwall

Meudon Hotel   *Telephone:* Mawnan Smith (0326) 250541

'Mawnan Smith lies in one of the most lush and sheltered corners of south Cornwall, between the Fal and the Helford rivers. Switchback lanes plunge into wooded valleys and emerge at waterside hamlets or yachtsmen's creeks. Falmouth, with its huge harbour, busy shopping centre and excellent seafood bars, is near by. To the south are the small resorts and sandy coves scattered round The Lizard peninsula.

'*The Meudon* is a stylish country house hotel—an old Cornish mansion on to which has been grafted a wing of sleek modern bedrooms with private bathrooms, and every desirable mod. con. The spacious public rooms are all in the old mansion, a mellow building with mullion windows and massive granite pillars. But the marvel of *Meudon* is its garden—a lush ravine running down to a private sandy beach with enough rock pools to hold any child enthralled. Mimosa, eucalyptus, banana, flame trees and huge tree ferns flourish on *Meudon*'s sub-tropical slopes. The food is as stylish as the hotel; seafood a speciality; fresh lobsters and oysters from the nearby Duchy of Cornwall Oyster Farm are local delicacies on the menu. This is a haven of peace and discreet luxury.' (*Roger Smithells;* also *Brigadier Millman*)

Open: all year.
Rooms: 30 double, 8 single, 4 family—34 with bath, all with TV.
Several lounges (including bridge lounge and TV lounge), conference room. Eight acres of showplace sub-tropical gardens leading down to a private sandy beach with rock pools. Sailing, trout and sea fishing; tennis, golf and riding near by.
Terms: B & B: £17.50; meals: £2.25–£3.50.

MIDDLETON-IN-TEESDALE, Nr Barnard Castle, Co. Durham

Heather Brae Hotel *Telephone:* Middleton-in-Teesdale (083 34) 203

'Middleton-in-Teesdale is a modest market town in the heart of the magnificent North Pennines. A combination of leadminers' tracks and well-signposted farm paths across hill country make this a splendid walking centre. The wild flowers in Upper Teesdale are a marvel. You could get goggle-eyed bird-watching. There are awesome waterfalls. No place for marathon motoring; but within a day's excursion range are the Yorkshire Dales, the Lake District, Hadrian's Wall, Durham and the entrancing Bowes Museum near Barnard Castle.

'*The Heather Brae Hotel* stands on a hillside 1½ miles outside the town with stunning views over woods and moorlands to the high Pennines. First impressions are of a large, undistinguished country house adequately rather than sumptuously appointed. But this no-nonsense place proves more genial than it looks when you join the company in the bar where Mrs Streit presides; more genial still when you have dined, for your host, Dieter Streit (who later joins the company still wearing his cook's hat) turns out to be a chef of international repute who has abandoned the whirl of luxury living to practise his art in the peace of the Pennines. You retire content to your centrally-heated but moderately austere bedroom knowing that fate cannot touch you—you have dined tonight. A place to take bracing walks and return with appetite well whetted for princely meals.' (*Roger Smithells*)

Open: all year.
Rooms: 7 double, 9 single.
Garden; fine walking country around and interesting excursions.
Terms: B & B: £4.95; lunch: from £1.95; dinner: from £2.95.

MILTON DAMEREL, Nr Holsworthy, Devon

Woodford Bridge Hotel   *Telephone:* Milton Damerel (040 926) 252

You will need a fairly detailed map to find the tiny village of Milton Damerel, a mile off the A338 between Holsworthy and Bideford, 11 miles to the north. A car is essential, but it makes an ideal centre for exploring North Devon. *The Woodford Bridge* is a restful away-from-it-all country hotel—a thatched building converted from a 15th-century coaching inn standing in a well-tended garden. The food, reported 'marvellous', is served on fine Royal Doulton china in a pretty dining room. (*W. Davidson*)

Open: all year.
Rooms: 13 double, 4 single—9 with bath or shower, all with radio and baby-listening service.
Two sitting rooms (1 with TV), 2 bars; dances at weekends. Two acres of garden and woodland with the river Torridge running through; 4 miles of fishing water reserved for hotel guests (mainly brown trout, and dry fly only); riding on Exmoor and Dartmoor; 11 miles from the North Devon coast and safe bathing.
Dogs by arrangement, but not in public rooms.
Terms (excluding service and VAT):   B & B: from £7.00; lunch: £2.20; dinner: £3.50; half board (4 days minimum): from £10.
          Off-season rates: October–April.

MORETONHAMPSTEAD, Devon

Manor House Hotel   *Telephone:* Moretonhampstead (064 74) 355

A rather spectacular mock-Jacobean mansion, built in 1907 for the W. H. Smith family. It's set in the middle of Dartmoor, only seven miles from Widecombe-in-the-Moor, where you can enjoy the fun of the famous Fair if you happen to be around on the second Tuesday of September. 'The rooms are spacious, the food is out of this world, the management most attentive, the staff kind and anxious to please. There were guests of all nationalities present last August. I wondered how they had heard of the *Manor House Hotel*. The reply: "We were told that this was the *only* well-run hotel in Britain".' (*Mrs M. E. Polanyi*)

Open: all year.
Rooms: 48 double, 21 single—all with bath, telephone, radio and TV. Lift; 2 lounges, cocktail bar, card room, billiards room; film shows twice weekly during summer; 250 acres of grounds, with 18-hole golf course. The hotel owns fishing rights on the near-by river Teign (salmon and trout). Tennis (2 hard courts), squash court; riding and pony-trekking arranged.
Dogs by arrangement.
Terms (excluding service and VAT):   B & B: from £13.00; half board (minimum 2 days): from £15.00; full board (minimum 2 days): from £20.00.
Reduced rates in winter.

MORETON-IN-MARSH, Gloucestershire

Manor House Hotel   *Telephone:* Moreton-in-Marsh (0608) 50501

The village is pure Cotswold, spread out along the old Roman Fosse Way, and as centrally placed for exploring the region as one could wish. If not as awesomely beautiful as, say, Burford, it is also a great deal less plagued by tourist coaches. Like Burford, it boasts two undeniably good hotels, each built in mellow Cotswold stone and each with its own enthusiastic partisans (see *Redesdale Arms* below). *The Manor House* is the larger and grander of the two, with the main part well over 300 years old, with dormer windows, though there is a new wing discreetly added in 1972 to provide further accommodation and banqueting and conference facilities (the latter only in the off-season). A feature of the hotel is an old Moot Room used by the local merchants in former times to settle their disputes. There is also a much-cherished walled garden. The bedrooms are as comfortably modern as one would expect from a hotel of this class, but with a few less predictable touches: a fresh rose in a vase on the dressing-table, for instance, special soap and shampoo in the bathroom, and the like. (*Doris Dudley*)

Open: all year except 24 December–3 January.

Rooms: 29 double, 8 single—28 with bath, all with telephone, radio and colour TV.

Two lounges (1 with TV), bar; sauna. Four acres of gardens with putting green; riding available near by; Broadway Golf Course, 8 miles. No dogs.

Terms: B & B: £11.50; lunch: from £3.00; dinner: from £4.25; full board (minimum 3 days): £38.00.
Winter weekends (2 nights), November to March, half board: £25.00.

Redesdale Arms Hotel *Telephone:* Moreton-in-Marsh (0608) 50308

'By far the best hotel in the town. It manages to combine its hotel function without driving away the locals from the public bar, where there will be a fire morning and evening throughout the winter. The accommodation is simple: few rooms have baths and none has a telephone, but the beds are comfortable and the rooms well heated. Top class food (particularly the pâtés and roast duck) in the restaurant, and ample breakfast including local bacon and black pudding. Very friendly service, but rather a poor wine list. An excellent stop for a cheap winter weekend, as well as being a haven from the Stratford pilgrims in midsummer. Very English.' (*John Higgins*)

Open: all year.
Rooms: 11 double, 4 single—3 with bath.
Lounge, bars, TV.
No children under 5.
Terms (excluding service): B & B: £7.50; meals: £2.90–£4.55.

MORTEHOE, Nr Woolacombe, North Devon

Castle Rock Hotel *Telephone:* Woolacombe (027 187) 465

'On the North Devon coast, between Ilfracombe and Baggy Point, the tiny village of Mortehoe has its own small bay and is close to the wide and splendid (and safe) sand beach at Woolacombe. There is superb wild cliff scenery. *The Castle Rock Hotel* is at the foot of the village, at the very edge of the sea, with its own path leading to the rocky, turf-covered headland of More Point, owned by the National Trust. A big, spacious seaside hotel of the old kind and in the best sense. Nice bar, generous lounge and dining room, a games room, and big, airy bedrooms with marvellous sea views. Quite good food. Buffet lunch served on the Terrace in fine weather. Personally and cheerfully run by Anthony and Mair Elliot.' (*Penelope Turing*)

Open: 12 May–30 September.
Rooms: 24 double, 6 single—5 with bath, most facing the sea, all with radio; baby-listening services.

Drawing room, hall, TV room, bar, dance and games room, table tennis, bar billiards. Two-acre grounds with putting green. Sea bathing, good walking district.

Terms (excluding service):   full board (weekly): £72.

NEW MILTON, Hampshire

Chewton Glen Hotel   *Telephone:* Highcliffe (042 52) 5341
                                 Telex: 41456

'This charming and luxurious country house hotel of Georgian origins stands at the southern fringe of the New Forest; the stream that now forms the boundary between Dorset and Hampshire runs through the thirty acres of grounds and parkland. *Chewton Glen* achieves a standard of excellence through the personal enthusiasm and vigilance of Martin Skan and his wife who, like all the best hoteliers, combine high management skills with an obvious pleasure in caring for their visitors' well-being. Big log fires burn when days or nights are chilly; the main rooms are spacious and almost outrageously comfortable; the restaurant, softly lit and intimate, with fine linen and silver, blesses its diners with the kind of high quality cooking and imaginative menus, combined with impeccable service, that mark it as outstanding. There is no lift, but there are most elegant staircases to the two upper floors; and there are also ground-floor rooms which open on to the garden terrace. Bedrooms have blissful country views and are delightfully furnished with an impressive care for detail.' (*Diana Petry*)

Open: all year.
Rooms: 42 double, 1 single—all with bath, telephone, radio and colour TV.
Two main lounges, 2 small sitting rooms, bar. Thirty acres of grounds and parkland, with tennis court, heated swimming pool, croquet lawn, putting and badminton. The sea is half a mile away, with safe bathing from shingle beach; the New Forest with its innumerable walks (ponies of course, and deer too) spreads to the north. Fishing, riding and sailing close by; 12 golf courses within a radius of 20 miles.
Children under 7, and dogs, not admitted.
Terms: B & B: £15.25; lunch: from £3.50; dinner: from £5.00.
           Hotel used for conferences during the winter.

OXFORD, Oxfordshire

Eastgate Hotel   *Telephone:* Oxford (0865) 48244
The High

Built at the turn of the century where the original East Gate of the city stood. Victorian origins now well-seasoned with modern comforts. Many rooms face on to Merton Street and are reasonably quiet, and some have views of the dreaming spires. Attractive dining room with well-served meals. 'Recommended for those who want to stay in the centre of Oxford, with good food.' (*John Lister*)

Open: all year.
Rooms: 30 double, 20 single—some with bath, all with telephone, radio and TV, tea and coffee-making facilities; baby-listening service.
Lift; lounge, TV lounge, bars.
Dogs not allowed in public rooms.
Terms: B & B: £7–£9.00.
          Bargain rates for off-season weekends.

PORTLOE, Cornwall

The Lugger Hotel   *Telephone:* Veryan (020 132) 322

'Portloe is a mini-fishing village wedged into a ravine above a rocky cove in South Cornwall's Roseland Peninsula. It is a tiny, peaceful place frequented by painters, bird watchers, botanists and escapists longing to laze in a lovely setting. There is a fine stretch of unspoiled Cornish coast to explore; good shark and sea fishing from nearby St Mawes or Mevagissey; boat trips up the river Fal, and to Frenchman's Creek on the Helford river. *The Lugger Hotel* is a 17th-century inn at the water's edge, once, you may be sure, a smugglers' hideout. It has been transformed by the Powell family into a modestly luxurious retreat without losing its rough-hewn charm. Bright boats line the slipway below the hotel. The dining room, overhanging the rocky beach, practically puts out to sea. There is a snug bar, a sun terrace above the cove, and a long oak-beamed lounge. Fairly plushy bedrooms with private bathrooms, in adjoining cottages, have flower names and decor to match. The food is a pleasant blend of traditional English and Continental cooking. Early-morning and afternoon tea and post-prandial coffee are included in the prices quoted for board. A place to unwind in an authentic Cornish setting. Not suitable for young children.' (*Roger Smithells*)

Open: all year, except 21 December–21 January.
Rooms: 20—14 with bath or shower (6 rooms in annexe).
Lounge (with TV), sun terrace, bar, sauna. Immediate sea and rocky beach.
No children under 12; no dogs.
Terms (excluding service):   B & B: £8.00; lunch from £2.25; dinner: £4.00.

> Details of amenities vary according to the information—or lack of it—supplied by hotels in response to our questionnaires. The fact that lounges or bars or gardens are not mentioned must not be taken to mean that a hotel lacks them.

RAVENSCAR, Nr Scarborough, North Yorkshire

Raven Hall Hotel   *Telephone:* Scarborough (0723) 84353

Magnificently sited 600 feet above sea level, and with spectacular views of coast and moor, this large cheerful family hotel has only one major drawback: there's no beach within easy walking distance. But there are plenty of compensations on the spot for young and old (see below), all included in the weekly terms. For the really energetic, Ravenscar is one end of the celebrated Lyke Wake walk across the moors to Osmotherley, forty miles to the west. But a car is advisable, particularly if you want to visit Robin Hood's Bay and Whitby to the north, or Scarborough, eleven miles to the south. The hotel clearly puts itself out to give all the family a good time. There are laundry facilities and baby-listening devices, and —a compliment to the staff—they never seem to resent the 'little horrors'. The food? 'Very good and very plentiful. It's the first reasonably priced hotel we've been to where my 6-foot, 15-stone husband has been full!' (*Mrs C. Corrigan*)

Open: Easter to early November.
Rooms: 50 double, 10 single—20 with bath, all with radio/intercom and baby-listening service.
Ballroom, 2 lounges (1 with colour TV), 2 bars, billiards room; table tennis, many facilities for children; cinema shows weekly, dancing several nights weekly; conference rooms. 100-acre grounds, with 9-hole golf course, swimming pool, 2 tennis courts, bowls, 18-hole putting green, clock golf, children's playground. During the high season, sporting and social events are organised by the resident host. Riding and pony-trekking available near by; sand and rock beaches with safe sea bathing within easy motoring distance; sea angling at Whitby and Scarborough, freshwater fishing at Hackness on the river Derwent.
Dogs not allowed in public rooms.
Terms: full board: £125 weekly.
           Spring and autumn breaks and special weekend tariffs in April, May and October.

ROSTHWAITE, Borrowdale, Cumbria

Scafell Hotel   *Telephone:* Borrowdale (059 684) 208

Many consider Borrowdale Valley the most beautiful in the Lake District. *The Scafell Hotel* is in the heart of Borrowdale, almost beneath Great Gable and the Scafell massif. The river Derwent runs at the back, sounding delightful. For those without a car, Keswick is six miles to the north, and the Keswick-Seatoller bus passes the hotel.

'A quite small country-house-type hotel, and quite simply superb! Our room was exceptionally attractive, with pretty (not purely functional) bathroom; the service was friendly, courteous and efficient; and the food for this category of hotel was really excellent—in fact, one just could not eat it all. A full, very good English breakfast; packed lunch (which most people had) was always imaginative and varied; tea was set out in the lounge for you to help yourself, and there were always at least two sorts of home-made cake as well as biscuits, scones and jam; dinner was five courses with several choices at each stage, with imaginative and varied starters (including smoked salmon on one occasion), and savouries as well as puddings. Coffee was set out in the lounge for you to help yourself, Cona made, with cream and a dish of mints. We have stayed in many more pretentious establishments where the standard of food and service was not nearly so high.' (*Marcelle Heyman;* also *Mrs R. J. Bowden, Mrs M. E. Soper*)

Open: mid March–mid November.
Rooms: 10 double, 10 single—6 with bath or shower, all with tea-making facilities; baby-listening service.
Lounge, sun lounge, cocktail bar (no TV); 1-acre garden. Swimming and fly-fishing in the adjacent river Derwent; beautiful walks and hill climbing.
Terms (excluding service):   half board: £15.00.

ROWSLEY, Nr Matlock, Derbyshire

Peacock Hotel   *Telephone:* Darley Dale (062 983) 3518

Izaak Walton slept here, and this lovingly preserved mid-17th-century stone hostelry is still a well-to-do fisherman's dream rest, with guests having a seven-mile stretch of the Wye for trout fishing and a two-mile stretch of the Derwent for trout and grayling. It makes a splendid base for a Peak District walking holiday. And for those with an appetite for the great country houses, it is also well-placed: Haddon Hall, for which the hotel was originally a Dower House, is just a mile up the road, and Chatsworth, 'the palace of the Peak', is three to four miles across the fields. The hotel has a strong emphasis on creature comforts, with some fine antique furniture in the public rooms to enhance the atmosphere. Some of the bedrooms are in the original house, others in a modern annexe. The rooms to go for are those at the rear overlooking the gardens: the hotel is on a busy Sheffield road, and can be noisy at night. The gardens, incidentally, are a special feature, spacious and very beautiful, bordering the river Derwent, with old trees and superb flowers. The gardener is a champion sweet-pea grower, and in season guests find bowls of his prize-winning flowers arranged round the hotel. He also grows fresh herbs and some vegetables and salad items for the chef, who specialises in traditional British cookery. The restaurant, which is intimate and has walls thickly hung with prints and paintings, is much patronised by the neighbourhood as well as by the residents, and is usually crowded, especially in the high season. (*Carol Wright*)

Open: all year.
Rooms: 12 double, 2 single in hotel; 4 double, 2 single in annexe; 15

rooms have bath or shower, 14 have radio, all have telephone and TV.

Residents' lounge (with TV), public lounge, cocktail bar. Large garden running down to the river Derwent; 7 miles of exclusive fishing (rainbow trout) on the river Wye; 2 miles on the Derwent for trout and grayling.

Terms: B & B: from £7.50; dinner: from £5.10.
Winter breaks, October to April; occasional coach parties (meals only).

RUANHIGHLANES, Nr Truro, Cornwall

Polsue Manor Hotel   *Telephone:* Veryan (087 250) 270

A smallish white Georgian house in the Roseland peninsula surrounded by beautiful unspoilt country and beaches. In August, families predominate, but the hotel is equally popular out of the school holiday season with the more middle-aged and sedate. The food, service and standards of comfort all come in for praise, but clearly the specially congenial character of the hotel is set by the owners, Rex and Diana Dufty, who are on Christian-name terms with their guests, make a point of introducing their visitors and, in general, make them feel that their company is appreciated and, in the traditional phrase, 'nothing is too much trouble'. (*Ivy and William Barnes, W. A. and W. J. Williams*)

Open: Easter to end September.
Rooms: 10 double (including 4 family rooms), 3 single—4 with bath or shower.
Lounge, TV lounge, hall, bar; table tennis; 12 acres of grounds with putting and croquet lawns. Ten minutes by car to eight beaches with safe sandy bathing; sailing, boating, fishing (sea or river), riding, and four golf courses near by.
Terms (excluding VAT):   half board (4 days minimum): £10.25; buffet or packed lunch only served, except on Sundays.

ST MARY'S, Isles of Scilly, Cornwall

Bell Rock Hotel   *Telephone:* Scillonia (072 04) 575
Hugh Town

The Isles of Scilly, an archipelago twenty-five miles south-west of Land's End, has so far escaped the worst ravages of holiday developers. It's still possible, even in the height of summer, to find a beach to yourself, though not on the main island, St Mary's, only three miles long. Hugh Town is the chief centre of St Mary's and the port, both for boats to Penzance and for regular services to the other islands; there is also a helicopter service to St Mary's from the mainland.

'*The Bell Rock Hotel* is a place where the guest is neither the necessary evil, nor an impediment in the staff's normal way of life, but someone who is treated as being important, whose wishes really matter. Superb dinners with lots of choice—not a single item repeated in the week we were there; a cold sweets trolley which made us thoroughly greedy. We tended to return from boat trips to the smaller islands in the early afternoon, at a time when most hotels are moribund, but were brought a tray of tea as soon as we asked for it. The staff were uniformly friendly and cheerful. Two of them told us unasked in the course of conversation that they all lived in, had really comfortable living quarters, and were so well treated by the owners that there was an excellent atmosphere which they felt contributed to the smooth running of the hotel.' (*Mr and Mrs F. E. R. Peach*)

Open: early March–late October.
Rooms: 14 double, 3 single—15 with bath or shower; baby-listening service.
Lounge, TV lounge, bar; heated swimming pool with patio and sun deck (residents only); the hotel is 50 yards from two safe sandy beaches and the harbour; fishing, inter-island and round-island trips. The Heliport bus stops at the hotel door; the quay is 5 minutes away on foot. No children under 2. No dogs in the restaurant.
Terms (excluding VAT):   full board, including 3-course or packed lunch ('we are famous for our picnic lunches') and 5-course dinner: £14.00; half board: £13.00.
Spring breaks (March–7 May): 4-day and 7-day, £40.00 and £69.00.

ST MAWES, Cornwall

Tresanton Hotel
Telephone: St Mawes (032 66) 544

On a hillside overlooking the highly picturesque seaside village resort of St Mawes stands this smallish but distinctly luxurious hotel. There are, in fact, several houses on different levels accommodating the guests, all situated in a beautiful sub-tropical garden overlooking the sea. It's one of the dozen *Relais de Campagne* hotels in the British Isles, but there's nothing pretentiously grand in its style. Not cheap, but those who can afford the prices are likely to feel they are getting good value. 'Excellent service, four-star cuisine, and a real sense of the hotel being interested in your personal enjoyment.' (*Clare Slater*)

Open: 1 February–31 October, and Christmas week.
Rooms: 7 double, 13 twin-bedded, 10 single—27 with bath, all facing the sea.
Three drawing rooms, TV room, bar; 2 acres of sub-tropical gardens with sun terraces. The hotel has its own beach with safe bathing, private moorings for yachts, powered sailing boats for day cruising and fishing, including deep-sea and sharking.
No children under 12. Dogs not allowed in public rooms.

Terms (exclusive of service and VAT): full board: £17.00–£20.00; lunch: from £3.00; dinner: from £3.50.

SALCOMBE, South Devon

The Marine Hotel   *Telephone:* Salcombe (054 884) 2251
Telex: 45185

Few hotels can offer such a stunning view from its rooms as *The Marine*. Right on the water's edge, it provides a ringside seat on this colourful busy sailing estuary. *The Marine* is the largest and most sophisticated hotel in Salcombe, but has succeeded, where many grand hotels fail, in combining quality of service with size. The building itself is modern, and so is the decor. The bedrooms, too, many with balconies, have *all* the modern conveniences, but are also full of those little touches which delight the holiday-maker: a sewing kit, bathcap, foam-bath sachets, hanging rack over the bath for drying clothes, and so forth. Nor is the cuisine neglected: the same attention to excellence is apparent in the variety and quality of the food, and there is, in addition to the main restaurant, the Neptune Room, specialising in seafood. (*R. A. Nisbet, E. M. Sanders*)

Open: all year.
Rooms: 42 double, 9 single—all with bath, telephone, radio and TV. Lounge, cocktail bar, games room, solarium, indoor pool; dancing twice weekly in summer. Half-acre of grounds with lawn, heated outdoor pool, pool bar and dinghy park. Sailing, boating and fishing (the hotel has its own private slipway and landing facilities, and shingle beach); 2 golf courses near by.
No children under 7. No dogs.
Terms: B & B: from £17.50; full board: from £23.50.
Special winter rates and winter breaks.

SANDBANKS, Poole, Nr Bournemouth, Dorset

Sandbanks Hotel   *Telephone:* Bournemouth (0202) 707377

You won't need a car at this large, family-oriented, everything-you-want-under-one-roof hotel. The service and the food have come in for some criticism. But there are substantial compensations:

'The outstanding feature of the *Sandbanks Hotel* is its location. Only a lawn with roundabouts and rocking horses separates it from a beautiful sandy beach. In front, a road has to be crossed to reach Poole Harbour, ideal for collecting shrimps and cockles. Not far away is the Sandbanks Ferry, which carries cars to Shell Bay nearby, and foot passengers for 2p.! In the other direction is Poole Park, with a boating lake, swans to feed, and plenty of roundabouts. On wet days, there is a playroom supplied with toys, crayons and paper. A boon to parents is the Kiddy Bar, which serves meals to children, allowing their parents to eat in the restaurant in peace. Children love the diabolical menu of baked beans, Marmite, fish fingers, jelly, Ribena, etc. There's a free putting green on the front lawn, a heated indoor swimming pool, a sauna, a ballroom with entertainments of various kinds each evening: discos (twice a week), frog-racing, and bingo. Finally I should mention that the hotel has three washing-machines, an ironing room, two drying rooms, and a baby-sitting service. As the harassed mother of two under-fives, I appreciated these facilities enormously.' (*Elizabeth Hoodless; also Maggie Burley*)

Open: all year.
Rooms: 110 double (most with bath), 33 single (all with shower and toilet).
Ballroom, 2 lounges, TV room, games room; many special services for children, including baby-sitting. Heated indoor pool, sauna, solarium. Situated on the beach with lawns on the terrace wall; sun deck, area for children with swings and Wendy House. Boating, yachting, fishing, water-skiing, golf, riding and tennis near by.
No dogs.
Terms: full board (2 nights minimum): £17.00.
          Winter breaks, October–1 April.

SAVERNAKE, Burbage, Nr Marlborough, Wiltshire

The Savernake Forest Hotel   *Telephone:* Burbage (0672) 810206

'Burbage is a village five miles from Marlborough, close to the 4,000-acre Savernake Forest which, unlike most royal hunting forests, is a real forest, with trees. There are idyllic picnic sites, woodland trails for walking or riding, a cathedral-like Grand Avenue. Beyond lie the under-estimated beauties of the Wiltshire downlands: a galaxy of archaeological sites—Avebury, Silbury Hill, Old Sarum, Stonehenge; stately homes galore—Littlecote, Donnington Castle, Longleat, Wilton House, Sudbury Castle, and the enchanted gardens of Stourhead.

'*The Savernake Forest Hotel* stands on the woodland fringes, a solid Victorian building of slightly forbidding aspect, built by the Marquis of Ailesbury in 1863. Nothing forbidding about the interior, which has been discreetly, completely and fairly lavishly modernised. It is spaciously comfortable and run with cheerful efficiency by the Morris family —father, mother and son. The great glory is the food. Margaret and Lee Morris are their own dedicated chefs, specialists in the preparation of traditional English fare—14th-century onwards. The menu, liable to bring on a crisis of indecision, includes such temptations as potted Savernake venison (cooked slowly with gooseberry wine and herbs), hot, stuffed anchovy eggs (1695 recipe), oyster chicken (oysters, mushrooms and chicken blended in cream and wine sauce), lobster bashaws, Savon partridge, crab nippies, Barthelmas beef ... The menu changes weekly. The hotel has a wine bar and a buffet serving a distinguished selection of snacks. A good choice, this, for a gourmandising weekend at any season of the year.' (*Roger Smithells*)

Open: all year.
Rooms: 10 double, 4 single—5 with bath or shower, all with tea-making facilities.

Lounge, lounge-bar, wine and buffet bar, conference room; 2-acre grounds. Close to the Kennet and Avon Canal—free coarse fishing to guests; 3 golf courses near by.

Terms (exclusive of service): B & B: £8.00; lunch (*à la carte*): £1.75; dinner (*à la carte*): £4.50.
Mid-week breaks (all year) and weekend breaks (except summer).

SEAHOUSES, Northumberland

The Dunes Hotel *Telephone:* Seahouses (0665) 720378

'*The Dunes* is not particularly prepossessing from the outside. The stark, grey stone building has rather the air of an orphanage. The teak panelling in the dining room is ugly, and the lighting in the TV lounge is not good enough for those who want to read their books during the commercials. But apart from these minor things, there is virtually nothing else which can be said against this truly excellent hotel.

'We have stayed there with our two children four times and always return as if to home. There are many things about it which make it ideal for children's holidays. First of all, only a road and a strip of grass separate the hotel from a magnificent beach, with sweeping white sands, rocks, and an exciting tumbling sea—a perfect beach for sand-castles or rock-pools or beach cricket. Out to sea there are the picturesque shapes of the Farne Islands, of great interest to bird-watchers; to the north-west, the dramatic bulk of Bamburgh Castle on its headland. Such is the curious angle of the coast that at night one can watch from *The Dunes* the sun setting in splendour behind Bamburgh Castle, while the light-houses flash from the Farnes. No hotel could have a more beautiful out-look. The whole of this coast is quite enchanting and very unspoiled.

'There is a large flat garden in front of the hotel, well suited to all kinds of children's games. The hotel is spacious, so that one need not feel shut in on wet days. There are four lounges, as well as a glassed-in sun lounge, so that there always seems to be a place where children can play without disturbing other guests. We have had the same large bed-room every time, which is very comfortable, and again, spacious enough to be played in. There are also plenty of bathrooms—no need ever to queue. Downstairs, there are washing and ironing facilities, a drying room, and plenty of clothes-line space for wet bathing things.

'The hotel is admirably looked after by two ladies, Miss Smith and Miss Bach who, in a quiet unobtrusive way, provide an excellent service. They seem willing to produce tea, snacks and so on at any time, serve drinks, and lay on a special children's tea at 5.30 pm. Food at *The Dunes* is invariably good, and the meal-times reasonably elastic. There is no nightlife as far as I know, but one is usually very sleepy after dinner from the bracing sea air. I think the best recommendation I can give it is that we have stayed there in all weathers, and after four visits, still speak of it as if it were synonymous with Paradise.' (*Angela Bull*)

Open: Easter–October.
Rooms: 16 double, 8 single, 2 family—4 with bath.
Four lounges (including TV lounge), games room; garden; situated immediately opposite the big sandy beach.
Terms (excluding service):   B & B: £6.00; half board (weekly): £59; full board weekly: £66.00.

SKELWITH BRIDGE, Nr Ambleside, Cumbria

Skelwith Bridge Hotel   *Telephone:* Ambleside (096 63) 2115

'Skelwith Bridge is little more than a bridge, a hotel, slate works, craft shop and a few houses, typical of the gentle side of the Lake District. It is the kind of place that clusters and nestles. In this case the buildings cluster on the banks of the river Brathay by the road westwards from Ambleside to Coniston. They nestle at the southern foot of Loughrigg Fell in low-lying, well-wooded country. There are scenic highlights: Skelwith Force, when the Brathay is in flood; sunset at Loughrigg Tarn (a good pre-dinner walk); autumnal mornings along the river with the tops of the trees showing golden in the sunshine just above the mist. You may even see a few horned Jacob's sheep. The road forks at the *Skelwith Bridge Hotel*, the less busy road running to Elterwater and Great Langdale. The main reason for staying at *Skelwith Bridge* is the friendliness of the hotel and it is unfortunate that the brochure's photographs of the interior are garishly offputting. That is not the impression when you are staying there, either in the public rooms or in the bedrooms. The hotel, which started as an inn in the 17th century, is as genuinely welcoming now as it was in the 1930s. The food is good, the menu varied, and there is no attempt to turn meals into a performance. The people who stay there seem mainly motorists but in other respects, a varied lot. A certain middle-class cosiness does set in over after-dinner coffee, but those who wish to escape it can drink in the public bar with the locals, or trail up the road to the crowded pubs at Elterwater.' (*Andrew Bicknell*)

Open: mid February–November.
Rooms: 18 double, 6 single, 1 family—4 with bath.
Three lounges, TV room, cocktail bar, buttery bar; ½-acre garden.
Terms (excluding VAT):   B & B: £7.50; buttery lunches; dinner: from £3.60; half board (weekly): £71.00.
          Winter bargain rates.

If you know of a good hotel that ought to be in the Guide, please write it up for us <u>now</u>. Procrastination is the thief of the second edition.

STAMFORD, Lincolnshire

The George　　　　　　　　*Telephone :* Stamford (0780) 2101
St Martins

Princess Anne slept here! Not to mention many other distinguished
personages in the equestrian world who regularly patronise this highly
traditional coaching inn at the time of the Horse Trials at near-by
Burghley House. Dating back to the 16th century, the hotel is full of
inn-ish character, with lots of flower tubs in the cobbled courtyard. It
also boasts of a monastery garden where performances of Shakespeare
are given in the summer. The hotel has a reputation for the quality of its
accommodation (note: front rooms tend to be noisy), but has also earned
high marks for many years for its cuisine, both English and Italian, and
for an unusually interesting wine list. (*Mary Cunynghame, W. R. Paul*)

Open :　　all year, except Christmas Day.
Rooms :　　28 double, 15 single, 4 family—26 with bath, all with tele-
　　　　　　phone, TV on request.
Residents' lounge, bars, conference room; ½-acre Monastery Garden.
Terms :　　B & B: £8.00; meals: £5.05–£7.55.
　　　　　　Winter weekend breaks.

STRATFORD-UPON-AVON, Warwickshire

Arden Hotel　　　　　*Telephone :* Stratford (0789) 69022 & 3874
44 Waterside

Timbered country house hotel in lawns overlooking the Avon and the
Royal Shakespeare Theatre. Under the personal management of the
owners, Mr and Mrs Anker, whose competence and friendliness have
been highly praised. 'The standard of the cuisine is without reproach;
the dining room staff courteous, helpful, and exceptionally well-trained.
A reunion with these people is an integral part of one's visit.' (*C. A. G.
Theobald*)

Open :　　all year.
Rooms :　　42 double, 20 single—40 with bath; all with radio and TV,
　　　　　　tea and coffee-making facilities, baby-listening services.
Foyer and residents' lounge, lounge/bar, separate TV room, terrace
restaurant. One acre of lawns and gardens; fishing and boating across
the road; theatre tickets obtained (though booking ahead is recommended); meals arranged to suit performances.
Terms :　　B & B: £9.50.

If you consider any entry inadequate or misleading, please let us
know <u>now</u>.

STUDLAND BAY, Dorset

Knoll House Hotel

Telephone: Studland (092 944) 251

'Once you've made the effort to get on to the Isle of Purbeck, either queuing interminably for the ferry at Sandbanks, or nose-to-tailing it through the narrow main road of Wareham, the self-styled "Gateway to the Purbecks", the rewards are considerable. Some of the prettiest country in the West, a handsome golf course, most comfortable villages, admirable ancient monuments such as Corfe Castle, and, of course, *Knoll House Hotel*. It's one of those places at which departing guests make their bookings for next year as they check out, and part from staff and fellow guests with ardent promises of frequent contacts in the grey winter months and heartfelt assurances of "see you next summer". So newcomers in the high season (that is, the school summer holidays), may find a certain cliquéness among guests at first. But not for long: most of the regulars are civilised people who welcome new blood to their annual house-party.

'Why do the regulars keep coming back? Well, the place is comfortable. Beds that you can really sleep well in, bathrooms with ample hot water and lavishly towel-supplied (not all that common in this country), and vast quantities of food which doesn't pretend to be *haute cuisine* but which is ideally suited for families. That really is the key of course. *Knoll House* is for people with children. During the summer school holidays, in fact, you won't get a booking unless you've got children of school age. The place is geared to them; not only the ample, agreeable food, but the way it is served. All main dishes are brought to the table for the parent to dish out—none of that tedious leaping about by waiters which can make even the most equable of children fractious. They don't mind if a family arrives in the dining room in dribs and drabs either; so the children can eat first, and leave you to eat *à deux* in peace. There's a nursery staffed by nannies, by the way, for very small children. Lunches are especially recommended: a vast array of help-yourself hors d'oeuvres, a cold table of Victorian splendour (cold rare beef, cold pork, hams, haslet, raised pies, brawn, pâtés, and heaven knows what besides, all cooked by a strong-minded but very friendly chef) and salads galore. And the puddings—oh, the sinfulness of *Knoll House* puddings! Gâteaux St Honoré, Charlotte Russe, a positive gallimaufry of calories. There's also a well-stocked English cheese board. And you can eat as much as you want of it all. You can see the children fatten before your eyes. Yourself, too, dammit.

'What else does the place offer? Pleasant public rooms and a broad handsome terrace under tall Dorset pines and overlooking the splendours of Studland Bay (it is said that Churchill met Eisenhower here, and sat on the terrace to share a Lease-Lend drink, during the war, when the house was a private home). There's a heated outdoor swimming pool. There's a children's swing park, including a large mock-up of a pirate ship complete with walkable plank; there are tennis courts, a 9-hole golf course, riding stables, pleasant gardens, a nature reserve for the observers of local flora and fauna (the fireflies are *very* special), and, of course, the beach. A walk either through the nature reserve or the gardens belonging to the Fergusons' house (of which more anon), brings you to a bay lined with clean, white sand and backed by dunes; great for swimming and boating and fishing (the local sea bass are splendid and the chef at the hotel usually cooks a young fisherman's catch if he's asked nicely). In summers like that of 1976, the place feels like the most Mediterranean of resorts, without the hubbub and the smells, but with tides. At the eastern end of the beach you can swim and sunbathe in the nude. It's the people in swimsuits who look odd up here. (Watchers of Dave Allen and the Goodies on TV know Studland Bay beach well; the seaside sketches are all filmed there.) Further afield, there's the small town of Swanage, very Edwardian seaside; beauty spots such as Lulworth Cove, and Dancing Ledge; mind-improving places such as Kimmeridge, famous for fossils, and the Bovington Tank Museum for the warlike; and for the literary, this is, of course, the edge of Hardy country; for buyers of antiques and old books, Dorchester and Sherborne are a reasonable drive away, and if you're a painter, the whole area is studded with studios, where you can look, gossip with the incumbent and often buy very successfully.

'Back to the hotel; it's owned and run by the Ferguson family, parents and offspring, and staffed by young people filling the University vacation by earning a little money for themselves. So the place is *very* middle-class, which isn't meant to be an insult. It's just a statement of fact. The Fergusons certainly have the middle-class virtue of treating their customers as private guests, so much so that if someone has a need for an extra bed when the hotel is full (someone's friend coming down for the weekend, say), they'll very likely be put up in the Fergusons' mini-stately home, Studland Bay House, across the road. Taking it all round, it's a splendid place for a family holiday. Lots of children for yours to hobnob with (you hardly see them from dawn to dusk. Bliss!). Pleasant people to talk to. Time to rest. No hectic nightlife (there's a disco twice a week but it's really for the kids), but local life such as the Church Fête, the Studland Flower Show, and the Conservative Garden Party if that's your fancy. As one who lives a hectic life for fifty weeks of the year, *Knoll House* is a two-week haven in the summer. See you next year?' (*Claire Rayner*)

Open: 16 March–16 October.
Rooms: 54 double, 57 single—80 with bath, all with baby-listening service.
Four lounges (including TV lounge), cocktail bar, writing and bridge room, nursery playroom, separate children's dining room, 2 games rooms; dances in season. 100 acres of grounds with tennis courts, heated outdoor swimming pool, riding stables, playground, cricket ground, 9-acre 3-par golf course. Safe sandy beach accessible direct from the hotel grounds, $\frac{1}{4}$ mile; Isle of Purbeck Golf Course, 2 miles.
Terms (exclusive of VAT):   full board: £99.00 weekly.

Important reminder: terms printed must be regarded as a rough guide only as to the size of the bill to be expected at the end of your stay. For latest tariffs, check when booking.

TALLAND-BY-LOOE, Cornwall

Talland Bay Hotel   *Telephone :* Polperro (050 38) 228

An attractive white Cornish country house, in parts dating back to the 16th century, well-converted into a medium-sized hotel 150 feet above Talland Bay, which itself is about halfway between the picturesque (and resorty) Looe and Polperro. Being Cornwall, the caravan sites can't be far away, but you won't catch a glimpse of them from the hotel, which is in a completely rural setting with magnificent views from many of its rooms. A country lane running past the hotel takes you down to the sea, but those who prefer to stay as put as possible have a 40 × 20 foot swimming pool literally at the lounge door, and large well-kept grounds in which to sunbathe in seclusion. The public rooms are spacious with plenty of deep armchairs as well as some pleasant antique furniture and wood panelling. And the food? 'As a gourmet and gourmand I cannot praise the cooking too highly: plenty of variety and imagination, home-made bread, and, of course, a lot of really fresh fish.' (*Edward Booth*)

Open :   all year except January.
Rooms :   13 double, 7 single—all with bath or shower, some with radio. Two lounges (1 with TV), bar, games room (with table tennis); 2½ acres of grounds with heated swimming pool, putting lawn and 'many quiet corners'; sea about 600 yards below the hotel—access by car or on foot through fields; rock and some sand, safe bathing and boating (most of the time).
Terms (excluding VAT) :   B & B: £9.10–£11.60; half board (4 nights minimum): £12.10–£14.60.
Winter bargain rates in November, February and March; Bird-watching and Artists' Holidays.

TAVISTOCK, Devon

Bedford Hotel   *Telephone :* Tavistock (0822) 3221
1 Plymouth Rd

'Tavistock makes a fine centre for Dartmoor, but is also strategically and pleasantly placed for anyone planning to catch the morning ferry to Roscoff, being half an hour from the docks at Plymouth even in the rush hour. The *Bedford* is built on the original site of the famous Tavistock Abbey. After the Dissolution of the Monasteries, the Dukes of Bedford acquired the lands of Tavistock Abbey, and in the 18th century most of the original buildings were taken down and the house rebuilt in its present solid, crenellated style. The bedrooms are not perhaps as up to date as some would wish, being high-ceilinged and a little ponderous. One of the bars, once a billiard room, has stained-glass windows. Otherwise there is nothing staid or starchy about the place. Trust Houses Forte may have a distinct sameness about them, but you can be sure of good value for money. However, the *Bedford* not only has the amenities one would expect from a Trust House, but also an extra abundance of friendliness and well-cooked and well-served meals.' (*Christopher Portway*)

Open: all year.
Rooms: 17 double, 14 single, 6 family—21 with bath.
Lounge, bars, TV room.
Terms: B & B: £8.75; meals: £2.70–£5.00; full board: £12.50–£16.00.

ULLSWATER, Cumbria

Sharrow Bay Country House Hotel
Telephone: Pooley Bridge (085 36) 301

A quiet road runs along the eastern shore of Ullswater from Pooley Bridge, eventually petering out on Martindale Common, and one of the small bays on its course is Sharrow Bay. But to many people, both in Britain and abroad, the name *Sharrow Bay* means not an indentation in the lake shore, but a splendid hotel with a remarkable view of this most romantic lake. Built originally as a desirable residence, the house has many of the characteristics of an Italian villa: flowery terrace with statuary, elegant furnishings, antiques, *objets d'art* and books, all in an incomparable setting above the lake in woodland gardens with lodge and cottages and waterside walks.

'Here you will be not only peaceful but pampered. The meals are a villainously stern test for those guests who hope to leave at least not heavier than when they arrived. It is hard not to dwell on the food, which is superb and for which Francis Coulson is internationally famous; but just as important is the skill with which he and his partner, Brian Sack, unobtrusively make you feel most welcome and at home through all the day. A highly civilised and most distinguished hotel.' (*Tom and Christine Seddon;* also *Roger Smithells*)

Open: all year except December and January.
Rooms: 23 double, 6 single—19 with bath/shower, telephone, radio and TV (some of the accommodation is in cottages or the Lodge Annexe; Thwaite Cottage has its own small kitchen and dining room).
Three drawing rooms where drinks are served as there is no separate bar. The water reaches the terrace wall, and there are 12 acres of gardens and woodlands; ½-mile of lake shore with private jetty and boathouse; lake bathing (cold!) and fishing from the shore; boats for hire near by; steamer service in season across the lake.
No children under 13; no dogs.
Terms (excluding VAT):   half board: from £19.50.

Warning: prices quoted are 1977 prices.

VERYAN, South Cornwall

The Nare Hotel
Telephone: Veryan (087 250) 279

'Perched on the cliff edge, overlooking a long beach and over a mile from the nearest village. With the beach, its own heated swimming pool, a sauna, a tennis court and other facilities such as a games room with snooker and table tennis, families in the holiday season probably find no need to leave the hotel once they arrive. Out of season it is an ideal spot for gentle (or otherwise) walks and for exploring the area between St Mawes and St Austell. First-rate menus with a wide choice, but an emphasis on fish. The most memorable female head waiter I have ever encountered: she controls the dining room with absolute but quiet efficiency, and drills inexperienced staff in her own standards of friendly service. The best recommendation for the hotel must be the number of visitors who return year after year.' (*Gordon Smith*)

Open: all year except November (restricted service December–February).
Rooms: 31 — 23 with bath, 3 with shower.
Three lounges (one with TV), games room, sauna; dances Friday and Saturday in season. Garden with heated swimming pool and tennis court.
Terms (excluding service and VAT):   B & B: £7.50–£9.50.

WATERMILLOCK, Cumbria

Leeming on Ullswater Country House Hotel
Telephone: Pooley Bridge (085 36) 444

A handsome Georgian house, seven miles from the M6 Penrith junction, in beautifully landscaped and wooded grounds leading down to the lake side. The hotel has an unusually high proportion of staff to guests (37 trained or in training) but, says the brochure endearingly, 'the atmosphere of friendly informality owes as much to the guests themselves as to the young and courteous staff'. Here is how one of the guests returns the compliment:

'A very comfortable house which exudes "welcome". The staff are helpful and understanding; they are not servile, but they care. The dining facilities and the cooking are excellent. The decor and furnishings are in quiet good taste. The hotel reflects the personality of the owners—Mr and Mrs Carlsen. Since my first visit a year ago, I have stayed there often to get away and be "mothered".' (*George Yarwood;* also *C. N. Maplethorpe*)

Open: all year.
Rooms: 16 double, 2 single — 12 with bath or shower, all with radio and telephone.

Drawing room, Blue Sitting Room, library, bar; occasional dancing and musical evenings. Thirteen acres of grounds with formal gardens with fountain surrounded by informal gardens with shrubs and rare specimen trees; also paddock and woodlands with lake frontage; jetty for boating, fishing, swimming; pebble beach, moorings.

Terms (excluding service):   rooms: from £7.00; lunch: from £3.00; dinner: from £4.00.

Reduced terms during some winter months.

WILLERSEY HILL, Nr Broadway, Worcestershire

The Dormy House   *Telephone:* Broadway (038 681) 2241

'Broadway is certainly one of the jewels of the Cotswolds, but for many people it's just a bit too precious. There's something inevitably self-conscious about a showcase village—every house listed, not a hair out of place. And, in the season, the charabancs, with their polyglot loads, descend like locusts on the plain. *The Dormy House* has the benefit of being a stone's throw from Broadway—a mile by footpath, two by road —but well away from the noise and bustle. It's on a quiet lane, high up on a hill commanding the village and the Vale of Evesham beyond. The façade is unimpressive, but the house itself, dating from the 17th century, is full of character—there's not just one lounge, one bar and one dining room, but a whole collection of rooms to sit and eat in, almost all with inglenooks and generous log fires. There is a score of bedrooms in the house, and a further half-dozen in an annexe outside; the former are the more comfortable, though a bit short on sound-proofing.

'The hotel prides itself on its restaurant and does a busy trade in the evenings among the gourmets of the neighbourhood. The prices are highish by Cotswold standards, but not out of the way for this quality of cooking and the enterprising nature of the menu. There are no set meals at lunchtime, but the bar serves a wide range of hot and cold snacks at very reasonable prices. There's an excellent wine list. The service is always friendly and informal. One connoisseur of Cotswold hotels, who prefers them small, reckoned this the best of the lot. It would be a good place for a week or more, as a centre for walking or touring, but it could also be used as a night stop for theatre-goers at Stratford, a dozen miles down the road. The all-inclusive winter weekend breaks, though costing a bit more than similar deals at other hotels, offer more too: the "package" folk have the run of the *à la carte* menu just like the full-paying guests.' (*H.R.;* also *Anne Edwards*)

Open: all year.
Rooms: 21 double, 5 single—all with bath and telephone; radio/TV on request.
Two sitting rooms, 2 bars (no TV); 1½ acres of grounds. Broadway Golf Club adjoins the hotel, other courses are near by; hunting twice a week during the season.
Terms: B & B: £11.00; dinner: from £4.70.
    Winter weekend breaks, November to March.

WILLITON, Somerset

The White House Hotel   *Telephone:* Williton (0984) 32306

'A good-looking Georgian country house in a delightful unspoiled part of the West Country where, even in high summer, one can wander away from crowds on Exmoor or the Quantock Hills. The area is not at all commercialised and is a paradise for the walker. The beaches are *not* the best the West Country has to offer, but the golden sands of North Devon are within an hour's drive if one must visit the occasional beach. This year I swam in the Exmoor rivers rather than join the beach crowds. But it is the hotel itself which makes me return year after year. It is small and family run, with a personal touch. Mr and Mrs Smith themselves do the cooking (breakfast and dinner only), now helped by their teenage daughter who waits (barefooted) at table. Food is their particular passion, and though there is no grand *à la carte* menu, there is a daily choice of three or four dishes at each course, some simple for the less adventurous, but always one exciting dish (*à la* Elizabeth David, Jane Grigson, or Robert Carrier). There are fresh white and wholemeal rolls made by Mrs Smith daily, and her daughter now makes the most scrumptious sweets as this is *her* weakness. The bedrooms are all individually furnished and everywhere is spotlessly clean. The only reservation I have about writing about this place is that I'd rather keep it to myself.' (*Miss P. Sutters;* also *Mrs Stella Rushton*)

Open: May–October.
Rooms: 13 double, 1 single—5 with bath or shower (light sleepers should ask for rooms facing side, back, or over the courtyard).
Two lounges (1 with TV); garden. Two miles from the sea with beaches mainly of shingle and rocks, but sand at Minehead, 8 miles.
Terms (excluding VAT):   half board: £9.20.

WILMINGTON, Nr Hinton, Devon

Home Farm Hotel   *Telephone:* Wilmington (040 483) 278

The only hotel in this Guide with a blacksmith's forge in its grounds. A horse, however, is not essential, but a car would probably be a good idea. Honiton is three miles away, and the nearest beaches (and good cliff walks) six miles off. Some people find this an agreeable place to break a long journey to the West. The hotel may well have another singular claim—its thatch. It is, in fact, a 16th-century thatched farmhouse, well-modernised but retaining plenty of traditional features—beams galore, inglenook fireplaces, antique furniture, copper, brass and the like—set in a large pleasant garden. The food is reported 'outstanding'. (*Mrs J. G. Rowlerson*)

Open: 14 February–1 January.
Rooms: 8 double, 1 single—3 with bath, some with radio.

Lounge (with TV), ante-room, bar; 3½ acres of grounds. Sea, with sand and rock beaches and safe bathing, 6 miles.
Dogs admitted 'if well-mannered'.
Terms (exclusive of service and VAT):   B & B: from £8.00; lunch: from £2.25; dinner: from £3.00.
Winter breaks, 1 November–30 April.

WINDERMERE, Cumbria

Beech Hill Hotel   *Telephone:* Windermere (096 62) 2137

An exceptionally well-sited hotel on the eastern shore of Lake Windermere, about three miles south from the bustle and scrum of the town itself. Modern terraced extensions have been grafted on to a Victorian gabled building, allowing most of the bedrooms, the restaurant and the bar to look out on a breathtaking view of lake and mountains. Well-kept lawns slope down to a floating dock, useful for the boating, sailing and water-skiing fraternity. It's a hotel with lots of fringe benefits (see below) but it also has that indefinable extra quality: 'It is one of the few hotels where, on entering, your pressures disappear. The food we found to be splendid, and the whole atmosphere has a warmth which is unfortunately all too rare.' (*Margaret Scott*)

Open: all year.
Rooms: 45 double, 5 single—all with bath or shower, telephone, TV and radio.
Residents' lounge (with TV), cocktail bar, games room with snooker and table tennis, sauna and solarium; Friday and Saturday dinner dances; indoor heated swimming pool; ¼-acre gardens leading down to the lake, with the hotel's own floating dock; sailing and water-skiing on the lake; steamer services and lake excursions.
Dogs: by arrangement.
Terms: B & B: £11.95; lunch: £3.00; dinner: £4.75.
Bargain breaks, 1 November–mid May.

Miller Howe   *Telephone:* Windermere (096 62) 2536

Visitors to *Miller Howe* have constantly, for many years past, reported a kind of ultimate hotel experience here—a quintessence of cosseting. Appropriately, this elegant country house hotel has earned almost all the symbolic accolades that the professional Guides can confer—red rosettes, chef's hats, crowns, stars—not to mention pestles and mortars and soup tureens. The location, for a start, is as peaceful and enchanting as you could hope to find short of the Elysian Fields. Miller Howe is the name of a hill on which the building stands, at the foot of the road to Bowness, and to the Kirkstone Pass, with only path-threaded National Trust land dividing it from the lake. Across the water are the outlines of the great fells—Crinkle Crags, Scafell, Great Gable, Pike O'Stickle and the rest. The size of the hotel doubtless contributes to its exceptional agreeableness. With only thirteen bedrooms, an intimacy of enjoyment is possible which larger establishments cannot hope to achieve. And those bedrooms are furnished with exceptional imagination as well as taste—with binoculars and hair dryers as well as with antiques and pictures. The public rooms are no less luxurious and individual. But, for many visitors, it is the quality of the meals—particularly the dinners —that contributes most to the glow of well-being which a stay here generates.

'There is no bar. Dressed as befits an occasion, you sit at ease before dinner in one of the three drawing rooms set about with deep, soft arm-chairs and sofas. You give your order for pre-dinner drinks to quietly efficient staff while reading the menu of the day (five set courses and a bewildering choice from the sweet trolley). Drink in hand, you can gaze across the lake and watch the sun setting as it dips behind the far shore, rugged with mountain outlines. The split-level air-conditioned dining room and its newly opened off-shoot seats 65 residents and visiting gourmets. Each night is an occasion—a first night—with soft (classical) music and lights dimmed when diners are settled and awaiting the coming of the first course. The imaginative cooking is by John Tovey, who combines the role of hotelier, chef-in-chief and greeter-of-guests, giving the impression that he is everywhere at the same time. He has diligently trained his staff, more than half of them having been with him for some six years. But the kitchen is his true home and here, aided by an enthusiastic team, he bakes his own bread, makes delicious pastry, dreams up new concoctions and uses local produce and flowers to their full advantage—flowers fill hall and rooms, appear on breakfast trays and even sit on top of dinner courses.' (*Diana Petry*; also *E. V. Hibbert, Doris Raby, Gladys Walker*)

Open: last Friday in March to 2 January following.
Rooms: 13 double—11 with bath/shower, all with radio; TV available. Four lounges including sun lounge/terrace. Garden from which paths lead down through National Trust land to Windermere with its steamer services, boats for hire, water-skiing and the like.
Children: 'Only those who would enjoy a five-course dinner catered for'. Dogs at the discretion of the management.
Terms (excluding service):   half board: £16.00–£20.00; packed lunches available.
Residential cookery courses in Spring and Autumn. Christmas and New Year House Parties.

WOODBRIDGE, Suffolk

Seckford Hall Hotel   *Telephone:* Woodbridge (039 43) 5678

'For anyone wanting a really relaxed stay in the country, *Seckford Hall* has much to recommend it. It lies just off the A12 between Ipswich and Lowestoft, but sufficiently far off the main road to be absolutely quiet.

You would certainly need a car, however, if you wanted to explore the lovely, gentle countryside (much of it designated an area of outstanding natural beauty). The hotel stands in three acres of grounds, with a lake and terrace where you can sit out with tea or drinks in fine weather. It is a noble Elizabethan manor house with much heavy oak and delicate linenfold panelling, modernised with a minimum of damage to the original structure, and furnished throughout with period pieces. There is central heating in the bedrooms, and log fires in two of the three lounges. There is also a comfortable bar where you can have snack lunches at reasonable prices. We found the service excellent and, although my room was on the second floor, a cheerful waitress served breakfast in my room. The menu offers a wide choice of food well-served in the panelled dining room.' (*Rita Ostermann*)

Open: all year.
Rooms: 16 double, 4 single—13 with bath, all with telephone, some with TV.
Several lounges and a good bar/lounge; 34 acres of gardens, parkland and lake. Fishing for trout in the private lake, horse-riding near by, 6 golf courses in the vicinity.
Terms (excluding VAT): B & B: from £6.50; dinner: from £4.50. Winter breaks: November to March.

YARMOUTH, Isle of Wight, Hampshire

The George Hotel   *Telephone:* Yarmouth (0983) 760331
Quay Street

'As the British Rail ferry from Lymington pulls over the Solent, the small gathering of buildings besides the masts of Yarmouth harbour gradually becomes distinct, and the most easily identifiable proclaims itself as *The George Hotel*. Right on the water's edge beside the old castle and the harbour, it has a delightful setting, with a small garden going down to its own pebbly beach; on the "town" side is a small square where the seasonal activities ebb and flow. The hotel is three centuries old, originally built by Charles II's Governor, and some of the bedrooms proclaim royal occupancy in the good old days. They are now comfortably modernised, some with private bathrooms. It is under the son and family of a previous owner; standards have risen commendably and the food is now an excellent feature of a visit. Staff are friendly and helpful even if often temporary local recruits. Incidental attractions include Fanny, a friendly spotty dog who loves everybody in Yarmouth, and two more reticent Siamese cats. Yarmouth is most delightful out of season, very quiet, no nightlife, nearest cinema in Newport. In peak holiday period the town and all its facilities are under siege from the sailing crowd, and the whole atmosphere is different. West Wight has great appeal, lovely walks, excellent beaches, quiet charm.' (*Margaret Aldiss*)

Open: Easter–October.

Rooms: 18 double, 11 single—8 with bath and telephone, all with radios.

Lounges, bar; ¾-acre garden with direct access to The Solent, and own small pebble beach; fine walks and plenty of good beaches near; golf at reduced rates on near-by course.

Terms (excluding service and VAT): B & B: £9.75; meals (lunch served only at weekends): £3.50–£5.00; half board: £13.20; full board: £15.50.

YORK, Yorkshire

Dean Court Hotel
Duncombe Place

Telephone: York (0904) 25082

Virtually opposite the Minster, this small, conveniently placed hotel has been considerably modernised. The public rooms have no specially remarkable features, but the bedrooms are comfortable, cheerfully furnished and practical, and have colour television. 'A modernisation directed towards attracting the American tourist; but what it doesn't mean is that the atmosphere and efficiency are of American and perhaps "cold" standards. All very warm and Yorkshire, in fact, as is the food— first-class Northern England fare. The kind of hotel you want to return to.' (*Frank Falkner*)

Open: all year.
Rooms: 11 double, 14 single—all with bath.
Lounge/bar, TV room, conference facilities.
Terms (excluding service and VAT): B & B: £9.00; meals: £2.80–£3.80.

Royal Station Hotel

Telephone: York (0904) 53681
Telex: 57912

'Conforms to the usual conception of British-Rail-Palatial but, some-what unexpectedly, graced with pretty formal gardens and shapely lawns. Enthusiasts for high Victoriana will also appreciate the painted ironwork of the central staircase which rises impressively through four storeys, and the moulded ceilings. A draw, too, to railway enthusiasts, who will find plenty of steam souvenirs in the Railway Bar. Fine views across the garden to the towers of York Minster; and the river is only five minutes' walk away.' (*Diana Petry*)

Open: all year.
Rooms: 91 double, 38 single, some suites—most with bath, all with telephone, radio and TV.
Lounge, 2 bars, coffee-shop; Steam Railway Cellar Bar (with decor of signal lamps, model engines, firing shovels, etc.). Large garden with formal lawns and flower beds.

Terms (excluding service and VAT):   B & B: £12.00; lunch: from
£2.65; dinner: from £3.80.

Prices quoted, unless otherwise specified, are for bed and breakfast
for a person sharing a double room with bath or shower in the high
season. We have also given half and full board prices per person in
high season when available.

Plas Maenan Hotel, Llanrwst, Gwynedd

Wales

ABERDOVEY, Gwynedd

Trefeddian Hotel   *Telephone:* Aberdovey (065 472) 213

Picture windows of this one-time school, now a family-run hotel, face
fine views of the sandhills and sea of Cardigan Bay; behind, it is sheltered
by hills. It would be easy to go little further than the hotel which seems
to provide plenty of restrained entertainment to keep its guests occu-
pied; and 400 yards' stroll to the sea is inviting enough for those who
prefer sand and salt water (surfing; but perfectly safe bathing for the less
experienced, on the incoming tide). The food, though with no pre-
tensions to *haute cuisine*, offers plenty of fresh local produce, including
salmon and crab. Most people opt for full board—four courses at lunch,
five in the evening—and feel they get their money's worth. 'The
Trefeddian has its faithful middle-class and middle-aged clientele who
return year after year. Plenty of amenities for children, though the more
rumbustious might find the prevailing adult air a bit prohibiting.' (*Mr
and Mrs P. Ratcliffe*)

Open: 1 April (or Wednesday before Easter)—24 October.
Rooms: 35 double, 13 single—30 with bath, all with radio and baby-
         listening service.
Lift; 2 lounges (1 with TV), bar/lounge, games room; heated indoor
swimming pool with balcony and changing rooms; 10 acres of grounds
with lawns, putting green, squash. Sand beach with surfing, 400 yards;
fishing and sailing on the river Dovey, 1 mile.
Terms: half board: £14.30; full board: £15.
         Bargain rates during the off-season.

75

Norfolk House Hotel   *Telephone:* Colwyn Bay (0492) 2128
Princes Drive

A medium-sized hotel, Victorian in origin but extensively modernised, close to the sea-front in one of the less populous resorts of North Wales.

'Startlingly better than the next best hotel that I have come across in Wales. I have stayed there regularly over the past five years and the standards have, if anything, improved from the 1971 high. The hotel scores because (a) the owner is personally involved; (b) the manager and staff are intelligent, pleasant, and unusually enthusiastic; (c) the decor, furniture and lighting is of very high sub-Heal's standard; (d) incidental detail is given great consideration—e.g. unlimited good coffee in the lounge after dinner, drinks cupboard "on trust", tea and coffee-brewing equipment in all bedrooms, home-baked bread rolls at dinner; (e) the cooking is imaginative, but not ridiculously ambitious, with consistently high quality; (f) prices are reasonable; (g) I have never found anything to complain about!—and this for me is rare, for I am difficult to please.' (*G. I. Cottiss*)

Open: all year.
Rooms: 30 double, 5 single—18 with bath or shower, all with telephone, radio, TV on request, tea and coffee-making facilities (light sleepers should ask for rooms at the back).
Three lounges; ½-acre gardens with putting green and sun patio; 200 yards from the sea, with sandy beach and safe bathing.
Dogs at the management's discretion.
Terms (no tips):   B & B: £8.00; half board: £11.25; full board: £13.50; meals: from £2.50–£3.50.

CRICKHOWELL, Powys

The Dragon Country Hotel   *Telephone:* Crickhowell (0873) 810362

A small homely hotel, in an early 18th-century house, close to the Black Mountains, the Brecon canal and the river Usk.

'Run by Judy Hindmarsh, with assistance from friends Ira, Pat, Stephen and Graham. If you want a fully-staffed hotel with maid service, forget it. But if you want charming people to look after you, pleasantly decorated rooms, dogs and children welcome, helpful friendly service, this is the place. If you like going into the kitchen and drinking tea at odd times, great. Interesting conversation. Spotlessly clean. Nothing ever too much trouble. If you book a single room with two single beds, and they get overcrowded, you are likely to be asked to double up. Breakfast between 8.30 and 9a.m. They are a bit disorganised at other times, but will arrange an early start if required.' (*Captain D. J. Bicker-Caarten*)

Open: all year.
Rooms: 8 double, 2 single.
Two lounges (1 with TV); an acre of garden; boating, water-skiing, sailing, riding, hang-gliding, fishing and pot-holing, all near by.
Terms: B & B: from £3.25; half board (weekly): £33.00; full board (weekly): £40.00.
    Off-season weekend breaks: £17.00. Mid-week breaks: £15.50.

GWBERT-ON-SEA, Dyfed

The Cliff Hotel
Telephone: Cardigan (0239) 3241

The position, high up on a headland overlooking the Atlantic and Cardigan Bay (sporting young seals often on view) is unsurpassable, and if you tire of fishing or swimming or riding or sailing or playing golf, this designated area of natural beauty offers superb cliff walks, with some 600 varieties of wild flowers spotted by keen floriculturists. Fifty-three bedrooms is, in fact, quite a modest number for a *de luxe* hotel with all or most of the trimmings. The standard of comfort is what you would expect, and the French chef, M. Woogue, is highly praised. Moreover —and this isn't always the case with the larger, posher establishments— the staff get high marks for extreme friendliness. (*Elisabeth de Stroumillo, D. D. Evans, L. Lewis Walters, L. J. and J. M. Davies*)

Open: all year.
Rooms: 41 double, 12 single—45 with bath, all with telephone, radio and intercom.
Three lounges (including 1 for TV), 4 cocktail bars; Saturday dinner dances in summer; 30 acres of grounds with heated swimming pool, 9-hole golf course, putting green and sandpit. Safe swimming in sandy coves and creeks, Sailing Club within ½-mile of the hotel, with jetties and moorings; 18-hole golf course at Cardigan; pony-trekking and riding available; 6 miles from 3,000-foot airstrip at Aberporth.
Children: 'We find children delightful' (brochure). Dogs provided for, but not allowed in public rooms.
Terms: B & B: £9.24; dinner: from £4.15.
    Mini-weekends and midi-breaks, October to March.

HAY-ON-WYE, Powys

The Old Black Lion
Telephone: Hay (049 72) 841

'Hay, on the borders of England, has been a declining market town, recently boosted by Richard Booth into becoming the world's largest second-hand bookshop. Booth stacks his books, collected from all over the world, into every corner of the town: the fire station, the cinema, the hospital, and in sundry shops as well; a bistro bookshop is now opened so that print addicts can eat and read at the same time. For those who are tired of reading, the country around, especially the Wye and the Brecon Beacons National Park, offer marvellous walking, fishing and touring country. Despite the growing pressure of tourists, the town has been short of places to stay. *The Old Black Lion* reopened in 1976. The inn has low beams and a creaking corridor; it is by no means an all mod. cons, with H & C in all bedrooms sort of place, but it should suit those who prefer character and companionship to the more prosaic creature comforts. One room, supposedly slept in by Cromwell, has a beamed gallery, with twin beds, and two more below; the door has been known to spring unnervingly open. But there's always plenty of hot water in the bathroom, there's central heating and comfortable beds with duvets. The proprietress mothers visitors with her excellent cooking, bread is home-made, and tea is served to residents in a pleasant print- and book-lined lounge. The bar/dining room is the centre for local gossip, and at lunchtime a good buffet is served.' (*Carol Wright*)

Open: all year.
Rooms: 4 double, 1 single.
Residents' sitting room (with TV), bar/dining room; small garden. Fishing (and some swimming) on the river Wye; wonderful walking country all around.
Terms (exclusive of service): B & B: £5.15; bar snacks.

LLANBISTER, Powys

Cwmllechwedd Fawr   *Telephone:* Llananno (059 783) 267

Peter Barnes, the owner of this dauntingly-named farmhouse hotel, is a keen naturalist, and his brochure, unique among the many we have examined, recommends the ravens, buzzards, dippers, herons, tawny owls and grouse, not to mention rarer species such as Montague's harriers, to be spotted in the locale. For those with a more predatory attitude towards their environment, trout fishing is available in the near-by river Ithon. Kilvert country and the prehistoric remains of the Moelfre hills are within easy reach, and this is, of course, first-rate walking country. The farmhouse is Regency in origin, set in rolling green hills, with the river Camddwr running through a meadow near the house. The bedrooms are roomy and airy, with lovely views across the valley; each has its own electric kettle and crockery for self-service brewing of tea or coffee. Mrs Barnes is the cook, an enthusiast and an expert in traditional Welsh cooking; to the best of her knowledge, *Cwmllechwedd Fawr* is the only farmhouse-hotel to specialise wholly in Welsh food. As much as possible is cooked on a bakestone suspended from chains attached to an old-fashioned stone fireplace. Cheese, butter, cream and bread, are all home-produced. Meals are served in a small but charming dining room to the accompaniment of Welsh harp music and Welsh choirs from the adjoining hall. (*Mrs V. Pearl, Margaret Jordan, Brandon Cadlusef*)

Open: all year.
Rooms: 3 double.
Two sitting rooms, hall bar; Welsh evening held weekly in adjoining cottage. Small garden and 250 acres of moorland. Dogs 'if well-behaved'.
Terms: B & B: £7.50; dinner: £3.25.

LLANTHONY, Gwent

Abbey Hotel   *Telephone:* Crucomey (087 382) 487

'*The Abbey Hotel*, deep in the Vale of Ewyas (or Honddu) in Gwent, is built from the west range of a ruined 12th-century Augustinian priory, with a bar serving real ale in one of the original cellars. Around it are a farm, which once included the Chapter House and other bits of the priory, a free car park, and a tiny, 13th-century church. From the neighbouring fields the woods rise steeply to the mountains towering on both sides. The whole area is imbued with that indefinably tranquillising serenity you find on many of the more remote monastic sites, especially on those where (as here) people have been worshipping for nearly 1,500 years. *The Abbey Hotel* is run by a relaxed Anglo-American couple, Susan and Lawrence Fancourt, who describe it accurately as a 'small hostelry'. There's no central heating, only one inside WC, and the few rooms are reached by an ancient stone spiral staircase. I had the top room last year (62 narrow steps up) with a Victorian toilet-set, a section of early 19th-century graffiti preserved on the wall, a knee-high view of the priory, and a huge four-poster with barley-sugar pillars. It was spartan but romantic. The Fancourts don't cater for lunching guests, though they'll gladly make up sandwiches, and the bar offers ploughman's lunch with excellent home-made bread and really good beer. But both the breakfast and the dinner, served in what used to be the priory's vaulted parlour, are not only imaginative but ample. Especially when you consider the price: last year it cost £5.00 (plus VAT) for dinner, bed and breakfast. Devotees of the *Abbey*, not surprisingly, book early in the year; and the Fancourts shut it from October to Easter.' (*Richard Findlater*)
Open: Easter–October.
Rooms: 3 double, 1 family.
Sitting room, cellar bar. Built in a wing of a former Augustinian priory, it has electricity, but no H & C in rooms, and no central heating. A place for tranquillity in fine walking country; hill-climbing in the Black Mountains.
Terms (excluding service and VAT): B & B: £4.00; bar snacks at lunch; dinner: *à la carte*, approx £3.50.

If you know of a good hotel that ought to be in the Guide, please write it up for us <u>now</u>. Procrastination is the thief of the second edition.

MAENAN, Llanrwst, Gwynedd

Plas Maenan Hotel   *Telephone:* Dalgarrog (049 269) 232

An old, agreeably converted country house overlooking the Conway valley, with spectacular views over the surrounding river and mountain scenery. What distinguishes this hotel from others similarly sited, is the determination of Enid and Allan Wynne Jones to provide as distinctive a Welsh experience as possible. The bedrooms are much like other hotel bedrooms, though the fabrics are local. Downstairs, Welsh antiques and furnishings are a striking feature of the decor, as the Welsh dishes are of the restaurant menu, though there is more conventional fare as well. Welsh entertainments (harpists, etc.) are provided regularly, and Saturday night is the occasion for a Welsh musical evening. The staff all speak Welsh as well as English and, say the owners, 'we all try to be as friendly as possible'. (*Mrs G. E. Cox*)

Open: all year.
Rooms: 15 double or family rooms—all with bath, telephone, TV, tea-making facilities, baby-listening service.
Residents' lounge, 2 bars; traditional *Noson Lawen* (literally a 'merry evening') held on Saturdays. Twenty acres of grounds; fishing, walking; 10 miles to nearest bathing beach.
No dogs.
Terms (excluding service):   B & B: £6.50; lunch: from £2.00; dinner: from £3.00.
Special winter rates.

PENRHYNDEUDRAETH, Gwynedd

Hotel Portmeirion   *Telephone:* Penrhyndeudraeth (076 674) 228
Telex: 61467

'Nothing could be more exotic than this improbable hotel-village in lush wooded and flower-decked grounds on its own private peninsula. And nothing—except its tongue-twisting name—could be less like Wales. It could have been transported straight from some rocky Italian coastal corner, piazzas, campanile, curly-tiled rooftops, turrets and all. During the day, tourists (at 60p. a time) come to gawp at the village and to buy Portmeirion pottery on the spot (you can buy it in some big stores, but that's less romantic), local crafts, antiques, and so on. The entire setting is idyllic: dense trees, massed rhododendrons and azaleas, the mountains of Snowdonia at the back, and dreamlike views across the deep-cut bay where, at low tide, waders pick about for food in the pinkish corrugated sand; and across the water, to the south, the Harlech hills sketch a purplish wavy skyline. Part of the accommodation is in the old mansion itself, once the home of architect Sir Clough Williams-Ellis, who realised the whole amazing complex. Here comfortable main rooms are furnished with antiques and deep armchairs; the dining room, in more formal style, with candlelit tables, has views of the Bay and serves good imaginative meals and well-chosen wines. In addition, there are luxurious rooms and suites in the many Italianate cottages and villas in the grounds. I once stayed in one called "Fountains" where you practically had to dash under a waterfall to reach it.' (*Diana Petry*)

Open: April–October.
Rooms: 34 double, 5 suites, 11 single—48 with bath or shower, all with
          telephone, most with colour TV.
Two lounges, writing room, bar; 3½ miles of peninsula, with woods, beaches, and sub-tropical gardens. Heated open-air swimming pool in grounds, swimming, riding, sea and freshwater fishing, boating, climbing, shooting, golf near by (Portmadoc—free for hotel guests; Royal St David's 18-hole championship course, 8 miles). The hotel is used for conferences and special event weekends. The hotel-village is a major tourist attraction.
Terms (excluding VAT):   B & B: £15.00; lunch: £1.95; dinner: from
          £4.00.

THREE COCKS, Nr Brecon, Powys

Three Cocks Hotel   *Telephone:* Glasbury (049 74) 215

'Perhaps best described as a restaurant with rooms, this small, creeper-covered inn on the A438 between Hay (four miles) and Brecon (twelve miles) dates back to the 15th century and has had bits and pieces added to it ever since. There are only seven simple bedrooms at the moment (the four at the back are quieter), but a further six are promised soon, with baths *en suite*. They will help to restore the balance somewhat: for the present, residents are far out-numbered by the visiting gourmets from many miles around. The food is outstanding: not cheap, but maintaining a standard of excellence over a long and tempting menu. A large party, choosing variously and swapping shamelessly, could hardly fault a single dish over three courses. There are simple dishes, such as local trout and salmon, but rich creamy concoctions predominate. The highlights by general consent were the Hot Shrimps en Croustade as a starter, the Entrecôte Poivre Vert and the Coq au Vin among the entrées, and the Coffee Chiffon Flan as a dessert; with a special mention for the chocolate pancake stuffed with crème de menthe cream as a surprisingly delicious innovation.

'The service, never obsequious, was entirely *comme il faut*. Healthy appetites were necessary to cope with a full meal, as helpings were emphatically generous. Pierre Hine, the *patron* (he is a member of the famous Cognac family), is much in evidence, while his wife is behind the scenes in charge of the kitchens; he looks like a club bouncer, but performs like what he is—a dedicated, highly individualistic hotelier. If you care about good food and don't mind fairly simple accommodation (and prices for the rooms and full English breakfast, are appropriately modest, too), the *Three Cocks* would merit a place on any itinerary in this signally beautiful stretch of country. The Wye runs a mile or so to the north, the largest second-hand bookshop in the world (Booth's at Hay-on-Wye) is four miles to the east, and the formidably grand Black Mountains loom up five miles to the south.' (*H.R.*)

Open: all year.
Rooms: 6 double, 1 single.
Residents' lounge (with TV), 2 lounge/bars; 7 acres of grounds; river bathing, fishing and canoeing on the Wye, riding and pony-trekking near by.
Terms (excluding service):   B & B: £4.50; lunch: £2.25 and £3.25; dinner: from £5.00.

WHITEBROOK, Gwent

Crown Inn   *Telephone:* Trelleck (060 082) 254

'The primary reason for including this inn in the Guide is the food. The setting in one of the most beautiful parts of the country—on the edge of the Tintern forest and a mile from the banks of the Wye—and the comfort, quiet and cleanliness of the rooms are all most commendable, but less interesting to write about than the food. The inn itself is a long, low, whitewashed building, rather antiseptic, and almost all vestiges of the original 1680 pub have disappeared. The bedrooms are rather small for a long stay, but a little bunch of fresh flowers, Guerlain soaps, new toothbrushes, toothpaste and face flannels in the bathroom, made us feel pampered. The bar, restaurant and little sitting room have all been given a familiar "country inn" decor (beams, chintz, hunting horns and spinning-wheel). Take care to sit by the window at breakfast if you want light enough to read, though in summer there is a sunny terrace for outdoor meals. The dashing little stream below the inn and the pasture and forest above put one in mind of the Lower Alps.

'However, the restaurant is the best reason for staying here. Sonia Blech, the landlady, is French and does all the cooking herself. Her standards are exceptionally high. She is only concerned with authentic classical French cuisine. She uses nothing but the best materials obtainable, which means that much of it is brought by her husband from London twice a week. She shuns the freezer, so this means that each dish is prepared from scratch daily, including her bread, pastry, tuiles, brioches and croissants. As much of the fruit and vegetables as possible is grown locally or from her own garden. Her monthly *Menus gastronomiques* are sold out weeks ahead. The restaurant has won her accolades in other Guides. Bar-room meals are given just as much care: fresh cheeses from Soho, excellent salads and pâtés from the kitchen. There is an interesting wine list and local-brewed beer and cider. Prices are very reasonable if one compares the quality of the food and the standards of cooking with anything in London. *The Crown* is certainly a place which no gastronome should miss. I would even plan a route through Wales to include it, but the richness of the diet might make it imprudent to stay for more than a few days.' (*Susan Campbell*)

Open: all year.
Rooms: 7 double, 1 single—6 with bath, 2 with shower, all with radio.
Lounge (with TV), bar; 3 acres of gardens and pasture; 1 mile from the river Wye (fishing permits arranged with notice).
Children: 'no restriction, but children under 12 will be bored.' No dogs in public rooms.
Terms: B & B: £6.50; meals: from £5.50; restaurant extensively used by non–residents.

Details of amenities vary according to the information—or lack of it—supplied by hotels in response to our questionnaires. The fact that lounges or bars or gardens are not mentioned must not be taken to mean that a hotel lacks them.

Scotland

AYR, Strathclyde

Belleisle Hotel　　　　　*Telephone:* Alloway (0292) 42331
Belleisle Park

Formerly the seat of the Glentaner family, this hotel has a variety of attractions to offer (see grounds below). It is two miles from Ayr Racecourse and a mile from sandy beaches; and hotel guests have access to no less than two golf courses close by: 'those who feel unnerved at the prospect of the highly trapped championship course can enjoy the flattering subtleties of the second course', as the hotel's brochure puts it. The interior has been done up in an opulent way, with a highly decorative Louis XIV-style restaurant.

'I have been travelling for the past six months all over Scotland. As a rule I try and stay in 3-star hotels. I have found the quality within that category to range from unbelievably bad to good, and I have found one exceptional hotel, the *Belleisle*. Large rooms, modern baths, colour TV, good food (service a bit slow), friendly staff, and very reasonable terms by present-day standards. As a Scot would say: value for money.' (*Theodore B. Dobbs*)

Open: all year.
Rooms: 15 double, 3 single—16 with bath or shower, all with telephone, radio and colour TV.
Cocktail lounge bars, golfers' bar, coffee shop; dinner dance on Saturdays; separate wing for banquets, conferences, etc. Ten acres of gardens with an aviary, a deer park, and a Pets' Corner; 10 minutes' walk to river

85

and sea with safe sandy bathing; 2 golf courses handy.
No dogs.
Terms: B & B: £8.50; lunch: £1.75–£2.00; dinner: £2.00–£2.50.

BADACHRO, Nr Gairloch, Highland

Shieldaig Lodge Hotel   *Telephone:* Badachro (044 583) 250

'*The Shieldaig Lodge* stands on its own on the southern arm of the deep-cut Gair Loch, with its lawn going down to the sea. No beach or bathing there, but good beaches are close by. The surrounding country, with impressive mountain and sea views across to southern Skye, is ideal for walking, also for fishing. The hotel is a converted shooting lodge, and the rooms are all spacious; the decor is rather faded, but not unattractively so. The fact that there are three sitting rooms is a big advantage, as Badachro is a major drive from anywhere, and you are pretty well bound to stay in the hotel in the evenings. There is a very small but pleasant bar. There's no pretence to *haute cuisine*, but we always enjoyed the food. The hotel is managed sympathetically by a young couple, with two children and a Labrador. I would recommend the place for its agreeable relaxed atmosphere, adequate comfort and marvellous location.' (*John Lister*)

Open: April–October.
Rooms: 12 double, 2 single—3 with bath or shower.
Three lounges, cocktail bar (no TV); 3 acres of grounds with croquet lawn; fly fishing for trout and salmon, stalking for stags and hinds in season, 9-hole golf course at Gairloch, 3 miles; sandy beaches within easy reach by car.
Terms (excluding service and VAT):   B & B: £7.00–£9.00; dinner: from £3.75.

BALLATER, Grampian

Tullich Lodge Hotel   *Telephone:* Ballater (033 82) 406

'As we run a personal business, we would prefer our names to be mentioned somewhere in your write-up' was the note which proprietors Neil Bannister and Hector MacDonald attached when they returned our routine questionnaire. We are delighted to comply: if only all hotels cared as much about the personal touch, this Guide would be as long as a telephone directory. *Tullich Lodge*—1½ miles east of Ballater (dominated by memories of Queen Victoria and by near-by Balmoral), on a commanding site overlooking Deeside and the Grampians—is a decidedly individual hotel. Bannister and MacDonald bought this Georgian stone lodge nine years ago when it was run down and bankrupt and, through dedication and sweat, have achieved listings in the more discriminating Guides, though they are equally proud of not getting mentioned in others. Part of their success is in treating the place as a private house. They care a great deal about the character of the interior. There is a magnificent walnut-panelled dining room. The bedrooms still have vestigial bells labelled 'Maid' and 'Valet', and the attention to detail goes to the point of having Victorian trays for the breakfasts served in rooms. Food matters. There are home-made broths on the menu, game pâté, Dee salmon, roast lamb with rowan, haunch of venison, Finnan haddie; very little that isn't fresh, most of the vegetables and salads from their own garden. There is an interesting, reasonably-priced wine list, and an exceptional selection of malt whiskys in the bar. (*Derek Cooper*)

Open: April–December.
Rooms: 7 double, 3 single—8 with bath, 2 with shower; some rooms with telephone. All have fine, open views.
Drawing room, sitting room, bar; 5 acres of woodland garden; fishing, shooting and stalking on Deeside; golf, putting and tennis at Ballater; many other golf courses near by. Skiing at Glenshee, $\frac{1}{2}$-hour by car.
Terms: half board: £12.00; lunch: £3.20; dinner: £3.80; full board (weekly): £98.00.

BANCHORY, Grampian

Banchory Lodge Hotel   *Telephone:* Banchory (033 02) 2625

A fine, white-painted Georgian building, full of Victorian and Edwardian furniture and bric-à-brac lovingly collected by the founding owners, Mr and Mrs Jaffray. Perhaps most popular with the fishing fraternity as it is close to the confluence of the Dee and the Water of Feugh, and with fishing rights in the water directly opposite the hotel. But it also attracts guests with other country interests:

'Of all the many hotels in Britain and abroad that I have visited, I include *Banchory Lodge* among my very short list. I belong to a group of visitors with rather special needs, for we run dogs in Field Trials, which means that we make certain demands on hotels, including early breakfasts, packed lunches full of our own particular fads and fancies; teas in a hurry; and then, when we have completed the day's purpose, we can relax and be critical of our excellent dinner menu—and every time we are served with a meal *par excellence*. The hotel has a country house atmosphere, with its attendant facilities: drying rooms, log fires, well-polished antiques still in evidence, and nobody seems to mind if wet dogs are brought in after a day's training. It is a hotel which seems to like and respect its guests who, reciprocally, respect it and return again and again. COMPLAINT: only convector heating in the bedrooms. Since we are winter visitors, we temporarily freeze until rooms warm up; and the rooms tend to become stuffy if heaters are left on for a long period. But I realise there may not be an alternative way of heating without enormous outlay.' (*Patricia Frazer*)

87

Open: all year.
Rooms: 16 double, 2 single—most with bath or shower, all with radio and tea-making facilities; TV on request; baby-listening service.

Two lounges, bar, sauna; 12 acres of grounds. Salmon and trout fishing on the river Dee; golf courses at Banchory, Aboyne and Ballater; tennis, putting and bowling at Banchory; Glenshee ski slopes an hour's drive west.

Terms (excluding VAT): half board: £13.00.

BONNYRIGG, Lothian

Dalhousie Castle Hotel   *Telephone:* Gorebridge (0875) 20153

Another famous baronial seat that has successfully made the transition from ancestral home to modern hotel, *Dalhousie Castle*, about eight miles south of Edinburgh, and in its own parkland, was built in the 13th century and is owned by the Earl of Dalhousie. It still retains its castle-like atmosphere, with towers and battlements, and its thick stone walls lined with armour. But it also boasts a well-spoken-of restaurant, and decent-sized bedrooms, all with baths and some with balconies. WARNING: men are expected to wear jackets and ties in the public rooms in the evening. (*Christopher Maycock*)

Open: all year.
Rooms: 20 double, 4 single—all with bath and telephone, some with radio.

Morning room, library, Dungeon Bar; 7 acres of grounds.
Terms: B & B: from £15.00.

CRIEFF, Tayside

Strathearn Hydro   *Telephone:* Crieff (0764) 2401

'It must be an exceptional allure that attracts families for generations to this impressive hotel set in 650 acres of beautiful Perthshire countryside. Yet one only has to visit the *Hydro* to become its captive immediately. What is its fascination? Is it regal architecture, with its towers and turrets, a legacy from an era of great wealth and good taste? Is it the spaciousness of its 200 bedrooms and wide corridors? The magnificent drawing room which would do justice to a royal castle? Its unique lounge, large enough to seat 200 guests, surrounded with windows where you can appreciate the scenery without having to risk the elements? Could it be the fine ballroom where the Gay Gordons, Waltz, Eightsome Reel, Quickstep and Tango are danced with great delight several evenings a week, and the gay and sociable atmosphere that this creates? Could it be that, although the *Hydro* is not licensed, your own dinner wine may be drunk in the dining room and that corks will be drawn, bottles chilled and glasses provided? Could it be the delightful company of the private parties that guests arrange in their rooms? Or the great variety of sports available—indoor swimming pool, private cinema, two TV rooms, etc.? Is it the good wholesome Scottish fare that is so tempting that one happily puts on weight? Is it the cheerful and willing staff who work so conscientiously, and the considerate guests some of whom become close and treasured friends? One could go on and on. I can only suggest that you allow yourself the risk of becoming a captive by visiting the *Hydro*. I have been over fifty times in the past fifteen years.' (*Tony Ryan*)

Open: all year.
Rooms: 136 double, 72 single—72 with bath or shower, all with radio and baby-listening service, some with telephone.
Lift; 2 lounges, drawing room, ballroom (4 dance nights a week in summer—dinner jackets), cinema, conference room; heated indoor swimming pool, sauna, billiards room (2 full-sized tables), badminton court, table tennis room, nursery (swings, paddling pools, laundrette for families with small children). Fourteen acres of grounds, with 5 tennis courts, 2 squash courts, stables, 9-hole golf course, 18-hole putting green, croquet lawn, in an estate of 650 acres of farmland, woodland and gardens. 18-hole golf course near by; Gleneagles golf course, 12 miles. The hotel has its own site on Loch Earn, with boating, water skiing, etc.
Terms (excluding VAT): half board: £7.50–£10.10; lunch: £2.00.

DORNIE, Highland

Loch Duich Hotel   *Telephone:* Dornie (059 985) 213
Ardelve

'We stay here always for one or two nights when we are going to the north of Scotland or to the islands, which is two or three times a year. The hotel is eight miles short of the Skye crossing at Kyle of Lochalsh on the road to Fort William. We have been to many good hotels in Scotland, but this is the most pleasant we have ever found. It is only about forty minutes' motoring to Sandaig, the Camusfearna of Gavin Maxwell's books, where the otter's grave is easily found even though only traces of the house remain. The railway journey from Kyle of Lochalsh across to Inverness is reputed to be the most beautiful in Britain.

'The *Loch Duich* is primarily a smallish hotel with a bar, taking about thirty guests, but there is a village pub attached to the back. Meals all contain special Scottish dishes, marvellously cooked. It's an old stone building overlooking the Loch, with the Five Sisters of Kintail in the distance. Eilean Donan Castle is five minutes' walk away. The Loch is full of salmon. And the climate is mild: you rarely get snow at sea level, as the hotel is. All the bedrooms have an electric fire which is included in the (very moderate) tariff. Children are welcome. There is good lighting everywhere and plenty of bathrooms and WCs. The hotel is usually full: it pays to telephone first. When I tell the proprietor, John Snowie, that his charges are too low, he only says: "But my hotel is full".' (*Mr and Mrs John D. Moss*)

Open :   all year.
Rooms :   19.
Village pub attached at rear; garden; fishing available to guests.
Terms (excluding service and VAT) :   B & B: £4.50; meals: £2.50.

DURNESS, Highland

Far North Hotel   *Telephone :* Durness (097 181) 221

'Though John O'Groats is the furthest north one can go without leaving the mainland of Britain, a far more dramatic and less tourist-infested extremity of geography is Cape Wrath, the north-western limit of the country. The township which "serves" it is Durness, with a spectacular beach for those who like a touch of holiday normality with their wilderness. Sutherland (as this area was called before they abandoned all the old names) is the last great wilderness of Britain and the majesty of its countryside is equalled only by a remoteness that, God willing, will keep it thus. But for those who venture to this far-flung region there is a hotel available that fits the mood and character of the surroundings. *The Far North Hotel* is a mile out of Durness and is an ex-RAF radar station. Near by is Balnakeil craft village, its products part of the materials and skills of the ancient land. In spite of the somewhat odd, flat-roofed shape of the establishment, the hotel offers every comfort and a quality and quantity of food that the versatile Yvette Brown can devise for her clients, many of whom come back year after year. The interior furnishings and fittings were all designed by Yvette and her husband Paul who, when they are not running the *Far North*, are designers who also have an art gallery out of season in Yorkshire. Yvette is full-blooded English, but has lived in Scotland's outback for years and knows the countryside like the back of her hand. She also runs the ferry and Land-Rover service to Cape Wrath, some ten miles distant. This is a no-frills home from home, and this applies likewise to the terms which are moderate indeed.' (*Christopher Portway*)

Open :   mid May–early September.
Rooms :   9 double, 9 single.
Lounge with open fire (no TV), sun lounge looking out over mountains; 50 yards from the loch; ¼-mile from sandy beach.
Terms :   B & B: £4.25; dinner: £3.00; half board (weekly): £42.00. For the first 10 weeks of the season, there is a block-booking of bird-watchers.

If you know of a good hotel that ought to be in the Guide, please write it up for us <u>now</u>. Procrastination is the thief of the second edition.

EDINBURGH

Caledonian Hotel
Princes Street

Telephone: Edinburgh (031) 225 2433
Telex: 72179

Part of the essential Edinburgh scene, overshadowed by Edinburgh Castle and beside Princes Street Gardens where there is entertainment on summer afternoons. High class and handsome, and accustomed to dealing with people who, above all, appreciate their creature comforts. Meals of various sorts (*haute cuisine*, less fancy, and snacks) are served with the reverence due to good food. Afternoon tea in the stylish lounge is dispensed by motherly waitresses. High prices, but equally high standards. (*George B. Mair*)

Open: all year.
Rooms: 164 double, 48 single, all with bath or shower, telephone, radio and TV, baby-listening service.
Lift; main lounge, 3 bars, 3 conference rooms.
Dogs allowed but not in any of the restaurants.
Terms (excluding service and VAT): B & B: £17.15.
Bargain rates for winter-break weekends.

The George Hotel
George Street

Telephone: Edinburgh (031) 225 1251
Telex: 72570

Victorian-built and predictably palatial in the classical style. In the heart of Edinburgh's New Town, between two fine Georgian squares—Charlotte Square and St Andrew's Square. The additional bedrooms which have recently been added at the back of the hotel, have magnificent views over the Firth of Forth. A sympathetic blend of old and new has been achieved, giving a choice between conventional and modern. An expensive hotel, but value for money. (*Alice R. Milligan*)

Open: all year.
Rooms: 194—most with bath, telephone and TV.
Lift; spacious, gracious lounge, bar, conference facilities. Expensive eating in the main restaurant (dinner dances on Saturday nights); self-help cold buffet in the 'Perigord'.
Terms: B & B: from £10; lunch: from £2.50; dinner: from £3.50.

INVERNESS, Highland

Culloden House

Telephone: Culloden Moor (046 372) 461

'A sort of mini-Gleneagles, only more personal' is a shorthand way of describing the attractions of this beautiful 18th-century house, two miles east of Inverness, now converted into a 25-room de luxe hotel. It was built about 1772, twenty-six years after the Battle of Culloden, the last battle to take place on British soil, and Bonnie Prince Charlie is said to have spent the night before the battle at the castle which formerly stood on the site. It has a handsome Georgian façade, magnificent when floodlit, and backs on to the Moray Firth. The interior is in the Adam style. With its forty acres of parkland, its spacious public rooms filled with antiques, its expensively furnished bedrooms, its 'dignified' reading room, its 'elegant formal restaurant', it is a place for those who like a hotel in the grand manner. 'The food and the wine', writes one satisfied customer, 'must be among the best in Scotland.' (*John Duerden, Christopher Maycock*)

Open: all year.
Rooms: 25 double—all with bath and telephone; TV available.
Two lounges, reading room, sauna. Forty acres of grounds; salmon and trout fishing in the hotel's own stretch of the river Findhorn in season; stalking for red and roe deer in season; 18-hole golf course at Inverness, 2 miles; skiing at Aviemore, 1 hour by car.
Terms (excluding service and VAT): B & B: £15.00; meals: £4.00–£5.85.

KENSALEYRE, Nr Portree, Isle of Skye, Highland

The MacDonald Hotel   *Telephone:* Skeabost Bridge (047 032) 339

'A brand new hotel put up in 1976, privately owned by the MacDonalds —and the MacDonald tartan much in evidence. Spotless rooms with ravishing aspects over Loch Snizort, and panoramic views of the Cuillin Hills. Mrs MacDonald taught home economics in Glasgow for many years and her cooking is classical and correct. In the winter her buffets astonished the locals and her set dinners have been described as outstanding. Much of her success comes from the market garden run by husband Murdo who taught agriculture back in Glasgow. A cabbage at the MacDonald table will probably have been plucked only minutes before it's served and there are strawberries and peas in the plastic tunnels on the shore. Eggs are free-range and guests are free to bring their own alcoholic stimulants. The MacDonalds have no licence. Guests have been known to take their aperitifs in nearby Skeabost House Hotel (*q.v.*).' (*Derek Cooper*)

Open: all year.
Rooms: 7 double—all with shower; tea and coffee-making facilities; radio and TV on request.
Sitting room; garden with putting green; fishing excursions arranged, also trips to the Outer Isles. No bar (the hotel is unlicensed) but guests may bring their own wine to the dining room.
No dogs.
Terms: B & B: £8.00; salad bowl lunch: £1.80; dinner: £4.00. Reduced rates, October to March.

LEDAIG, Connel, Strathclyde

Isle of Eriska Hotel

Telephone: Ledaig (0631 72) 205

'Take a magnificently appointed early-Victorian magnate's former Highland home and position it on an islet measuring one mile north-south by half a mile east-west; surround the house with island-bespattered seas, green lawns, crimson beeches, and almost every type of tree which can grow in these latitudes; bedeck the ground with primroses, rhododendrons, daffodils, narcissi, azaleas and bluebells, and then organise colonies of badgers, visiting roe deer, a heronry and a herd of great shaggy Highland cattle, and you will have the basis for that exceptional atmosphere which characterises this almost unique hotel.

'Visitors by train are met at Oban station, eight miles away, but most people arrive by car and use it to explore some of the best scenery south of the Caledonian canal. Glencoe is forty minutes away. Loch Awe about the same. Fort William is an easy motoring hour distant, and Mallaig, across the waters from Skye, only another forty-five minutes. Loch Ness and the Nessie Museum and even Inverary are all within easy motoring along lovely roads. The hotel is also a splendid centre for boat trips around some of the Hebrides (departures daily from Oban). Weather tends to be better than in most places in Western Scotland, but it is at its best during April, May and June, while the autumn can also be relied upon.

'The owners, Mr and Mrs Buchanan Smith, supervise everything and are responsible for the house-party atmosphere. Visitors get the impression that the young hand-picked staff may well be family members. A highly professional permanent hotel manager contrived to "fit in" as though he were an elder son, and last time I was there the barman was a parson from a cathedral (though no one would have guessed it). Mrs Buchanan Smith is a Cordon Bleu cook. Breakfast is served on vast entrée dishes and is traditional, with choices of sausages, bacon, eggs and kidneys all in a row below gleaming helmet-like lids, while cereals, porridge, toast and various marmalades are on side tables. Morning coffee (filtered) is available in a large pot. Luncheon tends to be a cold buffet with hot soup. It also tends to be unforgettable. But not so unforgettable as the dinner!

'A good deal of the house is furnished in Victorian idiom and there are Eastern carpets and rugs, all of which contrive to give that enviable slight "shabbiness" which money simply cannot buy and which conveys so much warm atmosphere. Bedrooms are faultless, and reading in bed is easy on the eyes. There is a good selection of books in the library located in the bar. There is a pleasant Victorian-style drawing room with vast oriel windows and colour television.

'The hotel is, in my view, one of the world's really remarkable places. The only others with which I can make fair comparison are Aggie Gray's in Western Samoa, and Sam Lord's as it was ten years ago in Barbados. There is also a hotel in Swat, Pakistan, which has the same homely yet idyllic atmosphere, but they are few and very far between.' (*George Mair*; also *Brenda Moriarty, P. F. Lane*)

Open: April–November.
Rooms: 15 double, 6 single—all with bath, telephone and radio.
Drawing room (with colour TV), bar (with library). Private bridge to mainland; 270 acres of grounds with a formal garden, park and moorland; croquet (tennis court and billiards room planned for 1978), bathing from shingle beach, sea fishing, pony-trekking.
Dogs not allowed in public rooms.
Terms (excluding VAT):   B & B: £10.00–£14.00; dinner: from £6.50.
NOTE: the hotel makes a speciality of weekly terms. Full board: £120–£150.
Mini-breaks in November.

NEW ABBEY, Dumfries & Galloway

Criffel Inn   *Telephone:* New Abbey (038 785) 244

'The inn was chosen by my husband for an overnight stay as against the inn opposite (AA and RAC recommended) because the sun was shining upon it, and my goodness so it should. We lunched upon home-made lentil soup (perfection), fresh salmon and salad (the salmon tasted as though it had jumped straight out of the burn glowing outside the window on to the plate), home-made apple pie with fresh cream. It was served by the wife of the inn-keeper in a spotless white coat. The table appointments shone on to a crisp white tablecloth. After a long haul up a mountain, I was ready for afternoon tea. It was served to me on a tray comprising three small delicious pastries, and the china was exquisite fine bone Minton. Our dinner started with a creamy potato soup, roast pork, various fresh vegetables, and a superb sweet. Our coffee and a special liqueur whisky was served to us upstairs in a small lounge. Breakfast was porridge, bacon, eggs, sausages, tomato, fresh hot rolls and toast. Our bill: £14 odd. "Why aren't you AA and RAC recommended?" I enquired. "We haven't sufficient rooms," they replied. How absurd!' (*Sheila Richman*)

Open: all year.
Rooms: 3 double, 1 single.
Residents' lounge (with colour TV), public bar; garden with patio; sea and sandy beaches, 8 miles; golf course and fishing near by.
Terms: B & B: £4.40; half board: £7.00.

OVERSCAIG, Nr Lairg, Highland

Overscaig Hotel   *Telephone:* Merkland (054 983) 203

As remote a hotel as any in this book, Overscaig lies in isolated splendour in the wide-open expanse of moorland, loch and peat bog in Britain's most northerly county. Originally a coaching inn and driver's halt, it became popular last century with the fishing fraternity, and the hotel maintains continuous fishing records from 1887. Fishing is free to residents on Loch Shin, on whose shores the hotel stands, and the adjoining Lochs Ghriam and Merkland, and there are innumerable other fishing lochs within a few miles of the hotel. And it is, of course, a good base for touring, walking or climbing holidays too. There are plenty of such places all over the Highlands. What distinguishes *Overscaig* is the ambition of its owners, Jimmy and Sheila Hamilton-Hesse, to make the hotel as noted for its food as for its situation and amenities. *Overscaig*, in its present renaissance, only opened in 1976, but the Hamilton-Hesses had already made a culinary name for themselves at the Ferry Boat Inn at Ullapool. They specialise in Highland dishes: cullen skink, kedgeree, haggis, skirlie cloutie dumpling and the like. The local brown trout is baked in foil with butter; the West Coast large prawns in whisky and cream; salmon, sea trout and venison are also standard features of their menus. (*Derek Cooper*)

Open: all year, but limited facilities November–March.
Rooms: 11 double, 4 single—3 with bath or shower; also a self-catering cottage.
Residents' lounge, TV room, 2 bars; 250 acres of grounds with 4½ miles of frontage on Loch Shin; the hotel adjoins the Loch, with safe bathing, sailing and fishing (excellent trout, sea trout and salmon).
Terms (excluding VAT):   B & B: £7.00; half board (weekly): £67.00; packed lunches and bar snacks available; dinner (*à la carte*): approx. £3.50.

PORTREE, Isle of Skye, Highland

Coolin Hills Hotel   *Telephone:* Portree (0478) 2003

'The Victorian lairds, since they owned all the land, were in a commanding position to choose the best sites for their shooting lodges. In the 19th century, Lord MacDonald of the Isles built himself a modest box on the northern side of Portree Bay. Its magnificent drawing room faces across the water and the eye travels on up Glen Varragill to the full glory of the 1,000-metre-high Cuillin Hills. Arguably one of the best views from anywhere in the island. The MacDonalds' steam yacht, *Lady of the Isles*, is no longer anchored in the bay, and there have been some modern extensions, but the rhododendrons still bloom in early summer, and in high summer wild raspberries can be picked in the grounds. An ideal centre for touring, and safe for children. The other hotels in Portree tend to empty you straight on to crowded pavements and traffic.' (*Derek Cooper*)

Open: all year.
Rooms: 20 double, 7 single—12 with bath or shower.
Fine drawing room, TV lounge; 13 acres of grounds; bathing, fishing, sea excursions, walking and climbing, all at hand.
Terms (excluding service and VAT):   B & B: £6.50; lunch: from £2.50; dinner: from £3.00.

SCOURIE, Highland

Scourie Hotel *Telephone:* Scourie (0971) 2396

A small hotel, noted for its fishing, on the west coast of Sutherland. It attracts a faithful following. 'Many of the guests have been going there for fifteen or twenty years, and the generation before them. We have been going for the past five years and have found it most comfortable and homely, and we are accepted and made to feel at home even though neither my husband nor I fish. Ian Hay and his wife, who run the hotel, are always around to welcome their guests. The food is plain but good, and a very friendly atmosphere exists between the staff and the guests.' (*Mrs N. J. Forsyth Lawson*)

Open: 1 March–21 October.
Rooms: 14 double, 9 single—11 with bath or shower.
Two lounges, cocktail bar, public bar, residents' dining room, restaurant for non-residents. (No TV.) Half-acre of grounds. Fishing for brown trout offered on over 50 hill lochs; fishing for sea trout and salmon offered on 6 lochs; 500 yards from the sea, with a ½-mile of sandy beach, safe for bathing; sea-bird sanctuary.
No dogs in the dining room.
Terms: B & B: £7.90; half board: £10.80.

SEIL, by Oban, Strathclyde

Dunmor House *Telephone:* Balvicar (085 23) 203

'A characteristic gabled white farmhouse on the hill farm of Dunmor, with invigorating views over the sea and some of the islands of the Inner Hebrides. The island of Seil, in an isolated corner of Scotland, is joined to the Argyll mainland by Clachan Bridge ("The Bridge over the Atlantic"). Its hills, cliffs and rocky beaches make it excellent walking country, and Oban, with its steamer tours, is only half an hour away by car.

'*Dunmor House* is the sort of house I sometimes wish I lived in, and the view from the lounge window actually inspired me to draw it—which is something that doesn't happen often. The house is up a gravel path, past green pastures and a lawn full of rabbits. Inside, it is pleasantly informal. Mrs Campbell-Gibson's superb cooking was partaken in a jolly room that opened on to a somewhat draughty extension. Her fresh pears in tarragon cream were delicious, and the good thing about her short set menu is that it forces you to try new things that you wouldn't otherwise have ordered. When I asked for cream on my dessert, she apologised but said that the cow hadn't produced enough that day. The bedroom was warm, large and comfortable in a homely way. Snack lunches in the wooden bar room, with home-made soups balanced on our knees, were worth staying in for. You can go for long walks through the fields behind, or along to the little village of Easdale.

There you can wander down a narrow lane of terraced cottages one of which is stuffed full of home-made sweets and souvenirs. Hurry back in time for scones for tea. Sundry dogs wander round the house—we wanted to stay longer, but they were firmly booked.' (*Susan Grossman*)

Open: 1 May–15 October.
Rooms: 10 double, 3 single—1 with bath.
Drawing room, lounge (with TV). 1,000 acres of hill farm; safe sea bathing on gravel and rock beach close to the hotel; sea fishing and boat trips by arrangement; trout fishing available on several local lochs.
No children under 8 in the dining room for dinner.
Terms (excluding VAT):   B & B: £9.00; dinner: from £4.30; half board (7 days minimum): £13.00.

SKEABOST BRIDGE, Isle of Skye, Highland

Skeabost House   *Telephone:* Skeabost Bridge (047 032) 202

'*Skeabost House*, a comfortable rambling mansion with Edwardian billiard room, is panelled (by Maples) within, and crenellated without. From its tower you can look out across Loch Snizort to the Outer Hebrides. It's six miles from Portree on the Dunvegan road. It is approached down a long winding drive enshrubbed with rhododendrons; through the grounds runs the peat-brown salmon-rich waters of the river Snizort, the longest in Skye. On a summer evening, for fishermen and those who like peace and beauty, this is a reasonable substitute for paradise. Sheila Macnab, who trained in cookery at Atholl Crescent in Edinburgh, commands the kitchen. Her mother, Mrs Stuart, does all the baking for the afternoon teas and makes *Skeabost*'s famous soda bread. The soups are home-made here, the salmon is straight out of the river, and the hotel's modestly priced five-course dinners are among the best in the West. There are modern extensions to the hotel which have been discreetly done; log fires even in high summer. Book early.' (*Derek Cooper*)

Open: April–October.
Rooms: 16 double, 5 single—10 with bath, all with radio and tea-making facilities.
Two lounges, sun room, snooker room. Twelve acres of parkland; salmon and sea trout fishing on the river Snizort which runs through the grounds (the hotel owns 8 miles on both banks, free to guests); there is a resident angling coach.
Dogs not allowed in public rooms.
Terms (excluding service and VAT):   B & B: £7.00; lunch: £1.80; dinner: £3.30; full board (weekly): £72.50.

Prices quoted, unless otherwise specified, are for bed and breakfast for a person sharing a double room with bath or shower in the high season. We have also given half and full board prices per person in high season when available.

Mauld Bridge House

Telephone: Struy (046 376) 222

The smallest hotel in the book, but though the restaurant—called confusingly Kristine's Kitchen—attracts a lot of outside visitors and is Christine and David MacKenzie's main business, it would be incorrect to call this small country house just a restaurant with rooms. It's a highly personal, thoroughly comfortable mini-hotel in the Glen of Strathglass, twenty-one miles from Inverness, surrounded by awesome Highland scenery. 'Good food, good wine and good inns are my hobby, and I'm a critical judge of all three. *Mauld Bridge* is a great find in an area I know well. David and Christine MacKenzie are delightful people; their concern for the well-being of their guests is paramount. A gem.' (*Jean Carnegie*)

Open: all year, except 4 weeks (variable during winter).
Rooms: 3 double—all with bath.
Lounge, cocktail bar (no TV); 3½ acres of grounds on the banks of the river Glass. Salmon and trout fishing near by, riding and pony-trekking handy.
Dogs only by prior arrangement, and not in public rooms.
Terms: B & B: £5.00–£6.75; lunch: £2.50; dinner: £6.00; half board (weekly): £88.50.
Winter weekend rates, November to March.

Isle of Barra Hotel

Telephone: Castlebay (087 14) 383

Barra is a pocket-sized island surrounded by its own scatter of rock stacks and islets to the south of the main Outer Hebridean islands. Small enough to be walked round in a day, it's Hebridean scenery in miniature. Sea cliffs, the home of innumerable birds, rise to 700 feet and more, and there are inland hills to be climbed, though none much more than 1,000 feet. Often known as 'The Garden of the Hebrides', it is predictably rich in flowers and wild life; but it also has some delightful pale sand beaches. Transport to the island is by steamer from Oban or, when it's not foggy, by 'plane from Glasgow, which island-hops to Stornoway on Lewis, and back. No formal airport here—there's no space: the 'plane lands on a beach known as the Cockle Strand—between the tides. The *Isle of Barra Hotel*, opened in 1974, may seem a solecism in such a place, but in spite of its modern architecture, it doesn't spoil the scene and is a boon to visitors wanting civilised amenities as well as the notion that they are 'away from it all'. It overlooks a lovely Atlantic beach and one of the sea lochs that indent the shore. There's a pleasant restaurant. You are surrounded not only by comfort, but by views. (*Christopher Maycock*)

Open: all year.
Rooms: 41 double—all with bath and radio.
Lounge and TV room; swimming, surfing, fishing (loch and sea); seal and bird-watching, hill and cliff walking, collecting cockles on the Cockle Strand (avoid the 'plane); excursions to near-by islands and deserted islets, boats and weather permitting.

Hotel Report forms will be found on pp. 257-67.

The Moorings Hotel,
Gorey, Jersey

Channel Islands

GOREY, Jersey

The Moorings Hotel   *Telephone:* Jersey Central (0534) 53633

Gorey, tucked below the impressive medieval fortress of Mont Orgeuil,
is a little Honfleur-like port and resort, with lots of fishing and sailing,
and popular with French day visitors who come over by hydrofoil from
Carteret and Portbail. *The Moorings*, opened in 1949, is a small busy
hotel actually on the pier. The food is well-cooked, with lobster and
other seafood always on the menu. The rooms on the front overlook the
goings-on. Those at the back are quieter—also cheaper. (*George
Behrend*)

Open: all year.
Rooms: 7 double, 4 single—7 with bath, all with telephone and radio.
            Also a luxury penthouse suite.
Lounge, residents' bar, public bar; sand and rock beach with safe bath-
ing near by; 18-hole Gorey Golf Course, 5 minutes' walk.
Not suitable for young children. Dogs not allowed in restaurant and
bars.
Terms: B & B: £8.60; lunch: £3.00; dinner: £3.50; full board
            (weekly): £60.20; penthouse, B & B: £150 per week for 2
            persons.

Dixcart Hotel   *Telephone :* Sark 15

Sark, without crowds or cars, is a dependable haven of peace for the jaded urbanite and a paradise for naturalists. Only $3\frac{1}{2}$ miles long by $1\frac{1}{4}$ miles wide, it has 40 miles of coastline with many coves and wonderful cliff walks. There are boats every weekday from Guernsey and a couple of hydrofoils operate from Jersey; the *Dixcart* collects your luggage by tractor, and can arrange a horse-drawn carriage (75p.) to take you to the hotel high up in the centre of the island. It's an early 19th-century building, stone-built and partly creeper-covered. Swinburne and Victor Hugo are among the illustrious names of former residents. The food, according to one Channel Islander, is the best on the archipelago. 'A flowery and friendly old house with a unique atmosphere of insouciance and charm. The rooms, although small and simple, are comfortable. The charges are reasonable. Peggy Ravenshaw, who presides with loving attention, is deeply versed in the lore of the island. She is an original and amusing woman whose tact, gaiety and strength of character add greatly to the sum of things.' (*Winifred and Miranda Mackintosh;* also *George Behrend*)

Open :   Easter–mid October.
Rooms :   12 double, 7 single—6 with bath or shower.
Two sitting rooms, lounge, bar; 9 acres of grounds; the sea is five minutes' walk, with sandy beach and safe bathing; fishing; fine walks. Children 'not really encouraged but tolerated'! Dogs charged according to diet and size.
Terms (excluding service) :   full board: £13.50.

> **Warning: prices quoted are 1977 prices.**

Rathmullan House, Rathmullan, Co. Donegal

Ireland

BALLYLICKEY, Bantry Bay, Co. Cork

Ballylickey House Hotel   *Telephone:* Bantry 71

'A relatively small country house hotel beautifully situated at the head of Bantry Bay, and an ideal location for touring the West Cork and Kerry areas. The hotel is a founder-member of the *Relais de Campagne*, renowned mainly for its members in France—and there is a French atmosphere noticeable particularly in the restaurant where French chefs under the supervision of the proprietor, produce what is certainly a high standard of cuisine—with the emphasis on what is freshly available locally. We found the presentation of the fish in all forms to be out-standing. There is an excellent wine list at, by standards of most hotels today, very reasonable prices. I have spent very pleasant holidays here, and have found it warm, friendly and comfortable, avoiding the stereo-typed atmosphere of many hotels. The service is good, without being so professional as to be detached.' (*Martin Lanigan Urell*)

Open: mid February–November.
Rooms: 25 double—all with bath and telephone. Also 3 chalets in the grounds.
Two drawing rooms, 2 bars; 12 acres of lawns and parkland bordered by the river Ouvane; heated outdoor swimming pool. Trout, sea trout and salmon fishing in near-by rivers and lakes; 2 9-hole golf courses within a few miles; 2 riding stables where pony trekking is available, close by.
Terms (excluding service):   B & B: £8.50–£10.00; lunch: £4.10; dinner: £5.75; half board (3 days minimum): £14.25–£15.50; full board (3 days minimum): £15.50–£18.00.

Gregan's Castle   *Telephone:* Ballyvaughan 5

This converted manor house, set in its own grounds, is in the beautiful Burren area—wild and remote though only an hour's drive from Shannon Airport. 100 square miles in area, The Burren is a kind of botanist's and ornithologist's paradise; and for the archaeologist there are stone circles, megalithic tombs, cairns and dolmen; caves, too, in the slopes of Slieve Elva, one of the Burren mountains, 1,134 feet high. The field opposite *Gregan's* has orchids growing in it as casually as other people have dandelions in their back gardens. There is excellent shooting and fishing close at hand, and clean beaches (which you won't always find on Ireland's east coast). The hotel is run by Peter and Moira Haden who, as one enthusiastic guest put it, 'actually like people and demonstrate this in a simple, natural manner.' The cooking, which Peter Haden supervises personally, makes plentiful use of the local fish and the fresh produce from the garden. The fresh crab, the mussels cooked in Peter Haden's own style, and the clams grilled with garlic butter, are specially recommended, also the soups. The hotel pays attention to creature comforts and gives the impression of a friendly country house, with large open fireplaces, a budgie down the hall, and a good selection of books in the coffee room. Unlike many hotels, which try to cold-shoulder the locals, the Hadens welcome their neighbours who contribute generously to the conviviality of the bar. (*Lloyd Smythe, P. T. Coulborn*)

Open: all year.
Rooms: 14 double, 1 single—10 with bath or shower; baby-listening service.
Residents' lounge (with TV), picture windows overlooking Galway Bay, Orchid Lounge, cocktail bar, Corkscrew Bar (decorated with quantities of antique brasses); traditional music two nights a week; 13-acre grounds, with parkland and gardens. Safe, sandy beach within 4 miles; surfing further off at Fanore; boat trips in summer to the Aran Islands.
Dogs admitted, but not in bedrooms.
Terms (excluding service): B & B: £7.00–£10.00; lunch: £2.50; dinner: £4.50; half board (weekly): £55.00–£60.00.

DUBLIN

Royal Hibernian Hotel   *Telephone:* Dublin (0001 from UK)
46/8 Dawson Street   (01 from Ireland) 772991
                        Telex: 5220

From a modest start in the early 19th century as a stage halt, the *Royal Hibernian* has progressed to the status of Grand Hotel, with an elegant decor, smart clientele, and a high reputation for comfort and good service. Predominant among the decorative public rooms is the number of eating areas of one sort and another: the main restaurant is the attractive Lafayette Room; the secondary dining room is the new Rotisserie; there is a quick grill in the Bianconi in the basement; and the Buttery for snacks, which doubles as a bar. The hotel prides itself on the fact that its chef is always French, and the welcome traditionally Irish. (*Oliver Wright*)

Open: all year.
Rooms: 114 double and single—most with bath or shower, all with telephone and radio.
Several lounges, bars, a variety of restaurants and snack bars, conference facilities.
Terms: B & B: £14.00; lunch: £4.50; tea: £1.25; dinner: £5.50.

The Shelbourne Hotel   *Telephone:* Dublin (0001 from UK)
St Stephen's Green   (01 from Ireland) 766471
                        Telex: 5184

One of Dublin's 'institutions'. Long established and popular, it occupies an enviable position on a fine Georgian square facing directly across to St Stephen's Green. Service is Irish-traditional-formal-friendly. The wood-panelled circular bar has a men-only air in spite of its mixed customers, and it is usually crammed to capacity. The restaurant is elegant and formal; not so the busy Saddle Room, noted for its roast beef and other robust specialities; here everything is cooked and carved before your eyes, and served at dizzy speed. The staff seems to stay for ever and have long memories for regular guests, however long the intervals between their visits. (*Diana Petry*)

Open: all year.
Rooms: 137 double, 23 single, 6 suites—all with bath and/or shower, telephone, radio and TV.
Several lounges, bars (one serving hot and cold snacks); banqueting suites and conference facilities.
Dogs allowed, but not in public rooms.
Terms (excluding service):   B & B: £15.10.

LAHINCH, Co. Clare

Aberdeen Arms Hotel   *Telephone:* Lahinch 20

'The *Aberdeen Arms* is the largest and only Grade A hotel in this beautiful small seaside resort. It is owned and run by the Vaughan family. Miceal, the proprietor, a past president of the Irish Hotels Federation, personally supervises the dining room for all meals. His wife, Phil, who bakes all the delicious brown soda bread for which the hotel is famous, looks after the housekeeping and, like Miceal, believes the guests' enjoyment is of supreme importance and is undaunted by any problem which might threaten to mar a holiday. Eamonn, Miceal's brother, is Manager, trained at the Shannon Hotel School and at Heidelberg, and is in charge of the kitchen where he has earned a reputation for his soups and other specialities. He has a particular flair for seafood, and his Liscannor Broth and Pouldoody Plate are among his best endeavours. One daughter, Aileen, is responsible for the sweets, and her two sisters, Brid and Marie, serve. One comes as a tourist, is treated as a guest, and leaves a personal friend of the family.' (*Brid Corry*)

Open: Easter–mid October.
Rooms: 41 double, 5 single—most with bath or shower, all with telephone.
Four lounges (1 with TV), bar; 300 yards from Entertainment Centre, with heated outdoor pool, cinema, dancing and other facilities in season; 200 yards from a sandy beach, good for surfing; two 18-hole golf courses, one a championship course; sea fishing in Liscannor Bay, brown trout and salmon fishing near by.
Terms (excluding service): B & B: £5.50; dinner: from £3.75.

OUGHTERARD, Co. Galway

Currarevagh House   *Telephone:* Galway 82313

'The Hodgson family have been living in this mid-Victorian country house on the banks of Lough Corrib for five generations, and June and Harry Hodgson now run it as an unstuffy, personal hotel. It is set in 150 acres of its own grounds, and there is beautiful wild country around for walks and golf and riding near by, but it is particularly popular with fishermen. There's a book in the hall where you can enter the number of fish caught, and that is a characteristic of the "private house" approach of the owners. There are no keys to the bedrooms—not that one would be likely to take one's diamonds to this remote spot. The decor hasn't changed much since 1900: the beds are marvellously capacious, with heavy linen sheets; splendid bathroom fittings, lots of Edwardian furniture. There are huge baskets of turf and large open fires in the two reception rooms—and the public rooms and hall are so spacious that it is easy enough to be on one's own. The food is good plain home cooking, such as one would get if one were lucky as a weekend guest in the country. Excellent home-made brown bread for breakfast, for instance, and first-rate coffee, kept hot over individual spirit lamps. Trout from the lough for dinner, simply cooked with melted butter. This is not a place I would bring small children—it is full of the hush of grown-ups relaxing—but I know that the owner would be too polite to demur at the idea.' (*Mirabel Cecil*)

Open: Easter–5 October (approx.).
Rooms: 11 double, 5 single—5 with bath.
Two sitting rooms, TV room; 140 acres of park and woodland; 100

yards from Lough Corrib, 2 miles of foreshore belonging to the hotel; trout fishing, grilse in June/July, the hotel owns several boats; the Lough is unpolluted and safe for bathing; much other fishing in the vicinity. Sporting rights over 5,000 acres of moors near the house for grouse, woodcock and snipe in season; golf and riding near by.

'Children are tolerated but not encouraged. Consequently, should parents want to bring children, any reduced rate will be agreed on booking, and only if children share parents' room. No listening service or games'. Dogs by prior arrangement only.

Terms (excluding service):   full board (minimum 3 days): £13.00; full board (weekly): £84.00.

RATHMULLAN, Co. Donegal

Rathmullan House   *Telephone:* Rathmullan 4

The small resort of Rathmullan, on the sandy western shore of Lough Swilly, is in a landscape that seems almost tame when compared with the wild grandeur of the coast and mountains to the west. The lough itself is tree-lined and with grassy banks, offering good sea fishing; the surrounding hills provide fine walking country. *Rathmullan House*, in romantic lawns and gardens (it won the National Gardens Award in 1975), is a confident Victorian country house, long, low and bow-fronted, furnished with considerable taste and comfort, and family-run by people who know and respect what holiday-makers want. Log and peat fires burn in the drawing rooms and library; in the large dining room, fresh salmon and lobster are served regularly, and there is a charcoal grill in what was originally a kitchen. The atmosphere is far from stuffy, though it is the sort of place for families who don't have to economise. Children are welcome and cared for, and baby-sitting can usually be arranged. The bedrooms are all close-carpeted and prettily furnished, and most have either garden or lough views. (*Diana Petry, Oliver Wright*)

Open: Easter–October.
Rooms: 17 double, 4 single—9 with bath or shower. Also 20 self-catering family chalets in the grounds, with baby-sitting services.
Drawing room, library, coffee room, TV room; 50 acres of grounds with tennis, croquet, clock golf and badminton; direct access to the sea, with sandy beach and safe bathing. Fishing, boating, sailing and water-skiing; 3 golf courses near by.
No dogs, except in chalets.
Terms: B & B: £6.50; lunch: from £3.60; light lunches: from 75p.; dinner: from £4.75; half board (minimum 3 days): £9.75; half board (weekly): £62.50.

All prices include tax and service unless otherwise specified.

RIVERSTOWN, Co. Sligo

Coopershill Farm

Telephone: Sligo 75108

'An enchanted and enchanting piece of country: to the south stretch the dramatic Bricklieve Mountains and vast peat bogs; to the north is Sligo town and the sea; and a few miles further north again is Drumcliff, where the poet Yeats is buried, the scene glowered over by the ship-shaped mass of Benbulben, its profile visible for miles around. Coopershill itself is a perfect paradise of rest and delight. Designated a farmhouse, it is, in fact, a gracious Georgian building, four-square, solid, beautifully furnished and run by charming people. There is a wine licence and the food is excellent. Here you live as a guest might in a minor stately home. Except for the lure of the surrounding sights, which it would be criminal to miss, there is enough going on around the farm to keep you there for the duration.' (*Diana Petry*)

Open: Easter–September.
Rooms: 6 double, mostly four-posters—1 with bath.
Drawing room, playroom with TV, piano, record-player and table tennis. The hotel has 8 ponies and provides riding for children, also a donkey and cart. A river runs through the grounds, a boat is available and there is fishing for pike and perch; trout fishing near by; sandy beach at Sligo, 12 miles.
Terms: B & B: £4.00; dinner: £3.50; half board (weekly): £45.00.

SHANAGARRY, Co. Cork

Ballymaloe House

Telephone: Cork 62531

'I first went to this hotel years ago, when we dropped in for lunch and found ourselves staying several days. I went there for my honeymoon, and whenever we feel we deserve a treat, we go there again. It's a beguiling place. The Allen family who run it are in evidence everywhere— Mrs Allen is in the kitchen, various children driving tractors on the Home Farm, helping in the office, etc., and grandchildren eating in the dining room. The service is efficient and relaxed. On our way here for our honeymoon, we were delayed by a meandering Irish cow on the road and rang the hotel, who sympathised and promised that they would have a cold meal waiting for us when we arrived very late at night. There was a beautifully arranged cold supper with half-bottle of Pommard waiting for us in our room.

'This summer we stayed in the Gatehouse, a pretty white cottage a mile away at the end of the drive, with two rooms, a little kitchen and a bathroom. There are also lofts above the converted stables in the courtyard where you can stay very cheaply in simple whitewashed bedrooms and still enjoy the marvellous food in the main house. The hotel is as popular with the Irish as with the tourists. I would thoroughly recommend it for children: there are so many jolly friendly families staying there in the summer, that the kids all have a wonderful time together. The sea is about three miles away. The famous Shanagarry Pottery is a mile down the road, with Mr Pearse's pots (cheaper than in the shops) and his son's marvellous glass. There is also an Irish crafts shop in the grounds, which sells tweeds, woollens and pictures, also fresh produce; there were loganberries there last time, an unheard-of delicacy in Ireland. The house itself, which is 17th century (though with a 14th-century keep), is very pretty. The dining room is in splendid William Morris greens, and is called the Yeats room after its collection of Jack Yeats pictures. The decor may have got shabbier over the years, which rather becomes it, but isn't significant of any decline in the standard of the cooking. The menus are very imaginative, and make full use of the fish caught in Ballycotton Bay near by. The home-made bread is out of this world, and the mushrooms alone at breakfast are worth staying there for several days. Helpings are generous. There is an interesting cold buffet lunch, so it doesn't matter whether you are in on time or not. (Packed lunch is the same price as lunch at the hotel, but not actually worth it.) Dinner is slightly more of a dressed-up occasion than lunch, though not oppressively so.' (*Mirabel Cecil;* also *Len Deighton*)

Open: all year, except for occasional 2 weeks in winter, and 3 days at Christmas.
Rooms: 18 double, 2 single—10 with bath or shower. Several rooms are in the Gatehouse Annexe—less expensive and suitable for young people.
Three sitting rooms (1 with TV), playroom; 400-acre farm, with tennis court, swimming pool, 9-hole golf course, trout pond. Horses and ponies are available for the use of guests. Sea with safe sandy beaches, 3 miles; sea and river fishing by arrangement.
Terms: B & B: £6.25; lunch (residents only): £2.00; dinner: £5.50.

Length of entries is not an indication of comparative merit, but of the relative attractiveness of the contribution.

Part Two
The Continent, North Africa and Israel

AUSTRIA

DENMARK

FRANCE

GERMANY

ISRAEL

ITALY

MADEIRA

MALTA

MOROCCO

NETHERLANDS

PORTUGAL

SPAIN (including
the Balearics and the Canaries)

SWEDEN

SWITZERLAND

TUNISIA

TURKEY

YUGOSLAVIA

Austria

Hotel Bristol, Vienna

PÖRTSCHACH AM WÖRTHER SEE, Carinthia

Hotel Dermuth

Telephone: (04272) 2240

'In the centre of this lakeside resort, the *Dermuth* is classified as being in the B class. But I would have given it an A by the standard of accommodation, which was spotless, and the food, which was the best of Austrian cooking, presided over by the host's wife, who talked to all the guests personally. The hotel is partly modern, but there is also, as an exceptionally grand annexe, a baroque summer residence, sumptuously furnished, in a beautiful lakeside garden with Grecian statues. The whole area is rich in historical sites, and it is only a short drive into Yugoslavia and Italy.' (*R. H. Owen*)

Open: 1 May–30 December.
Rooms: 30 double, 17 single—21 with bath, 26 with shower, all with telephone.
Lift, 2 salons (1 with TV); 4,000 square metres of lakeside gardens; tennis courts, private landing stage to lake, with sailing and swimming; bathing beach 500 metres from the hotel.
Terms: full board: 350–90 Sch.

Sterling and dollar equivalents of foreign currencies at the date of going to press will be found under Exchange Rates on p. 243.

SALZBURG

Hotel-Restaurant Bayrischer Hof   *Telephone:* (0622) 72316/73840
Elisabethstrasse 12   *Telex:* 63291

'The *Bayrischer Hof* is a three-minute walk from the station, which to some is an advantage, but that means that it is a ten-minute bus ride from the centre of town, though I have never found that much of a draw-back. The actual hotel is small, but it has an annexe on the top (eighth and ninth floors) of the adjoining buildings, where one has a fine view over the mountains—about half the rooms have balconies. The annexe is ruled by a housekeeper who has been there at any rate all of the last five years and keeps it in a spotless condition and looks after the miscellaneous tastes of the inhabitants at breakfast. The restaurant is run separately from the hotel, but it has the approval of the Austrian equivalent of the *Good Food Guide*, and fully deserves it. In summer, the restaurant explodes into the garden where one sits under the trees. The food is quite as good as any I have had elsewhere in Salzburg, even at much more expensive places. There may not be much character about it all, but it is a pleasant place to stay in a town where tourists are otherwise regarded as an industry. You pay appreciably less than in the centre. Personally, I would not stay anywhere else.' (*George A. R. Bird*)

Open: all year.
Rooms: 31 double, 21 single—25 with bath or shower, all with telephone, some with radio or TV.
Lift, lounge, bar; garden for meals in summer.
Terms: B & B: 345 Sch.; full board: 495 Sch.

VIENNA

Hotel Bristol   *Telephone:* (0222) 529552
Kärntnerring 1   *Telex:* 01/2474

Personality, elegance, understanding service, and a high standard of cooking, make this one of the 'great' hotels, and as central as can be—overlooking the Ring, and facing the Opera House. Corridors and halls are filled with delightful antiques, brocade walls, chandeliers; bedrooms are spacious and furnished in the grand style. 'In the excellent panelled dining room—cuisine the best in Vienna—staff are on the elderly side: you feel they have been there for years. They give you the feeling of considerateness, dignity, efficiency: what it used to be like in the great old days.' (*Frank Falkner; also A. Kahane*)

Open: all year.
Rooms: 70 double, some suites, 49 single—all with bath and telephone, some with radio or TV; air-conditioned.
Lift; lounges, drawing rooms, bar, music room; piano concert nightly in the Bristol Restaurant. Opera, theatre and concert ticket service.
Terms: B & B: 675–850 Sch.

Hotel Dagmar, Ribe

Denmark

BRAMMINGE, Nr Esbjerg, Jutland

Bramminge Hovedgaard

Telephone: (05) 173325

'During a business trip to South Jutland in October 1976, I stayed at this hotel for two periods of five days. I travelled many miles by car each day so that I could return to its calm and congenial atmosphere in the evenings. It is a medieval manor house run by the Lord and Lady of the Manor who personally take part in cooking and serving meals, which are cooked to a high standard and agreeably served. The dining room and lounge in the manor house itself are spacious and dignified and contain many objects of artistic interest. The guest apartments, each quaintly named after some well-known personality, are in the adjoining buildings. Six of them have their own lounge and can be regarded as separate flats or cottages.' (*L. A. Clark*)

Open: 5 January–22 December.
Rooms: 12 double—all with bath/shower.
Two salons (1 with TV); 10 acres of grounds with a small river near by; riding facilities (the hotel has its own tackle room); swimming, 1 km.; fishing (for bream and roach) on the river Holsted (free to guests), and on the near-by Sneum and King's river (small charge).
Terms: Bed: 43–75 kr (breakfast extra).

Warning: prices quoted are 1977 prices.

Falsled Kro   *Telephone:* (09) 681111

'Kro means Inn in Danish and this one, in a tiny country village with a grassy garden backing on to the sea, is the most beautiful one I've ever stayed in. It was rebuilt in 1840 with beamed ceilings, a thatched roof and whitewashed walls, and has been extensively redecorated inside in impeccable taste that makes it feel like a very comfortable country house. The bedrooms are exquisite—each one different. All open on to a quiet stone courtyard with a trickling fountain and a trout pond. Even the smallest is vast, and as you open the door the extravagance and luxury of the decor hits you. All have Spanish ceramic tiles on the floors and walls, log fires, heavy drapes and four-poster beds. All have modern warm bathrooms, again with attractive tiles and nice little touches such as bathrobes hanging behind the door. Some rooms are on two floors with a rickety wooden balustrade separating the sleeping area on the half landing from the comfortable sofas and armchairs on the ground floor. There is a tiny bar and an elegant lounge, with a central hearth and deep leather chairs. After quails' eggs with our aperitifs, it was difficult to uncurl ourselves from the comfortable sofa to go into the restaurant, even if it had the reputation for the best food in Denmark. And deservedly so—the chef is French and he smokes his own salmon and hams and kills his own deer and game. A superb meal, then back to the lounge to watch the dying embers, with a bottomless cona coffee pot and thick double cream. It's exorbitantly expensive, with meals costing about £15 a head, though well worth visiting for the set lunches at about £6. Worth going miles out of your way for—except on a Monday, when the restaurant is closed.' (*Susan Grossman*)

Open: all year except January and February.
Rooms: 9 double, 2 single—all with bath and shower and telephone. Living room, coffee room; garden; direct access to the sea, with fishing, sailing and swimming.
Terms: Bed: 88–138 kr (breakfast extra).

JYLLINGE, Nr Roskilde, Seeland

Hotel Søfryd   *Telephone:* (03) 388011
Søfrydvej 10   *Telex:* 43145

'A small hotel halfway between Hillerod and Roskilde in the province of Seeland, on the shore of the Roskildefjord. Only a dozen bedrooms, but it has a large restaurant and a bar, the latter a bit pseudo-shipshape, but none the worse for that. Really beautiful views across the fjord, particularly as the sun sets across it in the west; small fishing boats setting out and returning, lights flashing off buoys and lighthouses; seagulls. The owner made us very welcome and told us a bit about the district. The great Danish boating season was just about to start, he said, but it was quiet this week. Later, we walked along the shore of the fjord and found an enormous marina full of the most expensive boat hardware I have seen anywhere.

'Rooms are comfortable, clean, well lit and furnished, small bathroom *en suite*, with a fantastic basin-cum-shower which you occasionally see in Northern Europe. The apparently fixed centre spout on the basin lifts out and becomes a hand-held shower fitting: the floor slopes gently to a drain. (You have to be careful not to saturate the loo-paper during this performance.) Food is excellent, well cooked, with a wide range of different kinds of food from traditional Scandinavian to standard French. Even special orders are taken, providing stocks of the ingredients are available, at very little extra cost. Fish, of course, is the obvious choice, and it couldn't be fresher. We enjoyed it all so much that we sneaked another day there later on, only to find a notice saying "Closed on Mondays" in Danish on the door. We went round the back to see what was going on, and the proprietor explained that it didn't apply to *friends and visitors*, but only to the casuals who wanted a meal. Great welcome, made us Danish sandwiches, sat with us in the bar and told us all his troubles. Oddly enough, a teetotaller, too. If you can afford to stay in Denmark and like fishing, boating, eating, drinking, or just being there, whether with the family, friends, or on your own, this is worth a try. But I would avoid the July/August season.' (*A. W. Pemberton*)

Open: all year.
Rooms: 16 beds—4 rooms with bath/shower.
Salon, bar; garden; fishing and boating on the Roskildefjord.
Terms: B & B: 80-110kr.

ODENSE, Funen

Hotel Windsor   *Telephone:* (09) 120652
Findegade 45

'Situated midway between the town centre and the railway station, this medium-sized hotel is in a quiet area with little traffic in the evening or night. Probably it would be a 2-star in the UK, but with what a difference ... We were welcomed personally by the proprietor, who had been told of our arrival by 'phone. After a pleasant exchange of greetings, we were shown to our rooms and given a voucher which entitled us to a free cocktail before dinner. Nothing exciting about the rooms—just good, standard hotel bedrooms. One unique feature was the triangular staircase between floors, making one complete turn round each side between levels. Comfortable sitting rooms on the ground floor, with unobtrusive and polite service for drinks, snacks, etc. (Let's forget the prices of the drinks ... that's Denmark, not the hotel.) Television was in a little annexe adjoining, and the set would even pick up UK stations, it was said (we never tried). Excellent restaurant: standard of food well above the norm for Denmark. Everything excellently cooked and served, and a head waiter who really knew his job. Even iced water on request on each table.

'In the later evening a pianist appeared, who could play almost anything from Pop to Chopin with considerable talent. Quite remarkable watching and hearing him adapt to the different groups of people who appeared from time to time: golden oldies for a coach-load of OAPs who appeared one night, *Jesus Christ Superstar* selection for a large party of youngish executives ... A good, clean, pleasant hotel of the kind you very seldom find in Britain any more, and an ideal base for exploring Hans Andersen's native town of Odense and the island of Funen of which it is the centre and capital.' (*A. W. Pemberton*)

Open: all year.
Rooms: 60—40 with bath/shower, all with telephone and radio. Salon (with TV).
Terms: B & B: 82-167 kr; half board: 145 kr.

RIBE, Jutland

Hotel Dagmar   *Telephone:* (05) 420033

'Ribe is one of Denmark's oldest towns and one of the best preserved. It's on the windy west coast of Jutland in typically flat Danish countryside. The town itself is delightful, with cobbled narrow streets of drunken old houses propping each other up. Many of them have "wing mirrors" outside so that their owners can see up and down the street without peering out of the window. In the spring you can see the fabled storks' nests perched on the rooftops. Don't miss the postbus that leaves, at low tide only, to drive across the sands to the near-by island of Mando. The *Dagmar* is in the central square. It was built in 1591, and is well in keeping with the rest of the town. The public rooms are of various shapes and sizes, rather ornately gilded in places, mostly old-fashioned and full of character, with low ceilings and chintzy armchairs. Some rooms are quiet (except for snoring residents) but others are patronised by "See Denmark in a Day" tours. Bedrooms in the old part of the hotel are museum pieces, though sleepable in. Furniture ranges from priceless antiques to random junk. Round the back is a new wing with thickly carpeted, net-curtained comfortable rooms with modern bathrooms. Rooms are quiet, service is cordial, and Ribe is charming.' (*Susan Grossman*)

Open: all year.
Rooms: 35 double, 7 single—20 with bath/shower, all with telephone and radio.
Two salons (1 with TV); fishing, riding and golf near by.
Terms: B & B: 123 kr.

> **Important reminder: terms printed must be regarded as a rough guide only as to the size of the bill to be expected at the end of your stay. For latest tariffs, check when booking.**

VEJLE, Jutland

Munkebjerg Hotel

Telephone: (05) 827500
Telex: 61103

'They often hold conferences at this hotel in a fairly isolated setting in lovely beechwoods above the fjord, and 3¾ miles by free hotel bus to the town of Vejle. It's a large hotel, outwardly a bit impersonal but with personal care and attention that puts it in the intimate class. Bedrooms are standard comfortable but a bit small, and the public rooms are spacious and airy with large areas of exposed brickwork and open hearths. But what makes this hotel special is its isolation, facilities, and the fact that it is almost entirely self-sufficient. It has its own farm, own butcher, baker, smokerie and vegetable garden. Guests are invited to inspect the kitchens and should do so. Down underground passages, past large larders full of hanging pigs and slabs of meat, past a smiling man in charge of the wine cellar inviting you to sample his many liqueurs, the cook making his irresistible Danish pastries and fresh cream-filled *petits fours*, through to the vegetable garden. Outside there are special trails for walking in the woods, horses, bikes, tennis, boats on the fjord, and a good golf course near by. You can walk down to the fjord below in about fifteen minutes. It's a splendid hide-away for those who want to relax, eat well and exercise, and a good base from which to explore a very lovely part of Denmark.' (*Susan Grossman*)

Open: 3 January–22 December.
Rooms: 105 double, 16 single—all with bath or shower, telephone and radio, some with TV.
Lift; lounges, bar (open until 1.30 a.m.), sauna, solarium, games room, conference rooms, indoor swimming pool; garden with tennis court, putting green; 12 kms from the sea, with sandy beach and safe bathing; fishing and boating on the fjord, 300 feet below the hotel; horses and bicycles available for hire; golf course near by.
Terms: B & B: 125 kr; half board: 155–80 kr; full board: 205 kr.

France

AIRVAULT, 79600 Deux-Sèvres

Auberge du Vieux Relais
Telephone: (49) 647031

'Old coaching inn in the quiet town centre, with magnificent Romanesque church—and a good base for exploring other wonderful churches
and châteaux in this untouristy part of France. Small bedrooms, but a
large bar patronised by locals. Smallish dining room which, like the
menu, is a bit too pretentious, but the food quite good, ditto wines, some
of which are interesting because local—from the Vendée. People very
pleasant. Antique shop in part of stables. I go there to sleep off Bordeaux
on my way home. Nowhere except bar to sit, except courtyard, but again
perfectly quiet with willing, friendly service.' (*Pamela Vandyke Price*)

Open: all year, except 1–16 October.
Rooms: 12—2 with bath or shower.
Bar; small garden.
Terms: B & B: 15–30 frs; meals: from 19 frs; half board: 40–60 frs;
full board: 55–80 frs.

ALGAJOLA, 20220 Île-Rousse, Corsica

Hôtel de la Plage
Telephone: (95) 607212

Algajola is a small village in the north-west corner of Corsica: just a few
shops and cafés and about four hotels. The back stairs of the *Hôtel de la*

Plage lead right on to a small beach, with a long beach adjoining; the former has some shade and its rocks at each end are good for snorkelling.

The countryside around is beautiful, particularly in the spring, but most visitors in the high season are content to spend their days basking in the sun. There's no nightlife to speak of, though one of the cafés has a disco. Calvi and Île-Rousse, ten and five miles away respectively, have a nightlife; there are daytime buses, but no public transport in the evenings. Algajola is not for those who like the bright lights. But it has other attractions:

'We have spent two weeks there in August every year for the last thirteen years, and generally find that about three-quarters of the guests have been there before, some as regular visitors for many years. The hotel is modestly appointed, but comfortable and very clean. The food is plentiful, varied and interesting, with generous use of the local herbs; there's always fresh fruit and often local goat and ewe cheese. What draws us back year after year? Above all, it is the family who run the hotel—two brothers with their wives and children. They are very pro-English. There is always at least one member of the family available to offer help, advice, or just friendly conversation; they will often sit down for a few words on the terrace at apéritif time, rarely accept a drink, but are just happy to make you feel at home. When you leave, it is quite usual to be seen off by half the family, several of the staff, as well as other guests.' (*K. F. Broom*)

Open: May–September.
Rooms: 40 double, 2 single—all with bath or shower.
Garden, and direct access to the sea and sandy beaches; underwater and boat fishing available.
Terms: half board: 55–60 frs; full board: 75–80 frs; meals: 22 frs.

ARDRES, 62610 Pas de Calais

Grand Hôtel Clément   *Telephone:* (21) 354066

'An old inn, with the bar and dining room much as they must have been for fifty years, lopsided stairs and small rooms which have, however, been made comfortable and equipped with bathrooms or showers, and WCs. There is a type of lounge apart from the bar, and a small garden. It is utterly quiet, the family who own it have done so for many years, and one is, after a few visits, staying *chez soi*. Telephone calls will be made for one, parcels left and collected, advice given—I think that the family all speak quite good English, although I speak French with them. Lots of English stay for the first or last night in France, because of the quiet—and the cooking. The dining room is completely plain, with a moulded plaster ceiling that looks like a superlative meringue. Madame does the ordering, Monsieur the cooking. The wine list is extensive, classic, and they buy their wines from good sources. The only possible disadvantage is that one tends to eat too much—the portions are definitely copious, but the quality is first-rate. The place goes in and

out of the "starred" category in Michelin, but I think is too unpretentious to appeal to the Michelin people these days—they go for olde
worlde stuff and far too much gastronomic chi-chi in my view. Belgians
and Parisians come here to eat seriously: seafood is very good, game and
the sweets are all excellent. I stayed once for Christmas and had the best
Christmas pudding I have ever had!

'Ardres is quite interesting enough to make it a centre for a few days'
stay—but, for the weekend visitor, the Gantelmes (owners) will fetch
you from the boat or hovercraft at Calais, only ten miles to the north on
the N43. The town is plain, the countryside a bit likewise, but there are
pleasing excursions and the whole atmosphere is definitely *French* in the
genuine way. And staying at the *Clément* is very much like walking into
a club.' (*Pamela Vandyke Price;* also *Adrian House*)

Open: all year, except 15 January–15 February.
Rooms: 18 double, 1 single—12 with bath or shower, all with tele-
           phone.
Lounge, bar, small garden.
Terms: B & B: 29–49 frs; meals: 33–62 frs.

ARLES, 13200 Bouches-du-Rhône

Jules César   *Telephone:* (90) 964976
Bvd des Lices   *Telex:* 400239

'In the main plane-tree-lined Boulevard des Lices, right beside a gallery
with a changing art exhibition and within walking distance of the Roman
amphitheatre. Formerly a convent, it is still an oasis of calm and cool-
ness, especially if you have just been trekking across the Camargue. You
are received (if you wish) with a well-chilled *champagne aux myrtilles*—
sheer Heaven!—while you consult the menu. And on the table is a pot
of *tapénade*, with lots of fresh butter and bread. Then the trolley of
crudités, a splendid still-life of raw vegetables in perfect condition. You
select those you want, and they are cut with a silver knife and presented
on your plate. Bedrooms are plain but comfortable, with great old-
fashioned baths, high ceilings, memories of slower, more gracious days.
Get a bedroom looking in on the still, dappled courtyard (once the
cloisters) rather than on the street. A park on the opposite side of the
road, a bit up the hill, is a good place for kids to picnic, or there are
plenty of restaurants for cheaper meals opposite.' (*Sheila Kitzinger*)

Open: 5 March–7 November.
Rooms: 60—all with bath.
Garden.
Terms: B & B: 69–85 frs; meals: 42–80 frs.

Hotel Report forms will be found on pp. 257-67.

AUBENAS, 07200 Ardèche

Hôtel La Pinède
Route du Camping

Telephone: (75) 352588

'A small isolated hotel, built between the wars, in a quite fabulous position above Aubenas on the river Ardèche. It overlooks the town, which is about a mile away, and is situated in its own large garden, full of flowers and trees. Garden seats are strewn about its own woods; an outdoor terrace provides a shady, cool place for drinks. Service is good and friendly. Food is excellent and not expensive.' (*Michael Bruce*)

Open: all year.
Rooms: 23 — 18 with bath or shower.
Large park with trees and flowers and terrace; tennis court.
Terms: B & B: 26-37 frs; full board (obligatory in high season): 70-85 frs; meals: 19-36 frs.

AVALLON, 89200 Yonne

Hostellerie de la Poste
13 Place Vauban

Telephone: (86) 340612

'One of France's really Grand Relais, an old posting house where they won't bat an eyelid if the whole family troops in in sweaters and jeans, provided they also look as though they'll appreciate (and pay for) the 2-star Michelin food as well as enjoy the hotel. The other visitors (so far as can be guessed from the restaurant), are mostly barons with their hunting dogs. Each room has its history, which means that, if you are alone, you can enjoy Napoleon and Empire, and salute imaginary crowds from the balcony in the morning. If you are accompanied, there's a fine selection of historic four-posters to choose from. Also bars, lounges, but no TV in the rooms. Avallon is still a convenient staging post, roughly halfway between Paris and Lyon on the A7. It is also an excellent base for visiting historic northern Burgundy, the Chablis district, and the lakes and hills of the Morvan.' (*Indrei Ratiu*)

Open: all year, except December and January.
Rooms: 25 — 23 with bath, 2 with showers; also 4 suites.
Lounges, bars; garden.
Terms: B & B: 80-140 frs; meals: 90-130 frs.

Prices quoted, unless otherwise specified, are for bed and breakfast for a person sharing a double room with bath or shower in the high season. We have also given half and full board prices per person in high season when available.

124

BANDOL, 83150 Var

Hôtel de L'Île Rousse
Bvd Louis-Lumière

Telephone: (94) 294686
Telex: 400372

Bandol is a busy, bustling, small resort town with lots of boats in its
harbour, popular with the French throughout the year, and increasingly
being discovered by foreigners as well. There is plenty going on around
the beach area: water-skiing, regattas, sand sports, and a casino and
dancing. Offshore (seven minutes by boat) is the island of Bendor, with
Zoological Gardens, exhibitions of local and other wines and spirits, and
a sailing and diving school. Something for everyone, in fact, which
accounts for the popularity of the resort in high season; best months,
when it is quieter, are May and June. Hotels have naturally increased in
number. The *L'Île Rousse* is the *de luxe* hotel of the place—modern,
with its own large heated swimming pool, and with exceptionally well-
furnished and attractive tile-floored rooms. It lies on a narrow street,
somewhat above the town, which is backed by wooded hills, and has its
own small cove and beach—a distinct advantage. Choose rooms facing
the cove, if possible; the ones looking on to the little street can be noisy.
'The service, ambience, and friendliness of all levels of staff are notable,
as is the first-class French cuisine in the restaurant.' (*Frank Falkner*)

Open: all year.
Rooms: 55 double—all with bath, telephone and radio.
Lift; large lounge overlooking the beach, separate TV room, nightclub.
Five acres of gardens with heated swimming pool; direct access to sandy
beach and safe bathing; tennis courts, riding, sailing; casino near by.
Terms: B & B: 115–75 frs; half board (minimum 3 days): 190–250 frs;
full board (minimum 3 days): 265–325 frs.

BARBIZON, 77630 Seine-et-Marne

Hostellerie du Bas-Bréau
22 Grande-Rue

Telephone: (1) 0664005
Telex: 690953

The Fava family have owned and run the *Bas-Bréau* for many years.
Once a modest inn, it is now an exceedingly posh one, on the main street
of this famous village in the heart of the Forest of Fontainebleau. Many
of the Barbizon school of painters stayed here; so did Robert Louis
Stevenson. Lucky the painter or writer who can afford this style of
luxury these days. All the rooms overlook the handsome terraced
gardens. 'Apparently a favourite hideaway for older Paris businessmen
and their younger mistresses, the *Bas-Bréau* is blatantly pretentious but
fun if you enter into the spirit of the thing. You pass through a charming
little old courtyard to the tiny reception desk at the side of the bar. Don't
let yourself be tucked away in their new motel-type block, but insist on
rooms in the older parts. The cuisine is high (as are the prices), but the
restaurant is full of flowers, the garden is pleasant in the spring and

summer, and of course it's an ideal base for exploring memories of the Barbizon School, antique shops and the marvellous forest, right at the end of the village school, on horseback, bicycle, or on foot.' (*Uwe Kitzinger*)

Open: all year, except 20 November–29 December.
Rooms: 28 double (including 9 suites)—all with bath, telephone, TV. Bar; terraced gardens.
Terms: B & B: 140–268 frs; meals: 110–40 frs.

LES BAUX-DE-PROVENCE, 13520 Maussane, Bouches-du-Rhône

(1) **Oustaù de Baumanière**   *Telephones:* (1) (90) 973307
(2) **La Cabro d'Or**   (2) (90) 973321
                                    Telex (both): Baucabro 420203

The ruined village and castle of Les Baux, on a high spur of the Alpilles, has become one of the show places of Provence. Formerly the seat of an ancient and powerful feudal house, it has had a long, romantic, often bloodthirsty history. The original dynasty died out in the 15th century, it fell into the hands of Protestants, and Richelieu had the castle and ramparts—'the eagle's nest', he called it—demolished in 1632. Now it is a ghost-city, and coach-loads daily pick their way across the grey jagged rocks of bauxite (hence the name) and through the spooky remains of medieval grandeur. You can stay, if you wish, in the old town, but the connoisseurs of high living will make for *Baumanière*, one of the great restaurants of France, or its younger (and cheaper) brother, the *Cabro d'Or*, under the same management. Both places should, properly speaking, be called restaurants with rooms, in view of the extensive non-residential trade. But what restaurants—and what rooms!

'Fantastic! Dramatic setting in rocks, tremendous volcanic natural architecture, with the valley far below. It is on a very steep slope, and fortunately our car broke down *just there*! You go for the experience and get it. *Baumanière* is expensive, lush, great fun to watch the other guests. Surprisingly, and always, whole French families turn up for meals, with six-year-olds delicately picking over the truffles, and then kicking their heels or taking a dip, while the adults enjoy course after course after course. This is a hotel with all the trimmings. The chef comes round to all the tables to know whether the food pleases, and he let on that he, too, was a vegetarian. So his vegetable cooking is superb. View Les Baux first. Then eat. Then lie down.' (*Sheila Kitzinger;* also *Freddie Freedman*)

Open: all year.
Rooms: (1) 15 double, 11 suites—all with bath, telephone and air-conditioning.
          (2) 15 double—all with bath and telephone.
Both hotels have swimming pool, tennis courts, and riding stables.
Terms: (1) B & B: 145 frs; meals: 95–140 frs; half board: 320–75 frs.

126

(2) B & B: 72-117 frs; meals: 45-90 frs; half board: 125-75 frs.

BEYNAC-ET-CAZENAC, 24220 St-Cyprien, Dordogne

Hôtel Bonnet   *Telephone:* (53) 295001

'*The Bonnet* has been popular with the English in the Dordogne for many decades. Wonderful to find this comfortable family hotel virtually unchanged (except for additional bathrooms) since a visit eight years ago. Madame Bonnet at eighty-six still takes her turn behind the desk. Chambermaids are genuinely friendly, and the service helpful all round. Rooms are not elegant, but tastefully furnished. Public rooms congenial, easy for relaxed Scrabble. Front rooms have wonderful river views but corresponding traffic and consequent noise. Very good restaurant, delicious inexpensive local wines, same friendly service, and better Roquefort than I found in a wildly grand 3-star restaurant. Nothing to do in Beynac except climb up to the half-ruined château, but splendidly placed as a centre for day trips throughout the Dordogne.' (*Elaine Greene;* also *Tom Congdon*)

Open: 15 March–15 October.
Rooms: 24 double, 1 single—23 with bath, 2 with shower, all with telephone.
Salon, bar; large creeper-covered terrace for meals above the river; two gardens. The hotel overlooks the Dordogne, with beach and bathing near by, also boating, canoeing and fishing.
Terms: B & B: 32-42 frs; meals: 35-60 frs; half board: 65-80 frs; full board: 80-100 frs.

CAP D'ANTIBES, 06600 Alpes-Maritimes

Auberge La Gardiole   *Telephone:* (93) 613503
Chemin de la Garoupe

'Since my husband and I first discovered this small hotel-pension, we have been back four times. It is on a quiet street, which is important as Cap d'Antibes can be busy and noisy. The beach is a ten-minute walk away, so you don't need a car if you only want a relaxing vacation. But if you do have a car, you are no more than an hour away from every important place to visit on the Riviera. The recommended beach, La Plage de la Garoupe, is one of the few sandy beaches on this stretch of the coast, and is lively and friendly with lots of French families. One disadvantage is that the rooms are not large and have no screens on the window, so that you can't read in bed after dark unless you are not bothered by mosquitoes. Not every room has a bath, but we found the place so marvellous that we were willing to put up with this minor discomfort. There are several very modern rooms, of course more expensive, but you need to reserve them early.

'The brochure cannot do justice to the wonderful food eaten on the vine-shaded terrace. Nor can it describe the hospitable atmosphere provided by the two women, both English-speaking, who own and manage the hotel. They worry about all the details, as does everyone's ideal mother, so that you have the feeling you are a house guest. We particularly liked the fact that the place is really French and is patronised by the local people as a restaurant. The hotel attracts French, Belgian, and some English and German. When we are abroad, we don't want to meet our own countrymen [the writer is American] and so far we haven't met any at La Gardiole.' (*Patricia Lievow*)

Open: 15 March–3 October.
Rooms: 20 rooms—10 with bath, 8 with shower, all with telephone. Lounge, bar. Small garden with vine-shaded terrace. Plage de la Garoupe is ½-km. away, with sandy beach; all aquatic sports, tennis, golf and casinos handy.
Terms: B & B: 60–72 frs; meals: 41-4 frs; half board: 101-14 frs.

LE CASTELLET, 83330 Le Beausset, Var

Castel Lumière   *Telephone:* (94) 906220

'Le Castellet is one of those lovely *villages perchés* that sit on pinnacles of rock, isolated and quiet, overlooking the bustle of the distant resorts on the Riviera. It is a few miles inland from Bandol and surrounded by peaceful country lanes and fields. You can drive up as far as the ramparts and then you must leave the car and go on foot. When I arrived in the sleepy air of a late afternoon and wandered round the narrow, cobbled streets, the village was deserted save for a few stray cats and elderly folk asleep in chairs outside their homes. There were small shuttered artisan shops, and a tempting *crêperie* that I vowed to return to. The *Castel Lumière*, almost part of the old ramparts, is a small hotel where the emphasis is more on the board than the bed. Nevertheless, though simply furnished, it is well worth staying in for the views, the food, and to escape from the noise of the coast. While I was there, the bedrooms were being repainted and I was lucky enough to get one newly done, with simple furniture and a tiled floor, and magnificent views for miles, with what looked like a sheer drop from the window itself. The dining room was set with as much care as if friends were coming to dinner, with roses on the tables, and an expectant air as if something great was about to happen—and it did. The chef-*patron* glided out of the kitchen with course after course of expertly cooked food, waited for approval of each dish with animated concern, and then waltzed back into the kitchen to prepare the next round. He and his wife obviously cared about their guests.' (*Susan Grossman*)

Open: all year.
Rooms: 8—all with bath/shower and telephone.
Terms: B & B: 47–81 frs; meals: 42–65 frs.

CHAMPILLON, Nr Epernay, 51160 Ay, Marne

Hôtel Le Royal Champagne   *Telephone:* (26) 512506

If you can afford it, the *Royal Champagne*, in a quiet position off the Epernay-Reims road, is as congenial a centre for exploring the Champagne country as you could wish. Many people only know it as a famous restaurant of *haute cuisine*, but it also has luxurious bedrooms in a chalet-type building in the garden. Mme Mercier (of that *marque*) is said personally to have supervised the furnishing. All the bedrooms have private verandahs, with a superb view over the vineyards of the Marne valley. (*Mrs M. E. Hartley*)

Open: all year, except January.
Rooms: 14—all with bath and telephone.
Garden and park.
Terms: B & B: 70-7 frs; meals: 70-100 frs.

CHASSEY-LE-CAMP, 71150 Saône-et-Loire

Auberge du Camp Romain   *Telephone:* (85) 490331

'A magnificently situated hotel in a panoramic setting. It is remote and ideal for relaxation. It is surrounded by Burgundian vineyards, and many illustrious *caves* are within easy reach. Though this is good walking country, a car is essential. The rooms are well-appointed and comfortable. The public rooms are adequate: in fine weather a verandah stretching the length of the building provides an idyllic setting for meals. The cuisine is excellent, and the proprietor combines a talent for the preparation of sauces with a gift for music. The latter he devotes to the playing, when duties permit, of a wonderful electronic organ which he makes almost to "sit up and beg" with a tremendous repertoire of melodies. The memories of lingering after dinner on a balcony in the warmth of a summer evening, against a background of his tunes floating through the air, is one which will long endure.' (*R. A. D. Bell*)

Open: all year, except January.
Rooms: 12—2 with bath, 6 with shower, all with telephone.
Garden; long verandah for meals.
Terms: B & B: 25-30 frs; meals: 25-35 frs; half board: 65-75 frs; full board: 70-80 frs.

CLERY-ST-ANDRÉ, 45370 Loiret

Hôtel Les Bordes   *Telephone:* (38) 807125

'Clery-St-André is a little town or a large village, just south of the Loire, about ten miles from Orléans. It has a huge Gothic church (rather nasty, in my view) and is within easy reach of many châteaux and pleasant places. The *Hôtel Les Bordes* is just outside the centre. It is an oldish country house, with some more up-to-date rooms in former stables. Extensive shabby garden, perfect for well-conducted children, and there is a swimming pool in the village. My room, in the main house, was modernised, with mini-bathroom—perfectly comfortable, utterly quiet. Family amiable. Large tatty bar, rambling dining room, food (several categories of menu) good bourgeois style, wine list short but adequate (Loire wines mostly, of course), people friendly. I shall go back there—it is cheap for what it offers, and the atmosphere is welcoming without fuss.' (*Pamela Vandyke Price*)

Open: all year.
Rooms: 20 double—9 with bath/shower, all with telephone.
Four salons, including a separate TV room, bar, garden.
Terms: B & B: 23-65 frs; meals: 20-55 frs.

CONQUES, 12320 St Cyprien-sur-Dourdou, Aveyron

Hôtel Sainte-Foy *Telephone:* (65) 698403

'Conques isn't on the road to anywhere, though it's a good place to stop if you're driving from the Dordogne to the Tarn. Medieval historians know it as one of the famous staging-points on the pilgrimage to Santiago de Compostela. Amazingly, this small village on a wooded hillside, two miles from the main road, with its slate-roofed houses and cobbled streets surrounding a massive and awesome abbey church, has retained the air of a sacred place and is wholly of the Middle Ages. The *Sainte-Foy*, the only hotel, is called after the martyred girl whose weird gold relic is still to be seen in the abbey museum. It's a fine medieval house, facing the great abbey, with a shaded courtyard in the rear and with handsome old furniture in the public rooms. There is no *à la carte*, but the hotel has a well-merited Michelin rating for good meals at a modest price. The service is exceptionally friendly, with the staff putting themselves out to accommodate families who want to share rooms or menus. There are plenty of good hotels of this class all over France. What makes this one exceptional is its location. It isn't a place for an extended stay, but Conques itself is so remarkable, especially in the evening when the abbey is floodlit and the daytime sightseers have departed, that it is well worth a special visit and a night stop.' (*H.R.*; also *Simon Browne-Wilkinson*)

Open: 15 May-1 November.
Rooms: 18 double, 2 single—12 with bath, 6 with shower, all with telephone.
Two salons (1 with TV); courtyard.
Terms: B & B: 35-58 frs; meals: 30 frs; half board: 70-120 frs; full board: 90-140 frs.

LA CROIX-VALMER, 83420 Var

Parc Hôtel *Telephone:* (94) 796404

'La Croix Valmer is an inland village of no particular charm, six kilometres from Cavalaire-sur-Mer, and near the attractive Côte d'Azur
villages of Ramatuelle and Gassin. The *Parc Hôtel* is on the outskirts of
the village, set back from the road, behind formal gardens and tall palms.
It's an imposing looking building, like a former stately home, with
terraces and an elegant cream-coloured facade. I parked the car and half
expected to see a cascade of liveried footmen tumble down the stairs and
remove my baggage. Instead, a very small chambermaid in black with a
white frilly apron and hat attempted to lift my bag, thought better of it
and led the way, for me to follow, to the reception. The hotel had only
one room left—and they apologised in advance. We climbed up several
flights of stairs that got narrower as we got higher until finally the little
chambermaid threw open the door to a tiny garret room. That room was
one of the most memorable I have ever stayed in. It was comfortable
enough and rather small, but the tiny window under the eaves opened
on to a view that could have inspired the French Revolution. It was the
sort of room that one could hide oneself away in for months and write a
book. The rest of the hotel was very different. Vast rooms with long
corridors with marble and mosaic floors. High ceilings and huge
tarnished mirrors. Very palatial but also very comfortably furnished,
and splendid grounds. Breakfast was taken on the terrace—and the only
disadvantage of the hotel was that it had no restaurant. Altogether an
inspiring place and very reasonably priced to make it an excellent base
from which to explore the surrounding countryside—or, write a book.'
(*Susan Grossman*)

Open: 1 April–1 October.
Rooms: 33—all with bath/shower.
Lift; salons; garden and terrace.
Terms: B & B: 51–64 frs. No restaurant.

LES EYZIES-DE-TAYAC, 24620 Dordogne

Hôtel du Centre *Telephone:* (53) 069713

With its cluster of prehistoric sites within walking distance, Les Eyzies,
dubbed *La Capitale de la Préhistoire*, attracts droves of tourists in the
high season. The Font-de-Gaume offers the most awe-inspiring cave
paintings still open to the public in this part of France, though the
number of visitors is strictly controlled, and long queues form early in
the morning and after lunch for the twice-daily quota. For those with a
taste for stalagmites, the *Grotte du Grand Roc*, rating two stars in the
Green Michelin of the region, is a mile up the road, and the fascinating
but boringly displayed National Museum of Prehistory is in the centre
of the busy village.

'My main reason for nominating the *Hôtel du Centre* is that it gives excellent value for money, is comfortable, has good food, and above all, is in a quiet location. I stayed there a week in July 1976 with my wife and our two late-teenage children. The four of us paid about £7.50 per person per night, half board. For this price, we had twin beds with bath, and an excellent five-course menu each night. The size of my family means that I must multiply all costs by four. I am therefore constantly looking for value for money, and feel that this was definitely achieved by this hotel, which was under the personal supervision of the proprietor.' (*Dr C. E. Morgan*)

Open: 15 February–2 January.
Rooms: 19 double—18 with bath/shower, all with telephone.
Swimming, sailing, water-skiing and trout fishing in near-by river; riding by arrangement; prehistory within walking distance.
Terms: B & B: 32–45 frs; meals: 28–60 frs; half board: 60–70 frs; full board: 80–90 frs.

Hôtel Cro Magnon   *Telephone:* (53) 539706

Les Eyzies boasts a pair of famous hotel-restaurants for those who want to explore the traces of prehistoric man in 20th-century civilised style, the *Cro Magnon* and the *Centenaire*. The former, on the quiet outskirts of what is in the season a bustling and crowded tourist village, is the older and more characterful of the two. 'An unusual and excellent hotel, with a special atmosphere because of its association with the discoverer of prehistoric sites near by. The founder was a prehistorian of the end of the last century, the discoverer of Cro-Magnon man, and the hotel contains rooms with the artefacts he dug up on display, and is itself cut into the actual side of a rock shelter. The grounds are beautiful in the summer, with the swimming pool an added bonus. The one-star restaurant fully lives up to its reputation each time I have visited it. The only snag is that it is full throughout the summer, and long advance booking is necessary in July and August.' (*Professor E. A. Barnard*)

Open: 2 April–9 October.
Rooms: 28—25 with bath, 2 with shower.
Two lounges; large garden, with swimming pool.
Terms: B & B: 56–88 frs; meals: 36–80 frs; half board: 80–110 frs; full board: 95–130 frs.

FLAGY, Nr Montereau-Faut-Yonne, 77156 Thoury-Ferottes, Seine-et-Marne

---

Moulin de Flagy   *Telephone:* (1) 4316789

'This was the last night of our honeymoon returning North, but it is also a good stop on the way south if you don't want to sleep in Paris, fifty miles up the road. The *Moulin* is a real 14th-century village water-mill in the quaint and silent greystone village of Flagy, not inconveniently far from the A6 motorway or the N5 at Montereau. The bedrooms are simple but very comfortable; there are only a few, so you need to book. The roaring mill stream won't keep you awake at night, but it is right beside you in the restaurant, along with a blazing fire in winter and a *cri-cri* somewhere in the wooden beams above. The mill's conversion was carried out by M. and Mme Mouvier. Monsieur's magnificent collection of Romanesque glass ikons adorns the restaurant walls. Madame ably if somewhat fearsomely presides over all. But this confers a chic and quality over restaurant and hotel that no visitor will regret. More a place to stay overnight than for an extended stay—unless *you* are on your honeymoon too.' (*Indrei Ratiu*)

Open: 3 March–23 January.
Rooms: 10—some with bath.
Garden.
Terms: B & B: 40–55 frs; meals: 40–50 frs; half board: 90–105 frs; full board: 135–50 frs.

FONTAINEBLEAU, 77300 Seine-et-Marne

Hôtel Aigle Noir　　　　　*Telephone:* (1) 4223265 or 4222027
27 Place Napoléon　　　　　　*Telex:* 600080

'The *Aigle Noir*, 200 yards from the entrance to the Palace, in the centre of Fontainebleau, was revamped in the winter of 1976, and now combines classic Empire decor with late-20th-century bathroom fittings. Fibre-glass padding gives an eerie silence in the corridors, though the rooms facing the square and the Château garden allow you to participate in the life of this small market town that remains international even after the departure of NATO, thanks to the European Institute of Business Administration. The buttercup-yellow restaurant serves exquisite dishes (at a price), preceded, if you wish, by a champagne cocktail flavoured with *myrtille* rejoicing in the name of "*Le Cardinal*"; try their fish soups, their wild boar—the ample and poetic explanations on the menu will tempt you to make your own choice in any case, but do not fail to leave room for (and order early) their famous apple tart, *Tatin*.' (*Uwe Kitzinger*)

Open: all year.
Rooms: 20 double, 4 suites, 6 singles—all with bath, telephone, radio and TV, mini-bars, and double glazing.
Two salons, lift; garden with outdoor dining room for fine weather.
Terms: B & B: 98–155 frs; meals: 60 frs.

If you can endorse any entry in this book, please do so <u>now</u>. We need a quick feedback on all our entries to help prepare our next edition.

Hôtel de la Halle   *Telephone:* (85) 443245

You are unlikely to come across this pleasant little Burgundy village except by intent. It lies on a minor road (N 481) between Chagny and Cluny, and its nearest town is Chalon-sur-Sâone, five miles to the east. *'Givry, ses vins, préferés par Henri IV'* says the sign as you drive in, and no doubt wine is still the chief draw of the village and the surrounding countryside, rich in the great names of the region. The *Hôtel de la Halle* takes its name from the old market hall on the other side of the Square —now restored, but no longer used as a market. It is an attractive old building, and its ten bedrooms, of varying degrees of comfort and price, are approached by a venerable spiral staircase. The hotel's restaurant is much patronised by locals. M. Christian Renard, the *patron*, who first learned his trade on an Atlantic liner, is an excellent chef. The guests are welcomed and looked after by his wife, Danielle, and their two daughters, Patricia (who is learning English) and Pascal. (*G. Garside*)

Open: all year, except 6 September–5 October.
Rooms: 10—2 with bath, 2 with shower.
Garden; swimming in near-by river.
Terms: B & B: 28–34 frs; meals: 20–30 frs; half board: 53–68 frs; full board: 70–83 frs.

GRÉOLIÈRES-LES-NEIGES, 06620 Bar-sur-Loup, Alpes-Maritimes

Domaine du Foulon   *Telephone:* (94) 093602

'When I arrived at this isolated spot, miles from anywhere, with views of the Gorges du Loup, I found that the family was out and that I was greeted by the dogs. The *Domaine du Foulon* is north of Grasse in thickly wooded countryside surrounded by green valleys and a river. The large old country house is simply furnished in Provençal style, and is comfortably run down so that you feel very much at home. I was pointed vaguely in the direction of the bedrooms by a friendly member of the family, and after a few misguided attempts at opening doors that led to wine cellars, eventually found a bedroom that didn't have an unmade bed in it. In fact, it was extremely comfortable—and had lovely views. The rest of the house was equally informal and lived-in. The sitting room had a large open hearth and deep armchairs (that seemed to be reserved for the doggy members of the family) and piles of old French magazines and books. The dining room overlooked the garden and we were summoned in for dinner and presented with a platter of enormous freshly caught trout, as well as home-made soup, chicken and dessert. The bar acted as reception, and there didn't seem to be a key to the bedroom. Altogether, a delightfully casual place. You can fish in the river, play table tennis and mini-golf, and walk for miles in the lovely countryside. There are swings and things in the rambling garden and no other habitation for miles.' (*Susan Grossman*)

Open: all year, except 15 October–15 November.
Rooms: 15—some with bath or shower.
Bar/reception, sitting room; garden; table tennis, mini-golf; fishing in the near-by river.
Terms: Rooms: 40-61 frs; meals: 30-50 frs; full board: 98 frs.

GRIMAUD, 83360 Var

Hostellerie du Cocteau Fleuri   *Telephone:* (94) 432017

'We arrived at Grimaud late one summer afternoon having driven up from Port Grimaud on the coast. Grimaud is one of the many *villages perchés* of old stone houses and tiny alleys—and at this time of year it was covered in geraniums. From the village you can just about see the coast hazily in the distance, and all around were vineyards and woods. The *Hostellerie* was a fairly new addition to the village—in a quiet, picturesque setting, very small and intimate with a relaxed use of natural materials. The house was cool and comfortable, with tiled floors, an open hearth and fresh flowers. The bedrooms were modern and with pretty curtains and covers in Provençal prints, with super-luxury bathrooms that were really rooms. Outside there was a small rambling garden full of colour and greenery. There's a small bar and a terrace and the general atmosphere of being a guest in a charming, cosy and comfortable French country house.' (*Susan Grossman*)

Open: 1 March–5 January.
Rooms: 14—all with bath/shower.
Bar and terrace; garden with swimming pool.
Terms: B & B: 82 frs; meals: 46 frs.

LAURIS, 84360 Vaucluse

La Chaumière   *Telephone:* (90) 29

'*La Chaumière* is a restful base for a few days in which to explore the vicinity: Lourmarin, Cadenet, the south flank of the Lubéron range, and the opposite bank of the Durance—the heart of Provence. The chief virtue of this modest little hotel is its view of the wide, serene and normally sun-filled Durance valley. You can sit by the restaurant's picture windows and be entranced by the sweep of the river's bend, with the Alpilles far over to the right; sunrise and sunset are the dramatic moments. *La Chaumière* is built into the old village walls atop a high cliff. Food is not exactly memorable, but it can be looked forward to, nicely served on attractive plate, and local Coteaux d'Aix wines to match. Some bedrooms in the main building (the annexe is just across a small courtyard) are spacious and welcoming, and some have sizable but slightly bedraggled terraces. You sleep in "Durance" or "Provence", not in numbered rooms, an agreeable little touch of old-fashionedness. Occasionally breakfast is brought up late, but for the most part, the young owners, M. and Mme Delporte, are correct hosts. Madame has a curious aversion to accepting even French francs travellers' cheques. "We have difficulty with them", is as far as her explanatory refusal goes.' (*Norman Brangham*)

Open: 1 March–12 November.
Rooms: 10—3 with bath, 7 with shower.
Terms (excluding tax): B & B: 38 frs; meals: 30–45 frs; half board: 55–78 frs; full board: 65–90 frs.

MARSEILLAN, 34340 Hérault

Le Château du Port   *Telephone:* (67) 772107

'One of several small fishing ports on the Étang de Thau, Marseillan is charming without being self-consciously picturesque. Local fishermen cultivate oysters and mussels in the Étang, a large salt lake separated from the Mediterranean by dunes and miles of sandy beaches. The beaches are approximately six kilometres away along a small but adequate road that skirts the corner of the lake. Mosquitoes were once a plague along the whole of this section of the French Mediterranean coast; constant spraying by helicopter has virtually eliminated the little pests.

'Marseillan is an old town quite different in character from the new resorts further east between Sète and the mouth of the Rhône—resorts which have only grown up since the effective "demoustification". It would make a good night stop for motorists on their way to or from the Costa Brava. The *Château du Port* is busy with yachting enthusiasts of several nationalities in season, and is quiet and gently nostalgic at other times. Winters, apart from occasional doses of the Mistral, are mild. The hotel is shabby outside, but several rooms, with private bathrooms, are superb. Their French windows overlook yachts and a few small fishing boats bobbing on the water below, tall mirrors reflect the scene, and a glass chandelier hangs from the ceiling. Deep *café-au-lait* panelled walls, picked out in gilt with swags of flowers, have been lovingly and skilfully restored by the proprietor's wife, an Englishwoman. The owner is as adeptly multilingual as most Dutchmen. Food in the French tradition is good, if not memorable. Prices are reasonable for the beautiful rooms and ideal situation.' (*Anne Bolt*)

Open: all year, except brief period in winter.
Rooms: 15 double, 2 single—2 with bath, 9 with shower, all with telephone.
Lounge with TV, small breakfast room. The hotel is on the quayside of the yacht harbour, with facilities for putting trailered boats in the water; sandy beach, 3 miles; sailing, water-skiing.

Terms: B & B: 51 frs; meals: 22–33 frs; half board (4 nights minimum): 80 frs; full board (4 nights minimum): 100 frs. (Half- or full-board prices include a carafe of local rosé wine.)

MERCUÈS, Nr Cahors, 46000 Lot

Château de Mercuès and Relais Cèdre   *Telephone:* (65) 360001

'Tremendous style and luxury in a historic château on a wooded bluff overlooking the Garonne, five miles north of Cahors. Belonged, for twelve centuries, to the Lord Bishops of that city. Superb food with marvellous use of truffles and goose fat. Timeless distinction. Quiet attention. A place for a third or fourth honeymoon, with the children receding into the distance, although we parked our five in a caravan just below the château walls, well out of earshot, and they had a happy time exploring. As well as the castle rooms, including some gorgeous ones in the turrets, there are "pavillons"—rather cheaper. Frightfully expensive. Give it to her instead of a diamond forever.' (*Sheila Kitzinger*)

Open: 1 April–31 October.
Rooms: 21 double in the Château; 27 chalets in the park (Relais Cèdre), from 1 July–31 August. All have bath, telephone and mini-bar.
Lift; 2 salons (1 with TV), chapel, orangery, tapestry room, music room, playroom, disco, art gallery, boutique. Private park with 2 tennis courts and swimming pool, and spectacular view from the terrace. Also 'the only international hunting ground in France' (brochure)—whatever that means. .
Terms: Château, B & B: 170–370 frs; Relais du Cèdre, B & B: 120–45 frs; meals 100–50 frs.

MEYRONNE, Nr Souillac, 46200 Lot

Café de la Terrasse   *Telephone:* (65) 375060

'This hotel, with its few rather plain rooms, is in a superb old monastery above the Dordogne river. In season, this corner of the river is over-popular, but in May, June and early July, it is a wonderful place to use as a base for exploring the region. Sarlat, Souillac, St Céré, and half a dozen superb châteaux are within striking distance for a day's outing, and you can fish and swim from Meyronne itself. Three very hard-working ladies run the hotel. The oldest, who does the cooking, must be nearly eighty, and she produces endless courses of delicious food from a kitchen as dark and tiny as a ship's galley. Round her the washing-up piles alarmingly high as she trots back and forth in her tennis shoes. The daughters, who run the hotel and serve in the restaurant, which has a vine-covered terrace overlooking the river, are tremendously nice and hard-working. They are often assisted by two black students of great charm. The rooms have been modernised by local craftsmen in basic but quite acceptable style. The lavatories are fairly appalling—airless and cold. The best thing is the food, and the other best thing is the bill, which is always extremely modest. The owners are not very good at correspondence, so if you want to reserve a room, it's best to ring.' (*Caroline Conran*)

Open: Easter–October.
Rooms: 8.
Terms: *Not available.*

MIRABEL-AUX-BARONNIES, 26110 Nyons, Drôme

Hôtel Le Mirabeau   *Telephone:* (75) 34

'A small, 18th-century Provençal mansion, the last building in Mirabel on the Nyons road, this hotel embodies the best characteristics of a modest Provençal Logis de France. The front of the house faces a small garden beyond which lies the prospect of an unspectacular but peaceful little valley and hillside. Restaurant, bedrooms and staircase, all have the ample solid proportions that make old bourgeois houses such a delight. It is a pleasure just to be in one of the large, low-ceilinged bedrooms, traditional red hexagonal tiles on the floor, old furniture, bedcovers and tablecloths that glow richly and welcomingly. It is no exaggeration to say that there is a sense of time standing still there. The restaurant is spacious, dim and panelled. On bright, hot days the cool half-light is a welcome relief. When busy, the restaurant is a cheerful bustle, and menus usually contain a regional speciality—I first was introduced to *tapénade* there. It is agreeable food, interesting, well served at tables set spaciously apart, and the wine list is adequate; at such times Madame Corbet supervises with swift competence. When business is slack, the room is a bit sepulchral, service is slow, and the food may lack sparkle.

'*Le Mirabeau* is inseparable from its surroundings. It is a place for peace and quiet. There is nothing much to do after dark and Mirabel is not one of the most attractive villages of the region. But there are walks, especially along the track to Les Pilles, ablaze with Spanish broom in June, through the olive groves, and across rough *garrigue* country. The tip-tilted Baronnies hills, the hamlets and chapels about the lower slopes of Mont Ventoux, Vaison-la-Romaine, Nyons, wine villages are half- or full-day car excursions away. Mirabel is poised delicately between rural Dauphiné northwards, and Virgilian Vaucluse to the south.' (*Norman Brangham*)

Open: all year.
Rooms: 8—4 with bath or shower.
Garden.
Terms: B & B: 42 frs; meals: 20-48 frs; full board: 75-85 frs.

MONTICELLO, 20220 L'Île Rousse, Corsica

Hôtel A Pastorella   *Telephone:* (95) 600565

'Very few Britishers seem to take their holidays in Corsica (which is good news for those of us who do) and most of those go on package tours which deposit them in tiny, concrete mini-Marbellas in the south; about as good a way of enjoying the island as going to Switzerland and renting a basement flat in Basle. The best way to enjoy this most hospitable and dramatically beautiful island is to tour, on foot, bike, motorbike or car, in the off-season; any time but that mad period from 14 July to 30 September. Most of the larger villages have some kind of a hotel and these are invariably cheapish, unluxurious and very clean. As far as food is concerned one has to lower one's sights a notch or two: nobody goes to Corsica for the food. But the Corsican range of homemade sausages is delicious, as is the cheese, and the bread—which is like a double cow-pat, grey, reminding one of what French bread *used* to be. Breaking the crust produces a report like a pistol-shot. The best of these small village hotels that we know personally is in Monticello, a medieval clump of dwellings which sits on a hill 600 feet above the port and beaches of Île-Rousse. The *Hôtel A Pastorella* is Corsican, not imitation French. It was built about fifteen years ago so the walls are thin and it can be a bit noisy, but it is clean, bright and happy. The food is plentiful and surprisingly cheap, always beginning with a real soup, moving on to something small and interesting like something stuffed with something else, then perhaps a plate of *charcuterie*, followed by a bit of meat, cheeses and fruit. The hotel is run by the Martini family—papa used to be a shepherd—and the meats come from a butcher in the family who lives up in the mountains. In other words, an unpretentious, very friendly, clean hotel with valleys and the sea in front of you, the mountains behind, and good family food to keep you going.' (*Frank Muir*)

Open: all year except November.
Rooms: 9.
Terms: B & B: 24-6 frs; meals: 25-30 frs; half board: 55-60 frs; full board: 60-5 frs.

MOUTHIER-HAUTE-PIERRE, 25920 Doubs

Hôtel Le Manoir   *Telephone:* (81) 870637

Mouthier is a typically beautiful village in the Jura on the river Loue. The hotel is in a wonderfully quiet position on a back street, and with its own garden. As its name suggests, it is full of character, being an old manor house. The food is excellent and, except for the wines, relatively not expensive. (*Michael Bruce*)

Open: all year.
Rooms: 16—5 with bath, all with telephone.

Garden on the river bank.
Terms: B & B: 28–43 frs; meals: 34–54 frs; half board: 60–75 frs; full
board: 70–90 frs.

NÎMES, 30017 Gard

Hôtel Imperator   *Telephone:* (66) 219030
Quai de la Fontaine   *Telex:* 490635

A splendidly spacious hotel, luxuriously appointed, and particularly
welcome as a retreat after traipsing round the Roman ruins which are
within walking distance. The hotel is opposite the enchanting *Jardin de
la Fontaine*, but with a maelstrom of a main road in between. Fortunately, it has its own entirely quiet and delightful *Jardin Provençal
Fleuri*, with Roman remains casually cropping up between the flower
beds, and with high walls shutting out the noise and bustle outside. The
public rooms all look out on the garden, and in decent weather meals are
taken under an awning on the terrace. The restaurant is celebrated, and
the wine list now better than ever. 'The *vol-au-vent aux morilles* are a
dream! Very good fish, superb desserts, and a splendid chariot of
cheeses, including a great variety of goat', rhapsodizes one enthusiast.
Accommodation is as good as you would expect in a grand hotel of this
class: high-ceilinged rooms, well-furnished, with first-class bathrooms
('everything works, and there is the odd gift thrown in'). Avoid bedrooms facing the road if you can. The only complaint: the solid old-
fashioned mahogany beds were 'too heavy to move into a more loving
proximity (though we did it).' (*Sheila Kitzinger, Paul Grotrian*)

Open: 20 March–31 January.
Rooms: 65—all with bath or shower, and telephone.
Lift; salons, conference facilities; large private park and garden.
Terms: B & B: 53–63 frs; meals: 50–80 frs; half board: 185–245 frs;
full board: 245–305 frs.

NOIRMOUTIER, 85330 Vendée

Hôtel Saint-Paul   *Telephone:* (51) 390563
Bois de la Chaize

'We had a delightful, relaxing, gastronomic holiday on this little island
in the estuary of the Loire. The hotel is quietly situated in beautiful
woods, a few minutes from a charming beach, and the atmosphere is
serene and informal. I had packed with a view to dressing for dinner,
but this was not necessary. My two wild boys, aged six and eight, chased
little French girls round the hotel's tennis courts till night fell and, short
of being advised to keep off the immaculate lawn (once), they were put
up with admirably by the staff, who were efficient, unobtrusive and, if
they spoke English, weren't letting on—except for the night porter, who

was most solicitous when one of the boys was sick in the night. The food was splendid. Every meal was breath-taking—oysters, crab, fantastic fishes, quail. The recollection stimulates the juices. Pretty good cellar, too. Breakfast is in your room—ours was both comfortable and pretty, and had French windows looking on to the *jardin fleuri*. The breakfast was coffee, hot chocolate, and home-made croissants and brioches, all piping hot, jams and marmalades and pale pink linen napkins. A hoopoe came to our window for crumbs. As a hotel it is *vaut le voyage* for the breakfast alone. And the bird! The French family we became friendly with there, would go nowhere else, a decision with which we would entirely sympathise.' (*Shelley Cranshaw*)

Open: 22 March–22 September.
Rooms: 42—31 with bath or shower; also 5 suites.
Large wooded garden with swimming pool and tennis courts.
Terms: B & B: 102 frs; meals: 45–60 frs; full board: 125–80 frs.

PARIS

Hôtel de l'Abbaye
10 rue Cassette, 75006, 6e

Telephone: (1) 5443811

A delightfully restored 18th-century residence tucked between St Germain des Prés and Montparnasse, furnished and decorated with simple elegance. Wide windows open on to a lovely little flagged court-yard with palms, pot plants and flowers, where breakfast or refresh-ments can be taken at ease (no other meals served). 'A charming pastoral "find" amid the bustle of the Left Bank.' (*Margaret Laing*)

Open: all year.
Rooms: 44 double—all with bath and telephone.
Sitting room, bar, interior courtyard garden for refreshments (no restaurant).
Terms: B & B: 80–99 frs.

Hôtel Bristol
112 rue du Faubourg St Honoré, 75008, 8e

Telephone: (1) 2669145
Telex: 280961

A first-class hotel of the old-fashioned type without modern gimmicks—no automatic TV in rooms (though you can obviously ask for one). It is next to the best shops in the Faubourg St Honoré (and the British Embassy) but it is an ideal place for peace and serenity: discreet and roomy—even in August. Good service and good food. (*Margaret Laing*)

Open: all year.
Rooms: 150 rooms and 50 apartments—all with bath and shower, and telephone; air-conditioning; lift.
Terms: B & B: 200–375 frs.

Hôtel Claude-Bernard
43 rue des Écoles, 75005, 5e

Telephone: (1) 3263252

'Near the Sorbonne in a street just off the Boulevard St Germain and worthwhile since it offers good service and is not pricey. It is not a modern building but bedrooms and bathrooms are spacious and reasonably well appointed. The lift is mini-size, but as there are only three flights of stairs, this is really no problem. It is run by a very pleasant family who speak English without the usual Parisian aversion to other languages. No restaurant, but an excellent Continental breakfast is served in a delightful little breakfast nook.' (*A. D. Traynor*)

Open: all year.
Rooms: 39—most with bath or shower, and telephone.
Lift; breakfast alcove (no restaurant).
Terms: B & B: 70 frs.

L'Hôtel
13 rue des Beaux-Arts, 75006, 6e

Telephone: (1) 6338920 and 3252722
Telex: 270870

The simply named *L'Hôtel* began life as a 'Pavillon d'Amour' constructed above cellars of remarkable proportions. It was here, in its more modest days, that Oscar Wilde took refuge, saying, 'I am dying above my means'; and so he did. In 1968, under its present owner, M. Guy-Louis Duboucheron, it began an existence which has charmed VIPs galore. The amazing stone cellars have been transformed into an air-conditioned wining and dining fairyland. Everyone who thinks they are anyone mingles in the Winter Garden, a luxurious piano-bar-restaurant. M. Duboucheron loosed his flair for decor on the place; he recreated Oscar Wilde's room, and installed Mistinguett's own furniture in her old bedroom. 'Expensive, though very special; the sort of place for a once-in-a-lifetime experience, with a girl friend.' (*Inge Haag*)

Open: all year.
Rooms: 27 double—all with bath, telephone, radio, TV and air-conditioning.
Cellar-bar restaurant; Winter Garden Restaurant; lift.
Terms: B & B: 137–247 frs.

Hôtel Inter-Continental Paris
3 rue Castiglione, 75040, 1er

Telephone: (1) 2603780
Telex: 220114

A 19th-century palace, but with plenty of modern attributes, just off the Place Vendôme and overlooking the Tuileries Gardens. A highly decorative and popular feature is the Garden Court, a delightful interior courtyard with central fountain and pool. 'Here an incredibly lavish hot and cold ad. lib. buffet is served; the lushest place for a relaxed open-air lunch away from the noise of traffic.' And this is only one sort of eating that goes on: in the Charcoal Grill specialities are served in a 17th-century setting; the Bistro is for quick lunches and after 10 p.m. it becomes a disco until 4 a.m. Other sorts of snacks and appetisers go on until midnight in the Café Tuileries. Decor, service and cuisine are superb—which is what you pay for. (*Margaret Laing*)

Open: all year.
Rooms: 500 single and double, of which 27 are suites—all with bath, telephone, radio and TV, fully stocked mini-bar; baby-sitting arranged.
Lift; air-conditioning. Grand Salon, 4 restaurants, bar-restaurant, bistro, disco, rooms for banquets and private functions. Interior courtyard landscaped to represent the four seasons, for lunch or candle-lit dinner (weather permitting).
Terms (excluding service and taxes):   B & B: 135–85 frs.

Hôtel Lancaster   *Telephone:* (1) 3599043
7 rue de Berri, 75008, 8e   *Telex:* Loyne 640991

Antique furniture, paintings, profusion of flowers, provide the intimate atmosphere of a gracious home. 'Small and beautiful, very select, very quiet, and lovely garden and charming dining room.' (*Inge Haag*)

Open: all year.
Rooms: 33 double, 10 suites, 14 single—all with bath and telephone; radio or TV on request; some air-conditioning.
Several salons where drinks are served, small bar. Facilities for private dinner parties and small functions. Delightful garden patio which many rooms overlook, used for meals in fine weather.
Terms (excluding service and taxes):   B & B: from 245 frs.

Hôtel Plaza Athénée   *Telephone:* (1) 3598523 and 2254330
25 ave Montaigne, 75008, 8e   *Telex:* Reservations, 650092
                                                 Messages, 290082

Bright canopies shade the windows and balconies of 'perhaps the most elegant of Paris hotels, though the bedrooms less so than the public rooms'. Round the corner from Dior, it has similar sophistication: impressive furnishings, flowers everywhere. 'The choice of restaurants is from the highest down to the coffee shop. First-class make-up mirrors—lit from below as well as above—so worth staying in if you only want to look your best for a special occasion.' If you can afford a river-facing suite, you will have an incomparable view of Paris across the water to the Eiffel Tower. (*Margaret Laing*)

Open: all year.
Rooms: 208 double, 35 of which have sitting rooms, 5 single—all with bath, telephone, radio and TV. Baby-sitting arranged.
Lift; some air-conditioning; 4 reception and banqueting rooms; Garden

Court used as summer restaurant; gallery tearoom.
Terms: B & B: 271 frs.

Hôtel Pont-Royal   *Telephone:* (1) 5443827
7 rue Montalembert, 75007, 7e   *Telex:* 270113

A medium-sized hotel in the thick of the Paris publishing world. An old
hotel, but completely overhauled and now lacks little by way of up-to-
date amenities. 'Some very nice apartments overlook the Paris rooftops.
The restaurant and bar are regular meeting places for writers and
publishers.' (*Inge Haag*)

Open: all year.
Rooms: 70 double (including some suites), 9 single—all with bath,
           telephone, radio and TV. All have refrigerators; suites have
           kitchenettes. Some air-conditioning.
Six main rooms; lounges, cocktail bar, conference and reception rooms,
lift.
Terms: B & B: 120–60 frs.

Hôtel Scandinavia   *Telephone:* (1) 6334520
27 rue de Tournon, 75006, 6e

On a street which runs from the Boulevard St Germain down to the
Luxembourg Palace and its attractive gardens. The hotel is a recently
converted and modernised 17th-century building. Bedrooms are agreeably decorated and well fitted out. There is a pleasant lounge; no
restaurant—only breakfast served, which is brought to your room. (*Guy
and Wendy Payen-Payn*)

Open: all year, except August.
Rooms: 22 rooms—all with bath and telephone.
Lounge.
Terms: B & B: 70 frs.

PERROS-GUIREC, 22700 Côtes-du-Nord

Grand Hôtel de Trestraou et de la Plage   *Telephone:* (96) 352405
Bvd Joseph-Le-Bihan

'Perros-Guirec is one of the more popular family resorts along the north
coast of Brittany. It has a generous supply of resort facilities: sailing
school, water and other sports, beach clubs, casino, and a wide range of
restaurants, cafeterias and crêperies. There is safe bathing from three
good sandy beaches and numerous small coves. The *Grand Hôtel de
Trestraou*, situated on the main beach, is a grand hotel in the traditional
meaning of the term. Built in the 1920s, it was modernised in the early

1960s. The rooms are enormous, the plumbing satisfactory, the service good. Its outstanding feature is the cuisine—a worthy mixture of French provincial cooking and local seafood: five-course lunches and seven-course dinners, with lobster for lunch on Sunday. Another attraction is the excellent "club" for children, which will entertain them with exercises, games and competitions from 10 a.m. in the morning until 5 p.m. at night, with only an hour's break for lunch. M. and Mme Denis, both of them teachers, take on this chore for a modest fee, with a tee-shirt thrown in. There is also supervised bathing. A disadvantage of the hotel is the slightly elderly clientele, who do not always appreciate the children around them.' (*Elizabeth Hoodless*)

Open: all year.
Rooms: 78—54 with bath or shower.
Lift; garden; the hotel faces the coast road, with beach opposite.
Terms: B & B: 65-72 frs; meals: 35-85 frs; half board: 114-42 frs; full board (obligatory in July and August): 118-54 frs.

PORT RACINE, Nr St-Germain-des-Vaux, 50440 Manche

L'Erguillère   *Telephone:* (33) 527531

'Port Racine has a small board beside the tiny harbour proclaiming it to be the smallest port in France. It is so small that Michelin lists the place under the next village, St-Germain-des-Vaux. As it only has ten rooms, the hotel is often full, for the attraction of the place is that it is utterly unspoiled. This is due to the presence, near by and out of sight, of France's "Windscale", Beaumont-Hague, which has placed a ban on development, whilst its situation, *north-west* of Cherbourg, ensures that it is on the way to nowhere whatever.

'The hotel itself faces south-east overlooking the harbour. A car in this out of the way place is essential, but it is only about half an hour's drive along the coast road with its 70 kilometres speed limit from the ferry at Cherbourg, or slightly less, if you know the way, via Beaumont. The main thing to do is nothing, though there is bathing, of course, and there are interesting drives round the Hague peninsula to Jobourg point, with Alderney five miles away, to Vauville Bay across to the south, and (40 kilometres) Carteret, whence you can visit Jersey for the day in summer. The main attraction is for those who yearn after the coast of England in the 1930s, with not a car in sight on the coast road outside the French season, perhaps. This part of the Manche Department looks so very English, and the roads are so twisty and narrow, with hedges, that one has to remember to drive on the right. There are also country walks along the lanes. The food is well worth the stay: seafood, sometimes farmhouse butter, Normandy steaks and cheeses. Comfortable rooms and gorgeous views over the Channel.' (*George Behrend*)

Open: all year, except January and February.
Rooms: 10—9 with bath or shower.
Garden overlooking the sea.

Terms: B & B: 37–47 frs; meals: 43–62 frs; half board: 76–81 frs; full board: 115–20 frs.

QUIMPER, 29170 Fousnant, Finistère

Manoir du Moustoir   *Telephone:* (98) 948080

'An enchanting old stone manor house, surrounded by parkland and forest, between Quimper and Concarneau, newly converted to the standards of a country house hotel, and charmingly furnished with attention to detail and a sense of period. Luxurious bathrooms. Public rooms not cosy, but interestingly arranged for striking art exhibition. Impeccably served breakfast. No dining room, but we were directed to a fine fish restaurant in the near-by tiny port. Totally remote and nothing to do, but so quiet and comfortable that one could happily spend several nights there if one wanted to visit places in the neighbourhood. Car essential.' (*Elaine Greene*)

Open: June–September.
Rooms: 19—all with bath; also 3 suites.
Gardens, parkland and woods.
Terms: B & B: 50–95 frs. No restaurant.

RAMATUELLE, 83350 Var

Hôtel Le Baou   *Telephone:* (94) 797048

Even at the height of the summer, the charming, friendly little village of Ramatuelle, in the hills behind St Tropez, retains its dignity and character, in contrast to the fairground atmosphere of the former jetset playground five miles below. *Le Baou* is an ultra-modern hotel—very small, but with the highest standards. Each of the rooms has a private patio overlooking the vineyards and the sea. Breakfast is served in the rooms; other meals are taken on the rooftop with breathtaking views all round. 'It can be recommended to those who like comfort, privacy, good service and good food. We had a memorable holiday.' (*C. V. Maplethorpe*)

Open: 15 March–15 October.
Rooms: 16—all with bath or shower and patio; air-conditioning.
Garden; rooftop restaurant.
Terms: B & B: 99–128 frs; meals: 70 frs; full board: 125–71 frs.

> **If you consider any entry inadequate or misleading, please let us know <u>now</u>.**

ST-JEAN-CAP-FERRAT, 06290 Alpes-Maritimes

Hôtel Le Clair Logis   *Telephone:* (93) 013101
Allée des Brises

'The *Clair Logis* is about 1¼ miles from St-Jean, the main village on the Cap, and a very lovely old family house. It felt so informal that it was like staying with relatives; half of the guests seemed to have lived there permanently and have little chores such as helping with luggage and looking after the garden. It's a beautiful villa with huge bedrooms each named after a flower—and mine had a balcony on two sides with the best views of the garden. The family prided themselves on that garden—full of exotic vegetation, orange and lemon trees, fruits and flowers that rarely grow in this part of the Mediterranean. At night, a heady perfume filled the air and I went to sleep to the sound of croaking frogs and singing cicadas. I had breakfast in the garden on a small table under my balcony—there was no restaurant and I couldn't see where breakfast would be eaten if it rained. Inside were two tiny rooms with lovely antiques, but hardly room to eat in. I left wishing I could stay longer—they could always have put me in charge of picking the oranges.' (*Susan Grossman*)

Open: all year, except 1 November–15 December.
Rooms: 16—all with bath and telephone.
Two small salons; garden.
No dogs.
Terms: B & B: 43–6 frs. No restaurant.

Résidence Della Robbia   *Telephone:* (93) 013307/065269
Bvd Général De Gaulle

'Someone told me that there are over 50 millionaires with villas on this exclusive peninsula of land between Villefranche and Nice. You wouldn't know it though, as most of the villas are well hidden behind exotic vegetation and the wild Mediterranean pine that jostles for a foothold with the villas. There are few hotels on this bit of land and those there are, tend to be small and hidden away.

'The *Della Robbia* is a splendid mansion with a small-scale faded grandeur that must once have been an extremely desirable residence. Now the high cornices and huge mirrors are peeling a little and tarnished, but parts have been renovated well and some of the bedrooms, though small, have an almost palatial splendour. Several have highly ornate frescoed ceilings and are small museums, though very comfortable. The garden is pretty and you can sit out under the vines, admiring the Riviera view. There's a small and modern TV room and a reception area in the well of the stairs. St-Jean with its yachts and winding one-way streets is near by and you can swim off rocks not far from the hotel.' (*Susan Grossman*)

Open: 20 December–30 September.
Rooms: 12—all with bath and telephone.
Salon, TV room, garden.
Terms: B & B: 46 frs; meals: 32–40 frs; half board: 79 frs; full board:
           111 frs.

ST PAUL-DE-VENCE, 06570 Alpes-Maritimes

Auberge La Mas des Serres   *Telephone:* (93) 328110
                                       Telex: Orem 470 673/902

Formerly a Provençal farmhouse, and now half-way between a hotel and
an inn, *Mas des Serres* is about a mile and a half below St Paul-de-Vence
in the foothills that slope down towards the Mediterranean. The six
bedrooms, each called after a different flower, are individually decorated.
Four, in an annexe, have their own small private garden. The reception
rooms, with log-burning Provençal fireplaces, lead out through French
windows on to a vine-covered terrace and a lovingly tended garden.
Everything about this small hotel is characterised by the taste and sensi-
bility of its owner, Madame Saucourt. (*Margaret Walker*)

Open: 1 February–31 October.
Rooms: 6 double—all with bath, shower and telephone.
Two salons (no TV); garden, vine-covered terrace. Golf courses, tennis
courts, riding stables near by. Sea, 7 kms.
'Not exactly suitable for children.'
Terms: half board (preferably for minimum 3 days): 223 frs.

SAVIGNY-LES-BEAUNE, 21420 Côte d'Or

Hôtel L'Ouvrée   *Telephone:* (80) 215152
Route de Bouilland

This modernised hotel is quietly set in a pleasant garden on the outskirts of the village and on the edge of the proprietor's own vineyards.
The autoroute A6, though close, is effectively out of earshot. Beaune is
only four miles up the road, and many of the famous names in Burgundy are within easy reach. It is in the heart of Burgundy, and is also
at the beginning of a small valley leading to Bouilland, which is so
scenically pleasant that it is known as *La Petite Suisse*. A number of the
bedrooms are set round a delightful patio on the first floor. The rooms
are clean and extremely comfortable; the service, friendly and helpful;
and the food is marvellous Burgundy cooking. (*R. A. D. Bell, Michael
Bruce*)
Open: all year, except from 1 February–15 March.
Rooms: 23—22 with bath or shower.
Garden.

Terms: B & B: 37–47 frs; meals: 30–62 frs; half board: 80–96 frs; full board: 102–18 frs.

SIORAC-EN-PÉRIGORD, 24170 Dordogne

Hôtel Scholly   *Telephone:* (53) 296002
Place de la Poste

'The Dordogne is a very large district, stretching from Riberac, if you like, down to the area south of the river known to the locals as the Périgord Noir (it was once famous for its dark forests). The *Hôtel Scholly* is a perfect centre for enjoying this region. "*Loin du bruit*" is the claim on the advertisements by the roadside; odd, since the hotel over-looks the railway line and is in the much frequented Place de la Poste, but justified: the bedrooms face mostly on to the garden at the back and those which do not, are not unduly disturbed by the modest traffic. (Trains are rare and unobstreperous.) Another boast of the *Scholly*: "Le Patron mange ici." Monsieur Scholly comes from Alsace, but he has been in the Périgord for over thirty years and he has studied the local cuisine carefully, though he still sells Alsace wine (in pitchers) and makes Alsatian specialities. There is little sense in staying at the hotel unless you want to eat there, and the restaurant is not cheap, though (half-) pension rates make it cheaper than it would be for a passing client. (Supper on the terrace in summer.) The hotel has recently been renovated in the neo-Périgordine style, and the new wing boasts private baths (and 'phones) in every room. These new rooms are comfortably furnished (plenty of double beds, but specify) and more expensive than those in the old wing, which do not all have baths, and can be booked at a much more moderate rate. The hotel is run by the Scholly family and children are welcome. Madame Scholly likes the English, sympa-thises with the *chute de la livre* and is disposed to temper the wind to the shorn *Britanniques*. The Dordogne is just down the road and there is a decent public beach, with a diving board, etc. Limeuil, Trémolat, Mon-pazier, and other places of repute and interest are within easy distance. Excellent walking. It is best to write and state requirements (and even budget) well ahead of time. The region can be particularly agreeable in late September or October, even into November, though there is not, of course, any swimming then, except for the intrepid.' (*Frederic and Beetle Raphael*)

Open: all year.
Rooms: 32 double—28 with bath or shower, all with telephone.
Salon, TV room, terrace, garden.
Terms: B & B: 63 frs; meals: 38–82 frs; half board: 95 frs; full board: 116 frs.

Length of entries is not an indication of comparative merit, but of the relative attractiveness of the contribution.

149

STRASBOURG, 67000 Bas-Rhin

Hôtel Gutenberg   *Telephone:* (88) 321715
31 rue Serruriers

'Once the preserve of the British Parliamentary Clerks to the Council of
Europe, who always pinch the best, this has now lured most of the
British members away from the grander hotels. No really logical reason;
just absolute genuine Alsatian atmosphere and comfort.' (*Lord Beaumont of Whitley*)

Open: all year.
Rooms: 50—25 with bath or shower, all with telephone.
Lift.
Terms: B & B: 24–49 frs. No restaurant.

TANCARVILLE, 76430 St-Romain-de-Colbosc, Seine-Maritime

Hôtel de la Marine   *Telephone:* (35) 948915

Twenty miles from Le Havre, this smallish post-war hotel is obviously
a useful night stop to or from the Southampton ferry. It has a remarkable and practically isolated position almost underneath the great toll
bridge of Tancarville, and on the water's edge. The prices are moderate,
the food is 'outstandingly good', and the management is cheerfully
accommodating to those arriving late or who need to leave at 7 a.m. in
the morning to catch their boat. (*M. E. Hartley*)

Open: all year, except 15 January–15 February.
Rooms: 14—8 with bath or shower, all with telephone.
Salon, TV room, bar, terrace; garden.
No dogs.
Terms: B & B: 26–35 frs; meals: 47–84 frs.

THÉOULE, Miramar, 06590 Alpes-Maritimes

Hôtel Tour de L'Esquillon   *Telephone:* (93) 903151

'Miramar is one of those small French coastal villages that you've driven
through before you've realised it, and the few hotels in the vicinity are
—like the *Tour de L'Esquillon*—isolated. It's about midway between St
Raphael and Cannes on the stretch of coastline that becomes dramatically attractive with craggy reddish cliffs dropping steeply to a rocky sea-
shore. Although the main road runs past its door, the *Tour de L'Esquillon*
is the sort of place to stay in if you want peace and quiet. It's small, run
efficiently, and has an intimate atmosphere that makes you feel you are

staying in a private house. The outside is covered in bougainvillaea and it's built into the cliffside with a cable car—with attendant door-opener —making frequent journeys to the sea below. There, you can bathe off the rocks and sunbathe, and there's a lunchtime restaurant as well as various sports things. Not surprisingly, they don't accept children under five. Inside, there's a bright and sunny atmosphere and the villa is furnished in a classic though comfortable style. Ask for a room on the sea side, as those near the road can be a bit noisy.' (*Susan Grossman*)

Open: 12 February–10 October.
Rooms: 24—all with bath.
Garden, with private cable car giving direct access to the beach; lounge. No children under 5.
Terms: B & B: 72–92 frs; meals: 55 frs; full board (obligatory in high season): 200–30 frs.

TRELLY, 50660 Manche

Hôtel de la Verte Campagne   *Telephone:* (33) 476533

Right in the middle of nowhere, this old 18th-century Normandy farm-house, now converted into a small country restaurant with rooms, makes an ideal first stop coming from Cherbourg, 80 kilometres to the north, along the Normandy coast. It is only 12 kilometres from Coutances, with its haunting Gothic cathedral, and the popular little seaside resort of Granville is 23 kilometres to the west. The proprietors are charming and helpful, even to children wanting only to camp in their paddock. The dining room is tiny, but prettily done with red lampshades and curtains and a lot of wood, and the excellent cuisine is done by the family themselves. (*Uwe Kitzinger*)

Open: all year, except 15 November–1 December.
Rooms: 6 double, 1 single—3 with bath or shower, all with telephone.
Two salons, bar; rose garden and paddock; nearest beach, 12 kms.
Terms: B & B: from 32 frs; meals: 26–50 frs; half board: from 35 frs; full board: from 70 frs.

VILLEFRANCHE-DE-ROUERGUE, 12200 Aveyron

Hôtel Terminus   *Telephone:* (65) 451788

'Villefranche is a 13th-century town attractively situated on the Aveyron. Though without any outstanding historical monuments, it retains much medieval atmosphere and the Chartreuse and the Church of the Black Penitents are both worth visiting. It has a lively market-place which has changed little since the late Middle Ages. The neighbouring countryside has attractive riverside walks. Villefranche is 72 kilometres north of Albi by road and is on the minor railway line from

Toulouse to Brive. The town is quiet, with a population of about 12,000, and has virtually no nightlife.

'The *Hôtel Terminus* has an unprepossessing exterior and its nearest approach to a lounge is a café area with stone-topped tables. The upper corridors are usually lit by one 40-watt bulb. The bedrooms are comfortable, however; they are spacious and well-lit, and many of them have at least a shower. The cuisine, of excellent country type, is of outstandingly good value, with good fish, meat, ham, fresh vegetables. It is a family hotel where the father looks after the kitchen and his daughters wait at table—where their first task is to bring you a carafe of iced water. Butter for breakfast is not wrapped in silver paper.' (*Robert Shackleton*)

Open: 1 April–15 October.
Rooms: 23—12 with bath or shower.
Terms: B & B: 22–38 frs; meals: 18–60 frs; half board: 45–55 frs; full board: 55–65 frs.

Details of amenities vary according to the information—or lack of it—supplied by hotels in response to our questionnaires. The fact that lounges or bars or gardens are not mentioned must not be taken to mean that a hotel lacks them.

Germany

BADEN-BADEN, 7570 Baden Württemberg

Brenner's Park-Hotel
Schillerstrasse 6

Telephone: (07221) 23001
Telex: 781261

'Baden-Baden has been called the queen of spas. In the 19th and early
20th centuries it was to Europe what Bath was to England in the 18th
century, and it still retains its character of elegance and the glamour of
famous personalities. Much of its success today as a resort as well as a
fully modernised thermal establishment comes from Baden-Baden's
natural setting. It stands at the north-west corner of the Black Forest,
built in the folds of wooded hills close to the Rhine valley and with its
own local vineyards. The little medieval town stands on a hill from
which the handsome 19th-century resort spreads downwards to the
gardens which fringe the little river Oos. Here is the Kurhaus with its
famous Casino.

'*Brenner's Park-Hotel* is almost as much a part of Baden-Baden as the
Casino itself, and stands only a few minutes' walk away, overlooking the
river. The hotel was in the Brenner family for nearly 100 years, during
which it steadily improved and was constantly enlarged. Today it is no
longer a family affair but has very carefully retained "style" while adopt-
ing modern amenities. After the size and grace of its public rooms the
visitor's first, strongest and lasting impression is the excellence of
Brenner's service. Courtesy and deference to the guest's wishes are a way
of life here, and a refreshing change from the easy familiarity of staff in
many modern hotels. Apart from the normal double and single bedrooms, all beautifully furnished, there are "junior suites" which consist
of a lobby, a large bathroom, a luxurious L-shaped room with twin beds

in an alcove, and a splendid amount of wardrobe space, mirrors, etc., and a balcony overlooking park and river. De luxe suites have a separate sitting room. The Schwarzwald Grill provides first-class cuisine.'
(*Penelope Turing*)

Open: 1 March–15 November.
Rooms: 83—all with bath or shower, and some suites.
Lift, lounges, bar, conference room; indoor heated swimming pool, sauna, solarium, massage facilities, Kneipp cure service, hairdressing salon. Large park with tennis courts, stables, golf.
Terms: B & B: 80–168 DM.; full board: 139–227 DM.

BAMBERG, 8600 Bayern

Hotel Garni Alt Bamberg   *Telephone:* (0951) 26667
Habergasse 11

'Bamberg is one of the showplace medieval towns of southern Germany, as atmospheric as Rothenberg and Dinkelsbühl, but less commercialised than either. There are several larger and posher hotels in the town than the *Alt Bamberg* (formerly known as the *Elefant*), but this would be a natural choice if you were seeking the *echt* Bamberg experience: you could imagine meeting Dürer in the cosy and reasonably priced restaurant or Hans Sachs in the foyer. The hotel is run by two charming young girls, the daughters of the former owner. The rooms are pleasant and airy and look out on to a winding old narrow street, full of other houses of the same period. There is very little noise, though you are only a short distance from the high Domplatz, with the town's beautiful cathedral, its world-famous Reiter sculpture, and its elegant Residenz.'
(*Lucy Kitzinger*)

Open: all year.
Rooms: 10 double, 11 single—13 with bath or shower.
Terms: B & B: 29.50 DM. No restaurant.

BAYREUTH, 8580 Bayern

Bayerischer Hof   *Telephone:* (0921) 23061
Bahnhofstrasse 14   *Telex:* 0642737

'Those who are fortunate enough to attend the Bayreuth Festspiel in August may well know more elegant and expensive hotels. I arrived there on a dark day in mid-winter, and accepted with gratitude the modest hotel booked for me by the University of Bayreuth (yes, there is one, two years old). It had a slightly old-fashioned air, as befitted its name, though not at all a faded look. It is central, in fact next door to Bayreuth's railway station, but quiet—I never heard any trains my entire stay. The rooms are small but well-equipped, with bathrooms *en suite*. I had a superbly comfortable big armchair with a foot-rest, not the miniature upright so often offered in medium-priced hotels. The usual duvet on the bed of course. Food is pleasantly served for breakfast —various kinds of bread, some cold meats, excellent coffee. Downstairs there is a Spanish-type cellar restaurant serving South German food, well-cooked and well-served—not, by German standards, expensive— and excellent local Franconian wine in those Hollywood-Medieval squat bottles. A courteous, unobtrusive and efficient hotel.' (*John Spencer*)

Open: all year.
Rooms: 62—most with bath or shower, all with telephone.
Lift; Hans Sachs Room, roof garden restaurant, Spanish room, con- ference room, indoor pool, sauna; garden with sun-terrace and small swimming pool.
Terms: B & B: 25–50 DM.; meals: 11.50–30.00 DM.

FREUDENSTADT, 7290 Baden-Württemberg

Hotel Waldeck   *Telephone:* (07441) 2441
Strassburgerstrasse 60

The famous Black Forest resort of Freudenstadt, dating back to the 16th century, claims more sun than anywhere else in Germany. In winter, it is popular with skiers; in the spring and summer, it attracts walkers, with more than 100 miles of well-marked trails in the neighbouring hills. 'The *Waldeck* is run with great care and generations of experience. The old proprietress comes into the dining room with a gentle greeting: "*guten Appetit*". All the same her eyes take it all in; the whole hotel shows it. The flowers and the china, skilful, bourgeois, a world of house- pride and fine linen—the exact opposite of factory-hotel keeping.' (*Edward Mace*)

Open: all year, except mid November–mid December.
Rooms: 67—all with bath/shower and telephone.
Lift, lounge, conference room; garden with tennis court; riding and fishing facilities.
Terms: B & B: 28–55 DM.; full board: 45–77 DM.

HAMBURG, 2000

Hotel Prem   *Telephone:* (040) 242211/245454
An der Alster 9   *Telex:* 02163115

In the city centre across the road from the picturesque Alster Lake. Quiet, old, small and family-run, decorative, too. Breakfast is served in a charming room opening on to a small garden behind the hotel. 'Not exactly cheap, but we paid a lot more in other cities for a lot less.' (*Jacqueline MacHale*)

Open: all year.
Rooms: 26 double, 23 single—42 with bath or shower, all with telephone.
Lounge (with TV), bar, breakfast-room; garden.
Terms: B & B: 65 DM.; meals: 14-16 DM.

HINTERZARTEN, 7824 Baden-Württemberg

Hotel Weisses Rössle *Telephone:* (07652) 1411
Freiburgerstrasse 38

'There is a local slogan in this holiday resort—"The guest is our king" —and this is certainly the ambience that pervades this little place set high up in the Black Forest. One has only to leave the immediate vicinity of the town to find oneself at the start of several thousand kilometres of walks, 300 kilometres around Hinterzarten alone, all clearly colour-marked with distances, at every forest or glade intersection. Hinterzarten is also only a few miles from some of the finest vineyards in southern Germany, particularly the Kaiserstuhl. The charming town of Freiburg is twenty minutes by car—and there is an attractive 9-hole golf course on the road to Freiburg. With a car you can also visit the historic clock museum at Furtwangen or the fascinating group of 16th- and 17th-century farmhouses in the open-air museum at Gutach. The best time to visit the area is in the spring or autumn, or in the skiing months—omitting the high summer season when accommodation and roads are very full. In winter every road and forest walk has to be snow-cleared by 7 a.m. so that walkers need not be housebound while skiers enjoy the slopes.

'The *Weisses Rössle* is first class in every sense of the term. Its most important asset is the attitude of everyone from the owner-proprietor, Hans Zimmermann and his wife, Urda, to the attendants at the swimming pool. There are three dining rooms, two mostly used by residents, and the rooms are all extremely well furnished. They serve a mighty German breakfast which makes lunch almost superfluous.

'The Zimmermanns have also arranged with eleven other regional hotels an unusual walkers' or motorists' holiday. The customer is transported free from Basle airport (one hour), put up at the *Weisses Rössle* for the first night, and thereafter has to walk (or motor, bus or train) to a different hotel between two and four wood/meadowland walking hours away each day, where his luggage will be awaiting him. At the end, he is taken to the airport. The total cost of everything except lunch and dinner for eleven nights was 330 DM.' (*Denis Morris*)

Open: all year.
Rooms: 67—some with bath/shower, all with telephone.
Lift; salon, indoor swimming pool, sauna, massage; terrace, garden with tennis court.
Terms: B & B: 30-85 DM.; full board: 81-117 DM.

LINZ AM RHEIN, 5460 Rheinland-Pfalz

Hotel Franz Josef   *Telephone:* (02644) 2332
Rheinstrasse 25

'The small town of Linz am Rhein is on the left bank of the Rhine about
39 miles from Cologne, and 23 from Koblenz. It is considered "*Die
Bunte Stadt am Rhein*"—i.e. "the beautiful town on the Rhine". A
feature is the multiplicity of "Fachhausen" or half-timbered houses,
many of them centuries old and all kept in wonderful condition. The
Rhine is fast-flowing at Linz, with a never-ending stream of huge barges,
with flags of many different nations. In summer, steamers offer a first-
class service to the castles, churches, vineyards and villages which line
the river. But the river is only one attraction. Behind Linz are rolling
hills, mainly afforested, hiding charming villages which the tourist
rarely finds. A car is useful if you want to explore the countryside,
though there is a rather sparse service of country buses which start from
the local railway station. For those who prefer to walk, there are many
woodland and forest tracks.
   'My wife and I were fortunate enough some twenty-three years ago to
be recommended to stay at the *Hotel Franz Josef*, and we have been
back every year since. It is not a hotel in the strict sense but, in my view,
the best Gasthaus in the town. English and French as well as German
are spoken. Old woodwork, old prints, mellow furniture, a fascinating
drawing of an old oak tree, with the trunk and branches tracing the
history of the Zimmermann family, who have been running the *Franz
Josef* for 200 years—all contribute to the atmosphere. Herr Zimmermann himself is the chef and is a superb cook. Knowledgeable locals
eat here. There is no raucous music, and no television. A modest menu.
Charming service by girls who always seem to have been there. Breakfast is a highlight: three or four different breads, cold meats in variety,
masses of butter, jam and marmalade, tea and coffee, all beautifully laid
out. The wine list is excellent, as one would expect in a country where
marvellous wines are made, and need not be expensive. There is also a
good locally-brewed beer.' (*F. C. Margetts*)

Open: all year, except 10–30 April.
Rooms: 4.
Terms: B & B: 17 DM.; meals: 11–20 DM.

MUNICH, 8000 Bayern

Bundesbahn-Hotel München   *Telephone:* (089) 558571
Bahnhofplatz 2   *Telex:* 0523174

'Situated on the southern part of the main Munich railway station this
is emphatically a convenience hotel, with direct access to the station and
with airport coaches dropping you at the door. Unexpectedly it is completely quiet—and elegant. It has rooms which are roomy—not always

the case with a modern purpose-built hotel. The smart restaurant on the first floor is open day and night.' (*Lucy Kitzinger*)

Open: all year.
Rooms: 226—most with bath or shower.
Lounge, cocktail bar, convention facilities.
Terms: B & B: 46 DM.

Hotel Deutscher Kaiser   *Telephone:* (089) 558321
Arnulstrasse 2   *Telex:* 0522650

'A very good hotel of the tall, match-box style, situated opposite the railway station, which is also the Air Terminal. But although so near to both, the rooms are quiet as the bedrooms are fairly high up, and the reception rooms further down are well insulated against noise. The whole atmosphere is very pleasant and the service commendable. The restaurant, on top of the high building, gives fine views over the city. Service is excellent and so is the food.' (*Sophie Dann*)

Open: all year.
Rooms: 165—single, double, and some suites—most with bath.
Lift; cocktail bar/lounge, wine tavern and café, banqueting rooms, ball-room.
Terms: B & B: 50 DM.; meals: from 22 DM.

Hotel Torbräu   *Telephone:* (089) 225016
Tal 37   *Telex:* 0522212

Quietly situated in the old part of the city, within pleasant walking distance of the Opera and main shopping areas. Family-run, it is popular with Bavarians. 'Bedrooms, though on the small side, have beds which are unusually comfortable, being longer and wider than single beds usually are. Lighting and switches are excellently placed. Bathrooms well appointed, but short, steep bath tubs—perhaps difficult for elderly people.' Tea includes all the usual rich German layer cakes. 'Food is *"gut Bürgerlich"*—large portions, not always particularly exciting, but at most reasonable prices.' (*Hans Lemming*)

Open: all year.
Rooms: 60 double, 44 single—about half with bath, all with telephone; baby-listening service on request.
Lift; large lounge, 3 conference rooms.
Terms: B & B: 39-45 DM.; full board: from 70 DM.

If you can endorse any entry in this book, please do so <u>now</u>. We need a quick feedback on all our entries to help prepare our next edition.

WILDBAD IM SCHWARZWALD, 7547 Baden-Württemberg

Hotel Valsana am Kurpark   *Telephone:* (07081) 425
Kernerstrasse 182

'Wildbad, on the north-eastern edge of the Black Forest, some 40 miles west-south-west of Stuttgart, still functions as a spa: people go there to take the waters and other kinds of cure; and the holiday population contains a noticeable proportion of the elderly, arthritic, and infirm. German doctors can prescribe a cure in Wildbad on their national health service. Don't let that put you off the place. The small town has a beautiful, extensive and very well-kept Kurpark, where you can walk (the gradient of every walk is clearly marked), play tennis or miniature golf, or outdoor chess or draughts with giant pieces. In the season there are frequent concerts in the concert hall and the church. The town is small: the heart of it is only two long streets running on either side of a small, fast-flowing stream. Just behind the town rises the Sommerberg, a mountain (you can go up by funicular) whose top is an extensive and level plateau with miles of walking through the forest and occasional views into the valleys on either side, and with several good, comfortable and very expensive hotels of a conventional kind.

'The *Hotel Valsana*, however, is something quite different. It was opened in 1975, and stands at the end of the small town, on the edge of the Kurpark (fifteen minutes' walk to the centre of the town). The owner, Herr Rothfuss, is an architect by profession and designed the hotel himself. He and his wife run it in a friendly and slightly inefficient way. There is a television lounge, but not much else in the way of public rooms. The corridors are dark and gloomy, but the rooms are the finest hotel rooms I have ever seen. They are enormous in size and divided into two by a high partition—one half is the bedroom, the other a spacious and fully appointed sitting room, with sofa, two armchairs, table, writing desk, radio, television (an optional extra), and as much shelving and cupboard space as you would have in your own sitting room at home. Drinks cabinet; beautiful glasses. The large French windows give on to a private terrace, each of which is itself the size of the sitting room on the next floor down, whose roof it is; the whole façade slopes backwards in a stepped way. The terraces look out over meadows, then a stream, and then the Kurpark beyond, and they are equipped with garden furniture and deck chairs.

'The cuisine is competent but not yet remarkable; the Rothfuss family plan to make that the next area for improvement. Service was very slow, but, remember, there are good restaurants with more choice of dishes within walking distance. The piped music in the dining room is controlled, at low volume, from Mr Rothfuss's office: his tastes are Mozart, Haydn and 19th-century operetta. Large, heated indoor swimming pool with jet massage. Sauna an optional extra. In short, a hotel where you would feel at home, even for a longish stay. It was nothing like as expensive as the hotels on the top of the Sommerberg, and incredible value for money.' (*Ralph Blumenau*)

Open: all year.

Rooms: 34 suites—all with bath and telephone (see above for description).

Lift; television lounge; indoor swimming pool, sauna, massage; tennis, riding and fishing facilities.

Terms: B & B: 45–70 DM.; meals: 16–28 DM.

Most hotels have reduced rates out of season and for children. For details, you will need to write to the hotel direct.

Greece

To our dismay, we received no entries for Greece which we felt merited inclusion. There certainly are good hotels in Greece, and we should welcome nominations in time for the next edition.

The Rimon Inn, Safed

Israel

JERUSALEM

The Plaza Hotel
47 King George St

Telephone: (02) 221111
Telex: 25460

'This new 5-star hotel deserves every single star. A flower (a single rose!) is brought to you on your arrival. The rooms are luxuriously comfortable—well lit, beautifully furnished. Breakfast was delicious. Towels are changed twice daily, your bedroom light has been turned on when you return in the evening. Management and staff live up to one's most optimistic expectations of efficiency and friendliness.' (*Gertrud Dann*)

Open: all year.
Rooms: 414—342 with bath, 36 with shower, all air-conditioned and with TV.
Lift; health centre; private swimming pool.
Terms (excluding service): B & B: £I 200-40.

KINNERET LAKE, Sea of Galilee

Nof Ginosar Guest House

Telephone: (067) 22161/4

A recently built guest house adjoining a 500-strong Kibbutz founded in 1934, in one of Israel's beauty spots on the northern shore of the Sea of Galilee. You can use it as a stay-put holiday centre or as a base for exploring the innumerable historical and architectural sites in the vicinity: Capernaum lies to the north, Tiberias to the south, and there is much more. Visitors to the guest house are also welcome to look over the Kibbutz. Apart from ruins, relics and historic attractions, there are motor launch trips on the lake, and fine walks above the water, many by the trails used in olden days, through woods and patches of asphodel. The bedrooms of the guest house are decidedly spacious—you can easily fit in a third bed without overcrowding—have fitted carpets and are well heated, but with somewhat miserable lighting, unlike that in bathrooms and public rooms, where it is perfectly adequate. Wire netting over windows protects against flies or mosquitoes. 'The food is excellent and plentiful, the service very good and friendly.' (*Sophie Dann*)

Open: all year.
Rooms: 106 double—54 with bath, 52 with shower, all air-conditioned, with telephone; TV available.
Lounge/bar; gardens and woods; private beach on the shores of the Sea of Galilee.
Terms (excluding service):   B & B: £I 110; half board: £I 180; full board: £I 235.

SAFED

The Rimon Inn   *Telephone:* (067) 30665/6

'A long stay in Safed may not be everybody's taste. This ancient town on the edge of Galilee has a spectacular site on the top of a mountain, and in winter it's no place for tourists: cold, windy, with snow. But when it is really hot in other parts of Israel, it's very pleasant up there. The town itself looks scruffy and ruined. Some of the ruins date back to the great earthquake of 1837: whole areas of the town never seem to have been properly rebuilt since that disaster. The old town climbs up the top of the mountain. The uppermost part is the main street (one decent restaurant); the next level down is the ancient Jewish quarter, the centre of the sects that studied the Kabala from the 16th century until the earthquake; it contains some very old synagogues. The lower town was, until 1948, the Arab quarter; the Arabs fled from it and their houses have in many cases been converted to the picturesque showrooms of about forty Israeli artists who, during the summer, have permanent exhibitions there and of course sell their works, which vary from the kitschy to the distinguished. For foreign tourists Safed is at most a one-night stop; but this is a pity. It is impossible to soak up the atmosphere of the town in that time. And, if you have a car, Safed is a good centre for trips in the Galilee region, down to Lake Tiberias or west to Akko (the Crusaders' Acre). The town is resolutely non-metropolitan: no decent shops, no trips are organised from there (the nearest excursion centre is Tiberias, perhaps some forty minutes away), but that is part of its charm: you really are not in modern Israel here.

'The *Rimon Inn* is probably the only hotel in Safed where one would want to stay for more than a night or two. It is in the artists' quarter, and consists of a number of renovated old houses skilfully integrated into a hotel complex. Most bedrooms are like separate small one-room cottages, and several have a marvellous view over a valley to the bare hills beyond. The food is variable in quality: we had one very poor night, but other times it was quite good. Service varies from the effusive to the incompetent.' (*Ralph Blumenan*)

Open: all year.
Rooms: 36—33 with bath, 3 with shower, all with telephone, many with balcony or patio.
Partly air-conditioned; terraced garden with swimming pool (heated in winter).
Terms (excluding service):   half board: £1 190.

Warning: prices quoted are 1977 prices.

Hotel Residenza Turistica Su Gologone, Oliena, Sardinia

Italy

ARZACHENA, 07021 Sassari, Sardinia

Pitrizza
Porto Cervo, Costa Smeralda

Telephone: (0789) 92000
Telex: 79037 Cosme

'The Costa Smeralda is a rich man's playground developed by the Aga Khan in the north-east corner of Sardinia. No Sardinian actually lives there, and they tend to resent its isolated presence, but it has been skilfully and unobtrusively developed without destroying the beauty of the landscape. It's a ruggedly attractive area covered in pines and low maquis with deserted sweeping bays, many of them only accessible by boat. There are relatively few hotels and most of the Costa Smeralda is littered with jet-set villas—low, whitewashed buildings that blend in well with the rocky scenery, anonymous from the outside, lavish and luxurious inside, and each designed and built individually. The main resort is Porto Cervo with a busy yacht marina, shops and restaurants. The *Pitrizza* is a small exclusive hotel—not in the resort itself, but isolated on a quiet and lovely bay with a mountain backdrop. It is more intimate and discreet than its equally rich relations near by, and is made up of several small and comfortable bungalows each with its own lounge. The main part of the hotel houses the small drawing room and dining room, both elegantly furnished, with a piano, fresh flowers, and a country club atmosphere. Outside the sunken salt-water pool has been expertly sculpted out of the natural rock and is surrounded by rockeries and shrubs. To one side is a wide, sandy beach, with a stone jetty for guests who bring their own boats (which made me a bit cross, because I'd left mine at home!). It's ideal for a quiet escape in the sun, to be pampered but not ostentatiously so, in an atmosphere that is relaxed yet

exclusive enough to make each guest feel as if he were personally chosen.'
(*Susan Grossman*)

Open: 15 May–30 September.
Rooms: 23 double, 5 single—23 with bath, 5 with shower, all with telephone, air-conditioning; baby-listening service on request.
Clubhouse with salon, bar, piano/bar, terrace; flower gardens with salt-
water swimming pool; private beach with safe bathing and boating.
Terms: B & B: 25,000–44,000 L.; meals: 13,500 L.; full board:
70,000 L.

ASSISI, 06081 Perugia

Hotel Umbra   *Telephone:* (075) 812240
Vicolo degli Archi 6

Just off the main square, and reasonably removed therefore from the
bustle round the Basilica of St Francis, where most of the hotels are. The
Umbra is among narrow streets, very quiet, and with two different but
equally attractive small terraces open to residents. Meals are taken in a
vine-covered garden overlooking a nunnery. The *Umbra* offers the only
Michelin 1-star restaurant in the town, and there's no need to venture
off the menu for high-priced supplements; but the hotel is charming
anyway, with pleasant service and not expensive. (*Graham Child, Derek
Cooper*)

Open: all year except 1–15 November.
Rooms: 27—14 with bath, 4 with shower, all with telephone.
Salon, bar, garden.
Terms: B & B: 6,550–8,300 L.; meals: 4,500–8,500 L.; full board:
15,000–16,000 L.

BELLAGIO, 22021 Como

Grand Hotel Villa Serbelloni   *Telephone:* (031) 950216
                                          Telex: 38330

'Lakes Como, Maggiore and Garda have a special southern European
colour and romance, and Como has always been particularly beloved by
the British traveller: 19th- and early 20th-century novelists made it a
setting for lighthearted love stories about wealthy young people and
mysterious diplomats; amateur watercolourists painted innumerable
not very good pictures of it which adorned the walls of English homes.
If those generations have gone, the beauty which enchanted them has
not. Como remains a very lovely lake, surrounded by small smiling
towns and villages, fringed with graceful trees and a luxuriance of
flowers, magnolias, azaleas, roses, through the season. Exotic villages
look down into blue waters. Steamers zig-zag to and fro. It is still

possible to enjoy romanticism here. Bellagio is one of Como's nicest little towns, situated on the peninsula between the two southern arms of the lake with an attractive waterfront and picturesque narrow streets.

'The *Grand Hotel Villa Serbelloni* is an ideal place in which to re-capture the old mood of the lake and its elegant sojourners—for those who can afford luxury prices. It stands near the tip of the peninsula two minutes' walk from the quay, a large, handsome, reassuring building with pale yellow walls and red roofs. Inside there are palatial public rooms with brocaded furniture, beautiful rugs, fine paintings, graceful chandeliers, and cool vistas of broad marble corridors leading to terraces and shady trees beyond.

'Bedrooms are large and well-appointed. All the bathrooms have been modernised. The hotel has a private beach and a new heated outdoor swimming pool with a snack bar, so that guests can have a cold lunch there without going up to the terrace (where meals are served) or the main restaurant. Private motor and rowing boats and water-skiing are available. The hotel's cuisine is of high standard, as is the service. The *Villa Serbelloni* is personally directed by the owner, Mr Rudy Bucher, an Italian-born Swiss, and has been in the Bucher family for about a century. It is Rudy Bucher's personality which has created this hotel's rather unusual blend of friendliness, style and formal courtesy.' (*Penelope Turing*)

Open: 7 April–10 October.
Rooms: 93—89 with bath, 4 with shower, all with telephone.
Palatial lounges; terrace, gardens (with tennis courts and heated swimming pool) leading to private beach.
Terms: B & B: 14,200–31,200 L.; meals: from 11,000 L.; full board:
           26,500–46,000 L.

BERGAMO, 24100

Agnello d'Oro
via Gombito 22

Telephone: (035) 249883

'One of the great attractions of Bergamo, or of its Città Alta at least, is that it is so small that the visitor is spared the tourist's customary state of chronic exhaustion: its delights are all contained within a modest compass. The Piazza Vecchia was regarded by Frank Lloyd Wright as the most balanced and varied in the world; and the art critic, Eric Newton, found that he returned to Bergamo as often as to any other town in Italy. The ambience is perhaps the chief attraction, another is the views to the Città Bassa and beyond, a third is the art nouveau iron-work of the late-19th-century funicular terminus. But undoubtedly Bergamo's most notable feature is the Colleoni Chapel—the same Colleoni whose equestrian statue by Verrocchio is in Venice. The outside of the Chapel is an unpromising jumble, but Tiepolo frescoes, some fine monuments, ingenious marquetry and low-relief carving by Amadeo make the interior one of the most rewarding for its size in Italy.

'At Bergamo the place to stay is the 17th-century *Agnello d'Oro* (not that the choice in the Città Alta is a wide one). It's not very large, nor is it expensive, but you will find that the decor of the bedrooms has a personal quality which contrasts agreeably with the usual anonymity of hotel decoration. Outside a small fountain tinkles, and within you eat as you might in some particularly fortunate home. (Or if, as on a recent visit, the restaurant proves to be closed, you have only to walk up the street to the excellent open-air alternative in the Piazza Vecchia.)' (*Sam Carr*)

Open: all year.
Rooms: 16 double, 4 single—all with bath or shower.
Terms: B & B: 5,000–6,000 L.; meals: 5,500–8,000 L.; full board: 15,000–16,000 L.

CASTELLINA IN CHIANTI, 53011 Siena

Tenuta di Ricavo   *Telephone:* (0577) 740221

'A hotel which, in my opinion, fulfils every civilised person's holiday needs—that is, if you consider one heated and one natural outdoor pool an adequate substitute for the sea. This uniquely beautiful and peaceful haven, equidistant from Florence and Siena, reached from Castellina in Chianti, is situated in the most wonderful country with endless walking possibilities; the food is at all times good and plentiful, and during the high season, quite delicious; service is excellent and unobtrusive, clientele international and cultured. The place used to be a wine grower's settlement which was deserted and bought by Signora Scottoni for her own and her family's holiday home, and only after her husband's tragic motor accident did she turn it into a hotel, converting the stone cottages, adding and rebuilding, and furnishing each differently. A car is advisable if one wishes to take advantage of the endless sightseeing possibilities within such easy reach; but then again, there is the local taxi to drive one into Florence and Siena from where to go on local excursions by public transport. And I have always found other guests more than willing to give lifts, as are also the hotel staff if and when they go off shopping. I have spent two holidays there, and were you to ask me where I'd like to go this time, it would be back, at almost any time of the year.' (*Uli Lloyd Pack;* also *Tom Congdon*)

Open: 10 April–31 October.
Rooms: 23 double, 2 single—all with bath, 10 with telephone.
Salons; park with 2 swimming pools (1 heated).
Terms (excluding tax): full board: 21,000–28,000 L.

Sterling and dollar equivalents of foreign currencies at the date of going to press will be found under Exchange Rates on p. 243.

FIESOLE, 50014 Florence

Aurora   *Telephone:* (055) 59100
Piazza Mino da Fiesole 39

'One of the virtues of Fiesole is that it is near to, but sufficiently removed from, the tourists and cars that abound in Florence. But Fiesole has much modestly to offer of its own: a handsome Roman theatre, a fine Renaissance monument by a local sculptor, Mino, in the Cathedral, an Etruscan tomb as a reminder of Fiesole's origins, and a tiny picture gallery which would be of considerable consequence anywhere else except in Italy. Fiesole's greatest attraction, though, is its view of Florence, with Brunelleschi's Cathedral dome an unmistakable point of orientation.

'The *Aurora* was, in its day, good enough for Queen Victoria and, discreetly modernised, it is good enough for us, too. (But did *she* also enjoy the companionship of a lizard, as we did, on the ceiling of her bedroom?) The appointments are modestly unflamboyant and none the worse for that. What is pleasant is to have a very decent meal out of doors in the garden. Afterwards you could walk down the hill to Florence (although walking back would be another story), or take your car, but the most convenient way would be to take the tram which starts from the piazza behind the hotel.' (*Sam Carr*)

Open: all year, except January and November.
Rooms: 22 — 14 with bath, 6 with shower, all with telephone.
Salon, bar, air-conditioned restaurant; terraced garden.
Terms: B & B: 8,900–12,400 L.; meals: 6,000–9,500 L.; full board: 22,000–26,000 L.

FLORENCE, 50100

Hotel Berchielli   *Telephone:* (055) 211530
Lungarno Acciaiuoli 14

'A very efficient, friendly, well-maintained hotel on the banks of the Arno, half a block from the Ponte Vecchio, and central to all one might want to do in Florence. We spent our first night in a twin-bedded room on the river side—and slept little because of the incessant traffic noise which went on all night. Next night we moved to a room at the back of the hotel and gave up our private bath in favour of a small patio-porch adorned with potted plants, table and chairs (and laundry lines!) which was blessedly quiet and which cost less. The hotel staff, who all speak excellent English, will make concert and other booking arrangements for you and are generally helpful and sympathetic.' (*Lee Zeigler*)

Open: all year.
Rooms: 78—most double, 28 with bath, 8 with shower.

Lift; bar; no restaurant, but Continental breakfast served.
Terms: room: 9,000 L. (breakfast extra).

Pensione Pitti Palace   *Telephone:* (055) 282257/287022
via Barbadori 2

'In spite of its grand name this is, in fact, a pensione situated on the upper floors of a building just by the Ponte Vecchio, not too expensive, with a nicely set up dining room and a charming little sitting room. The bedrooms are pleasant and some have private bathrooms. The cooking is good. English is spoken.' (*Guy and Wendy Payen-Payn*)

Open: all year.
Rooms: 20 double, 4 single—14 with bath, all with telephone.
Lift; sitting room, TV room, roof garden.
Terms: bed: 11,350 L. (breakfast extra); meals: 5,000 L.

FONNI, 08023 Nuoro, Sardinia

Sporting Club Monte Spada   *Telephone:* (0784) 57154/57285

'Fonni is in the heart of Sardinia on the slopes of the highest mountain —Monte Spada. High enough for skiing in the winter and little changed since the days when D. H. Lawrence explored this remotely beautiful area and so vividly described it in his *Sea and Sardinia.* The town itself, 8 kilometres away, is quiet and peaceful; old houses with tiled roofs and pretty balconies, women in black, and little traffic apart from the occasional man on a donkey. The *Sporting Club*, as its name suggests, is a winter sports hotel that in summer is a cool retreat from the heat of the coast. It's built into the mountainside and surrounded by fairly gentle rolling hills, vineyards and fields, thistles and blackberries, forests of cork oak, bees and butterflies. I kept getting lost in its long corridors, as it's built on several levels down the hillside. The bedrooms were sparsely furnished, bright and modern and because of the slant that they're built on, disastrous if you flood the bathroom, as it all pours downhill into the bedroom. There are lovely views from the windows. The public rooms were simply furnished but comfortable and views from the dining room were superb. It's not a place to spend the whole of your summer holiday in, but a good base for exploring the little-known and wild Sardinian interior. And the *banditi*—so the locals assured me —never attack tourists.' (*Susan Grossman*)

Open: all year.
Rooms: 28 double, 2 single, 11 suites (for 4 people)—all with bath, telephone and radio.
Tavernette, American bar, Congress Room, playroom, art gallery, discotheque, boutique, separate TV room; large park with private lake (trout fishing), mini-zoo, heated swimming pool, tennis courts, riding

stables. Land-Rover safaris and excursions. Winter skiing (with Sardinia's only ski-lift near by).

Terms: Bed: 8,200 L.; breakfast: 1,200 L.; meals: 5,000–6,000 L.; half board: 16,000 L.; full board: 18,000 L.

GRESSONEY-LA-TRINITÀ, 11020 Aosta

Hotel Busca Thedy *Telephone:* (0125) 86136

'When some five years ago our usual summer alpine haunts had become unbearably crowded, we started looking round for something unspoilt, but still within our very limited family budget. The *Daily Telegraph* recommended the *Busca Thedy* as extremely good value, good food, in an area of outstanding beauty and historical interest. We went there and found all that and more. We have been there as a family and I have been there on my own, and in each case the welcome, courtesy and value for money were outstanding. The owner, Signor Busca, is proud of having been a frequent host to the former King Umberto, and the old part of the hotel reflects that era. The new part has been cleverly given a more relaxed atmosphere and is built in mellow pine, avoiding the excessively rustic. New arrivals are made very welcome, whilst guests returning for a second visit are treated like long-lost friends. The ambience is more that of a country house than a hotel, and very suitable for an energetic or a lazy holiday. The tennis courts are well-maintained, and there was a *"salone"* out of bounds to *"bambini"*. The food can best be described as high-class regional, the wine list mostly Italian with excellent house wines. The service is good but at the peak of the season sometimes slow. Otherwise the service is efficient, personal and unobtrusive. Language is no problem as Signor Busca speaks fluent English, French and German. The village council has restricted development very strictly, although some concessions have been made to the winter sports industry. There are no evening entertainments, but Gressoney St Jean (6 kilometres) has everything from a colourful market to nightlife.' (*Marianne Allies*)

Open: 15 December–15 April, and 1 June–15 September.
Rooms: 87—33 with bath, 10 with shower, all with telephone. Garden with tennis courts.
Terms: B & B: 6,250–8,000 L.; full board: 13,000–18,000 L.

IVREA, Lago di Sirio, 10015 Torino

Hotel Sirio *Telephone:* (0125) 423646

The town of Ivrea lies just off the autostrada from Aosta (and the Mont-Blanc Tunnel) to Turin, Milan, and points south. Many people use the *Hotel Sirio* as an attractive night-stop, but it could also be a good place to stay for an extended visit in a beautiful location a long way off the usual tourist map. It is a very quiet, smallish hotel, with many rooms overlooking Lake Sirio, which offers rowing, sailing, swimming and fishing. There are lovely views of the mountains, and plenty of good walks in the neighbourhood for those without a car; a bus service to Ivrea passes near the hotel. The rooms are pleasantly furnished and comfortable, and the service is very friendly. You eat on a large terrace, and the food is 'terrific'. The restaurant is well-known in the locality, and people come from long distances for a meal. Although the hotel is often used for wedding receptions and the like, the hotel guests are not made to feel neglected. (*Sheridan Russell*)

Open: all year.
Rooms: 33—11 with bath, 22 with shower, all with telephone. Lift; garden.
Terms: B & B: 7,300–8,000 L.; meals: 5,500–9,500 L.; full board: from 14,000 L.

MERANO, 39012 Bolzano

Hotel Pension Sittnerhof   *Telephone:* (0473) 23331
via Verdi 60

'Merano is in the heart of the Alps, in the beautiful Alto Adige (or South Tyrol), south of the Brenner Pass. Until the end of the First World War, it was Austrian, but then, along with the rest of the region, it was given to Italy. Most of the inhabitants still speak German, but many of the younger generation also speak Italian. The town is a world-famous health and holiday resort, with many elegant and very expensive hotels, a big Kurhaus with its gardens along a foaming mountain river, and some highly sophisticated shops. The best time to visit is in the spring, when all the apple trees are covered in white blossom, or in the autumn, dark blue with grapes and red with apples, and a wonderful smell. The summer is unbearably hot. The *Sittnerhof* is on the outskirts of the town —the last house at the end of a long street, at the foot of the hotel's own orchards and vineyards (ten minutes on foot to the centre, but a car is almost essential). It belongs to the Tyrolean family Brunner—parents, son and daughter-in-law. The father is a cattle dealer, the son a racing driver (with lots of silver trophies); the hotel is run, very efficiently and pleasantly, by the two Frau Brunners. The house is airy and light, with a wide staircase, and flowers everywhere. Most of the bedrooms have balconies with deck chairs, and a view of the mountains; bedside lamps, however, are no use to the insomniac. The food is good and plentiful, with a well varied menu.' (*Lucy Kitzinger*)

Open: all year.
Rooms: 20—18 double, 2 single—6 with bath, 14 with shower. Lift; salon, bar; lawns with swimming pool.
Terms: bed: 7,500 L. (breakfast extra); full board: 14,000 L.

MILAN, 20122

Hotel Francia Europa   *Telephone:* (02) 708301
Corso Vittorio Emanuele 9   *Telex:* 34083

'A hotel in the grand manner, right in the city centre, next to the Cathedral but, oddly enough for such a position, remarkably quiet. Inside rooms look on to a courtyard full of flowers and pot plants. Main rooms are spacious and elegant, the balconied dining room lit by a glittering chandelier and soft wall lighting. Flowers are everywhere: in the grill room, salon, bar and bedrooms. It is extremely well run and has a high reputation for style, service, and good food.' (*John Fox*)

Open: all year.
Rooms: 135—all with bath and shower, radio and air-conditioning. Large salon, TV room, solarium, bar; inner courtyard set with tables, chairs and sun umbrellas.
Terms (excluding taxes): bed: 17,500 L.; breakfast: 2,500 L.

Hotel Manzoni   *Telephone:* (02) 705700
via Santo Spirito 20

'This is a very pleasant, *quiet* hotel, rather modern in appearance, located just a block from the main street which leads to La Scala square, the elegant Vittorio Emanuele shopping arcade, and the Cathedral.' (*Lee Zeigler*)

Open: all year.
Rooms: 54—many with bath/shower.
Lift.
Terms: B & B: 10,000–12,400 L. No restaurant, but Continental breakfast served.

OLIENA, 08025 Nuoro, Sardinia

Hotel Residenza Turistica Su Gologone   *Telephone:* (0784) 47512

'You're unlikely to see many tourists in this part of Sardinia, near the hilltop town of Nuoro, and a few miles from the sandy beaches of the east coast. Oliena, with its cobbled streets and population of shepherds, is a typical mountain village in the semi-bandit country of the rugged and wild interior. Several miles to the east of Oliena is Su Gologone. We found it by accident—on a drive that was breathtakingly beautiful, through an Umbrian landscape out of Poussin or Claude Lorraine. We glimpsed oxen ploughing the fields through gaps in the cypresses, we passed loaded donkeys coming back from the fields, vines, olive trees and pine forests. Finally, at sunset, we reached the wooded ravine that gave Su Gologone its name. There, leading their flocks over the tumbling water, in and out of the willows, were the shepherds. Wild pigs lurked beneath the flowering oleander; a small group of shepherds sat and strummed their guitars and sang. The *Residenza Turistica* was the only building (apart from an old church) near this scene of rural splendour —a low whitewashed villa covered in bougainvillaea, run by a young Italian couple.

'The hotel had a surreal atmosphere that lifted it from its splendid Sardinian location to a setting from *The Discreet Charm of the Bourgeoisie*. When we first arrived, the owners looked vaguely puzzled as to why we were there at all. The front door was permanently locked and they were totally unaffected by their guests, talking and arguing as if they were on their own. The lovely outdoor pool surrounded by lawns was locked behind a wrought-iron gate and guests had to seek out a key before they could use it, and there was no service at all to speak of—if you wanted anything outside mealtimes you virtually helped yourself. We had a fabulous Italian tiled bedroom overlooking the isolated hills —and could hear the tinkling of sheep bells in the distance. Other rooms varied greatly and some were small and rather run down. The child of the house and sundry staff spent their evenings in the lounge with the television turned full on. The walls were covered in original paintings that seemed to have been left by guests who couldn't pay their bills, and each evening the local Sards gathered in the rough-looking bar and on the terrace and sang and danced together. The restaurant was justly famous throughout the island. You could eat outside, either in a courtyard at the back, or under the bougainvillaea on a terrace overlooking the pool. The menu was short and unchanging but everything on it was a local speciality: *Carta da musica*—a paper-thin unleavened bread; *panne fratau*—the same bread soaked in a herb and tomato sauce with grated cheese and a fried egg on top; raw smoked hams from the mountains and roast suckling lamb and pig. It was the sort of place that anything could happen in—and frequently does. While we were there a local wedding in full colourful regional costume took place in the small church and the reception lasted all day and all night at the hotel. On Saturdays the bread doesn't arrive until lunchtime and no one seemed to care about breakfast, so we ended up with a bowl of fruit picked from the garden. The house was always full of flowers and well looked after and it was a weird and eccentric place: when we came to pay the bill, they'd never seen a traveller's cheque and almost insisted that one was enough, even though it was for only £5 when the total bill came to £40. It's the only hotel that I've been to where, although the guests were perfectly adequately looked after, you got the feeling you didn't exist at all.' (*Susan Grossman*)

Open: all year.
Rooms: 31 double—all with bath and telephone.
Four salons (2 with TV), bar; gardens with heated swimming pool, tennis courts and basket ball.
Terms: B & B: 6,250 L.; meals: 5,000–7,500 L.; full board: 15,600 L.

ORTA SAN GIULIO, 28016 Novara

Hotel San Rocco   *Telephone:* (0322) 90222

Formerly a 17th-century monastery converted with skill and restraint into 'a very special hotel indeed'. Overhanging the lake and well away from the road, the setting is exquisite. All is calm: lapping water, flowers and old roofs in the foreground; mountains in the distance. Inside, the service is gracious, rooms spacious and food almost too tempting. The hotel is run by Signor Terxi, an hotelier of the old school, assisted by a young cheerful attractive staff. Access except by car is difficult—which is why hotel, town and lake are still untarnished by tourism. (*Jean Robertson, Edward Mace*)

Open: all year.
Rooms: 34—8 with bath, 17 with shower, all with telephone.
Salons, bar, air-conditioned restaurant; garden with terrace on the shores of Lake Orta.
Terms: B & B: 8,250–13,700 L.; meals: 8,800–10,000 L.; full board: 29,500–32,700 L.

PALERMO, 90142 Sicily

Villa Igiea Grand Hotel   *Telephone:* (091) 543744
Salita Belmonte 1   *Telex:* 91092

The *Villa Igiea* has been created from an ancient and noble villa built on the edge of the bay of Palermo. Grand is the *mot juste*. The bedrooms, corridors and public rooms are spacious and furnished with period and antique pieces. Marble floors abound. Service and food, indoors or out, on the delightful terraces, are of an excellent standard. The gardens stretch down to the sea walls and are quite spectacular. The setting is charming, with its prospect of the sprawling city and its port. There is normally a pleasant bustle to watch, but at certain times of day (and occasionally in the early morning) there is a cacophony of strident banging noises from a coaling device which carries across into certain rooms; these should be avoided. (*Frank Falkner*)

Open: all year.
Rooms: 92—89 with bath, 3 with shower, all with air-conditioning and
           telephone.
Salons; garden with tennis courts and swimming pool.
Terms: B & B: 16,000–24,000 L.; meals: 10,000 L.; full board: 37,000–42,000 L.

Important reminder: terms printed must be regarded as a rough guide only as to the size of the bill to be expected at the end of your stay. For latest tariffs, check when booking.

PANZANO IN CHIANTI, 50020 Florence

Villa Le Barone   *Telephone:* (055) 852013

A delightful small guest-house on a hilltop in the Tuscan hills, roughly halfway between Florence and Siena, surrounded by vineyards and olive groves. It used to belong to the famous Della Robbia family, and it still retains the feeling of an old family house. The Viscontis, who now own it, understand how guests should be looked after, and the food is excellent. You will certainly need a car here, but it's an easy run into Florence or Siena for daytime sight-seeing, and a joy to retreat to the tranquillity of the Chianti country in the evenings. (*John Fox*)

Open: 1 June–31 October.
Rooms: 9 double, 2 single—7 with bath or shower.
Two salons, bar; 2 acres of garden; 2 golf courses, 1 with restaurant and swimming pool, near by.
Terms: B & B: 11,500 L.; half board: 18,000 L.

PERUGIA, 06100

La Rosetta   *Telephone:* (075) 20841
Piazza Italia 19

'Perugia was where Perugino, Raphael's master, came from and there is a whole enchanting room decorated by him (the Collegio del Cambio) in the Palazzo dei Priori. That is only one of Perugia's many delights. There are, too, the Pisano sculptures on the Fontana Maggiore and those by Duccio on the façade of San Bernardino, the varied architecture of the blessedly car-free Corso Vannucci, the subterranean marvels of Sangallo's Rocca Paolina, the excellent National Gallery of Umbria, the cathedral, the churches ... Perugia, it is no secret, is one of the towns best worth seeing in all Italy. That aside, Assisi, Todi, Spoleto and Gubbio are all conveniently near.

'For somewhere to stay, *La Rosetta*, in the Piazza Italia, is quiet and, since it falls into the official Italian Category II, not excessively expensive. The food is the thing, as Michelin points out. The speciality of the house is pasta and you will be offered it in a great variety of tempting forms. No need to worry about getting fat as you will doubtless have been conscientiously sightseeing since breakfast. And, since greed is the order of the day, look out for a sweet in which profiterolles swim unseen in what appears to be pure whipped cream. If the waiters seem sometimes to show a certain hauteur towards the guests that is something which can philosophically be borne knowing that it is you, not they, who are eating and drinking.' (*Sam Carr; also Graham Child*)

Open: all year.
Rooms: 108—49 with bath, 35 with shower, some with radio and telephone.

Terms: B & B: 7,750–9,000 L.; meals: 5,000–9,000 L.; full board: from 18,000 L.

POSITANO, 84017 Salerno

Hotel Miramare   *Telephone:* (089) 875002
Telex: 77072

A small hotel of character owned by very Anglophile proprietors. The bedrooms are spacious, beautifully decorated and furnished with antiques, subtly yet adequately lighted, and provided with bathrooms of palatial proportions, with hand-made tiles. Each room opens out on to its own well-equipped terrace sheltered by overhead vines and with an unobstructed view of the beach some 100 feet below. The lounge is sumptuously furnished and well supplied with (Italian) periodicals in the *Vogue* class. The small but attractive cocktail bar is just off the lounge; prices are reasonable. There is good Italian cooking, elegantly served. As with most places in Positano, the *Miramare* is difficult to reach—there are 212 steps down to the sea, and 100 steps up to the road —but probably only the averagely fit should consider Positano for a holiday, beautiful though it is. A car is almost a handicap here, but there is a good local bus service and, in the season, regular boat and hydrofoil services to Salerno and Capri. (*Dr L. J. Morgan, T. M. Shelford*)

Open: 15 March–15 November.
Rooms: 15 double, 3 single—all with bath, telephone and balcony overlooking the sea.
Lounge, small cocktail bar; sand and rock beaches with safe bathing.
Terms: B & B: 12,500–16,250 L.; meals: 8,000–8,500 L.; full board: 19,500–28,500 L.

RAVELLO, 84010 Salerno

Hotel Palumbo   *Telephone:* (089) 857244

'The *Palumbo*, with a wonderful situation, 1,000 feet above the sea, and with superb views over the Gulf of Salerno, has been in the Swiss Vuillermier family for nearly a century, and has associations with Wagner, and many famous literary personalities and actors, as well as with members of the Allied Forces in the last war. The public rooms and our bedrooms were very comfortable, though the bath water could have been hotter. The dinner menus at first we found a little too simple and "English/Swiss", but as soon as we said that we would like something more Italian and different, the hotel produced delicious dishes, particularly fish. There were also excellent vegetables fresh from the garden. There was efficient personal attention and service from the staff. It was like staying in a very well-run large private house.' (*Michael Appleby;* also *Mrs Richard Black*)

Open: all year.
Rooms: 45—21 with bath, 1 with shower, all with telephone.
Garden.
Terms: room only: 5,700-7,400 L. (breakfast extra); full board:
16,500-18,000 L.

ROME

Hotel Forum
via Tor de' Conti 25, 00184

Telephone: (06) 6792446
Telex: 68252

'An unpretentious looking hotel opposite the Roman Forum; inside it
is elegant and comfortable, both in the public rooms and the bedrooms.
Some of the remains of ancient walls are actually built into the structure
of the hotel. The finest and most delightful aspect is the roof restaurant
and bar from where there is a magnificent view of the Imperial Roman
ruins stretching from the Colosseum on the one side to the Piazza
Venezia on the other. The cuisine is excellent—one of the best in Rome.
Free bus service to and from the airport.' (*J. D. Hamilton*)

Open: all year.
Rooms: 81—all with bath or shower, air-conditioning and radio.
Roof restaurant and bar.
Terms: B & B: 11,000-18,700 L.; meals: 7,100 L.

Hotel Oxford
via Boncompagni, 00187

Telephone: (06) 4751393

'Very well situated on a street which runs off the famous Via Veneto—
easy to go on foot to most of the places one wants to see. Recently
modernised (though not exactly our taste—mock antiques and the like);
but our room, though small, was clean and comfortable, and there is a
nice lounge. As for food, breakfast was a bit sparse, but dinner (we were
on half-board) was well cooked and plentiful, and there were good
carafe wines.' (*Guy and Wendy Payen-Payn*)

Open: all year.
Rooms: 45 double or triple, 7 single—all with bath, telephone, radio
and air-conditioning.
Lounge and TV room, bar, 2 restaurants. Modest nightlife: 'a piano-bar
with singer'.
Terms: B & B: 6,500 L.

Hotel Raphaël
Largo Febo 2, 00186

Telephone: (06) 6569051
Telex: 68235

'A quiet hotel, unobtrusively hidden behind creepers in a small, quiet side street not far from the Piazza Navona, which at night is one of Rome's liveliest piazzas. Very conveniently situated within easy walking distance of the main sights. The inside is air-conditioned and has an intimate atmosphere. It is very elegantly decorated in true Italian style, with sculptures, paintings, antiques and *objets d'art*. Bedrooms are less ornate but comfortable enough and also air-conditioned. But the nicest thing about it is the rooftop: a tiny area squashed between the tiled roofs, chimney pots and belfries of the surrounding buildings, with a pretty garden and magnificent views. Tables, chairs and sun umbrellas are set out—a lovely spot to escape the bustle of the city.' (*Susan Grossman*)

Open: all year.
Rooms: 85—all with bath or shower, telephone and air-conditioning. Lift, lounge, bar; small rooftop garden for refreshments.
Terms (excluding service and taxes): bed only: 10,000 L. (breakfast extra).

Pensione Scalinata di Spagna   *Telephone:* (06) 6793006
Piazza Trinità dei Monti, 17, 00187

Just at the top of the Spanish Steps, this is a modest, inexpensive and excellently run pensione. A drawback could be noise: 'An excellent restaurant, La Rampa, which is just below, stays open until midnight; and then there is the cleaning up, the arrival of cats, the garbage trucks —but one quickly learns to sleep through these disturbances. Besides, the location and the price cannot be beaten.' (*Lee Zeigler*)

Open: all year.
Rooms: 10 double, 4 single—some with bath.
Large flowery terrace for meals.
Terms (excluding tax): B & B: 8,500 L.

SAN FELICE CIRCEO, 04017 Latina

Hotel Maga Circe   *Telephone:* (0773) 528027

A first-class modern hotel, about half-way between Rome and Naples, at the foot of Mount Circeo and right on the sea. All the rooms are spacious and well-furnished, with plenty of wardrobe and desk space, as well as comfortable chairs and good lighting. The rooms facing the sea have picture windows opening out on to large balconies. The staff are attentive and friendly. When you come the second time, they remember that you take your coffee without sugar. The food eaten on a shaded terrace is delicious, except—a frequent complaint, this—for the coffee. (*Sophie Dann*)

Open: all year.

Rooms: 50 double, 25 single—all with bath, air-conditioning, radio
             and telephone.
Three salons (2 with TV), bar, lift, conference facilities; children's
playground. Tropical garden with salt-water swimming pool. The hotel
has direct access to its own rock beach with safe bathing, and its own
moorings for water-skiing, fishing and excursions. Tennis near by.
Centre for Physical and Dietetic Therapy attached to hotel.
Terms: B & B: 18,000 L.; meals: 12,000 L.; full board: 38,000 L.

SANTA CRISTINA VAL GARDENA, 39047 Bolzano

Hotel Dosses   *Telephone:* (0471) 76326

'I have stayed at this small family hotel at least sixteen times, usually in
late June or September, thus avoiding the high season when it is full of
noisy Italians. One of the advantages of this Dolomite resort is the easy
accessibility of no less than nine mountain lifts, thus making a car unnecessary. The hotel has been owned by the same family for generations,
the same high standard persisting, nothing pretentious, but nothing
second-rate. There are two disadvantages. Since the new building has
been added, I have occasionally seen food on trolleys passing to the non-
residents' dining room through the lounge. The small garden is across
the road, and exposed to passing traffic.' (*E. Sogno*)

Open: all year except October.
Rooms: 46—all with bath and telephone, many with balcony.
Salons, bar, terrace; garden.
Terms: B & B: 11,000 L.; meals: 3,500-4,500 L.; full board: 13,000-
             18,000 L.

SANTA MARIA ALBIANO, Valpromaro, 55100 Lucca

Villa al Castello   *Telephone:* (0584) 69971

'About 10 miles out of Lucca, an easy drive from Pisa, Florence, Siena,
etc., and innumerable small and delicious places. Ravishing situation in
the foothills of the Appenines—the house commands views of three
valleys full of olives and vines, and the chestnut woods begin just above
it. Exquisite walks start from its doorstep—but it's necessary to have a
car to get the full benefit of it. Lovely romantic garden with swimming
pool. Large old crumbly house, furnished throughout with antiques,
some of which have always belonged to it, some brought to it by the
present owner. Delicious food, very well served. Staying there is very
like staying in a private house. Four different rooms for sitting in, including a splendid frescoed *salone* and comfortable converted wine
cellar with billiard table. Snag: no separate tables in the dining room—
the host presides over a beautiful dinner table as though it were an
ordinary house-party. This could be tiresome if other guests uncon-

genial. Terms are for bed, breakfast and dinner; picnic lunches provided as an extra. Local wine included in the price with dinner, most of
it from the land attached to the house, and very agreeable. Host
(Nicholas Trevilian) most kind and helpful with advice about excursions
etc., and very good company. His partner, who is in charge of the
kitchen, is an excellent cook himself, and has very high standards of
service. Breakfast, by the way, is served when weather permits (which
it usually does) on a lovely patio with a fountain and a splendid view,
shaded by a vine pergola. Half an hour from sea—but the sea is at
Viareggio, which isn't very nice. Host not too good about correspondence: best to telephone.' (*Diana Athill*)

Open: all year.
Rooms: 4 double, 2 single—all with bath.
Drawing rooms, games room; garden with swimming pool.
Terms: *on application.*

SIENA, 53100

Palazzo Ravizza   *Telephone:* (0577) 280462
Pian dei Mantellini 34

Charming old converted palazzo dating from the 17th century, situated
in the old town, with much antique furniture and a lounge with library
which includes English books (some of them antique, too). It is a house
of great character: the staircases are wide, the landings spacious, the
bedrooms high-ceilinged. From some bedroom windows there are enchanting views down to the gardens (where one can eat breakfast) and
over the descending hill towards a monastery and a lot of lovely countryside. The Duomo and the Piazza del Campo are within walking distance;
prices are moderate, food sturdy, staff pleasant. (*Guy and Wendy
Payen-Payn; Lee Zeigler*)

Open: all year.
Rooms: 19 double, 9 single—13 with bath.
Several sitting rooms (1 with TV); very large garden.
Terms: B & B: 6,000–7,950 L.

SORRENTO, 80067 Napoli

Grand Hotel Excelsior Vittoria   *Telephone:* (081) 8781900
Piazza Tasso 34

Three huge houses and a Swiss chalet form a complex joined by a single-
storey addition. Be prepared for legwork along corridors or up marble
staircases. The reward is to be part of a pre-war film set—high ceilings
with mechanical fans, great awnings, 'Grand Hotel' furnishings, vast
private bathrooms, staff on call at every doorway, and nothing too much

trouble. The food is first-class on Italian dishes, so-so on other cuisines. The hotel, which is in the centre of the town, has very extensive grounds with a gate on to the main piazza. You can pick up buses to all the main tourist sites, and there is also a railway station not far away, so a car is unnecessary. The hotel has a lift to its own private beach, with access to the quay where the steamers leave for Capri and Ischia. (*Mrs R. Shuttleworth*)

Open: all year.
Rooms: 101—all with bath, telephone, and air-conditioning.
Large garden with swimming pool, and access by lift to private beach.
Terms: B & B: 11,250–18,350 L.; meals: 9,300 L.; full board: 25,700–34,400 L.

SPERLONGA, 04029 Latina

Parkhotel Fiorelle   *Telephone:* (0771) 54092

'Roughly halfway along the coast between Rome and Naples, Sperlonga is a cliff-top village with whitewashed stairways and winding streets. Rocks and profuse vegetation overhang; inland is the Lago di Fondi, and just to the north, the resort of Terracina—a fascinating region to explore. In one of the grottoes open to the sea at Sperlonga, came the Emperor Tiberius from his near-by villa at Gaeta—one of the most unusual archaeological sites in Latina.

'The *Parkhotel Fiorelle*, about 1 kilometre from the village, is by the sea in a large flower-filled garden, so planned that it is easy to find a secluded corner to sit away from other people. It is an exceptionally peaceful place, made more so by the aversion of the proprietors to transistors and guitars (which are not permitted). There is a decorative terrace for drinks; also a swimming pool, but with a lovely private sandy beach and ideal sea bathing so close, the pool seems almost superfluous. The hotel is run by a couple: he is a retired naval officer and takes care of the cooking; his charming Austrian-born wife looks after the running of the hotel and is very good company. The bedrooms are on the small side, but perfectly adequate and pleasant. One small criticism: the meals, though well cooked, are slightly on the sparse side.' (*Guy and Wendy Payen-Payn*)

Open: March–October.
Rooms: 33—7 with bath, 26 with shower.
Terrace; garden with swimming pool; private beach.
Terms: B & B: 4,900–5,800 L.; meals: 4,000 L.; full board: from 13,000 L.

If you know of a good hotel that ought to be in the Guide, please write it up for us <u>now</u>. Procrastination is the thief of the second edition.

TAORMINA, 98039 Sicily

Timeo

Telephone: (0942) 2380
Telex: 98062 Ashotels

Not the largest, but certainly one of the more celebrated hotels in Taormina, happily a few minutes' walk away from the centre and next door to the Greek Theatre. A rather formal hotel, quiet and traditional, with an exceptionally beautiful private park, overlooking the sea on one side and Mount Etna on the other. The hotel has been in the same family for over a century. 'One of the most pleasant hotels I have ever stayed in.' (*Fritze Quist*)

Open: all year.
Rooms: 55—42 with bath, 3 with shower, most with telephones and balconies.
Salon, writing room, library, bar; 40,000 square metres of park and flower gardens. The hotel has a private beach, with access by hotel bus to the sea.
Terms: half board: 28,000 L.; full board: 33,000 L.

Villa Sant' Andrea
Mazzarò

Telephone: (0942) 23125
or Maxotels (London): 01-727 1345
Telex: 98062 Ashotels Santandrea

There is no shortage of hotels of every class and character in Sicily's most famous holiday resort. This medieval hill-town (though now, alas, much developed) sits 600 feet above the Mediterranean and enjoys one of the most majestic views on earth, with the sun rising from the sea and setting (if you are there at the right time) into the very crater of Mount Etna. Those who like to be near the scene and the nightlife will prefer to stay aloft and take the funicular down to the coast for daytime beachwork. But many will choose to be based out of the turmoil of the town. Mazzarò (or Taormina Mare) gets the best of both worlds. It has the most attractive beach in the area, and the cable car can whisk you to the centre of Taormina in a few minutes for cultural exercises or shopping during the day, and to enjoy the *volta* and the discos after hours.

The *Villa Sant' Andrea*, British owned and managed, two minutes from the funicular and well placed in the ravishing crescent of the Bay, has been a draw for English-speaking visitors to the area for many years. Formerly a private house bought by a Cornish family who had been building Sicily's railways in the early 19th century, it still retains something of the flavour of an English country house, with a library full of books by Kipling, Edgar Allan Poe and Henty, and with fine English porcelain as well as Sicilian art in the deeply carved oak-panelled rooms. The dependable quality of the food served, except in bad weather, on a broad terrace overlooking the bay, as well as the spaciousness and elegance of the accommodation and the serenity of the location, are all praised. The hotel is still managed by direct descendants of the first owners, and this sense of continuity adds to the special charm and character of the house. 'Staying there is rather like staying with one's favourite uncle, in a friendly but in no way demanding house party. It's the sort of slightly old-fashioned hotel which seems to be fast disappearing, and I recommend it, at the risk of making it too popular.' (*Paul Miles; also Mrs Y. A. Fulton*)

Open: 1 March–31 October.
Rooms: 32 double, 5 single—all with bath or shower and telephone, many with balconies.
Three salons for use in spring and autumn. Summer spent outside. Large private sub-tropical garden; palm-terrace bar and restaurant overlooking the sea. The hotel has direct access to a private beach with safe bathing from fine shingle or rock; boating and water-skiing available.
Terms: B & B: 11,000–16,500 L.; meals: 8,500 L.; full board: 26,000–30,000 L.

TREMEZZO, 22019 Como

Grand Hotel Tremezzo   *Telephone:* (0344) 40446

'The most romantic lake in the world, as Como has been called, is shaped like an inverted "Y", and Tremezzo is on the western shore where the two lower arms fork, facing across to the central promontory and over to Bellagio on the far eastern shore. It is set in the region of the grand villas, mostly neo-classical, and near by is the famous Villa Carlotta, in a magnificent formal park, today used for congresses and concerts. The *Grand Hotel Tremezzo* has to be one of Europe's grandest holiday hotels —built about 1913, it has around 100 rooms still furnished in the original style, with bathrooms which are bigger than many double rooms in new hotels. The service has that rare balance of formality one would expect from a traditionally run hotel, with the smiling Italian friendliness of a staff who are evidently proud of the place. The proprietor, the son of the man who built the hotel, is quietly but fanatically pro-English. Weather permitting (and it invariably does) the meals are served on the outside terrace—one sitting per meal only—and the views over the lakes are outstanding, as indeed is the food. Meals are a gastronomic adventure. The Veneto house wine is recommended as are the raspberries from the hotel's gardens. There are games rooms (ping-pong, etc.) and an outdoor swimming pool; a television room—strictly no TV or radio in the bedrooms—and a disco/nightclub for teenagers and aging swingers. The English clientele tends to be middle-aged professionals resting. And all seemed well rested and well content.' (*John Duerden*)

Open: April–October.
Rooms: 80 double, 20 single—all with bath and telephone.
Sitting rooms, writing room, parlours, bar, TV room, disco/nightclub, lift. Large park with tennis courts and swimming pool. Private Lido on

the Lake, with water-skiing, fishing and lake excursions; 18-hole golf courses near by.

Terms: B & B: 12,500–14,000 L.; half board: 18,000–21,000 L.; full board: 20,000–23,000 L.

VENICE

Pensione Accademia   *Telephone:* (041) 37846
Dorsoduro 1058–60, 30123

'A delightful old villa with its own cool and pleasant garden, facing a relatively quiet side canal, yet only a few yards away from the Grand Canal itself. It is within easy reach of the Accademia, also of the water-bus services. The walk to the bridge goes past the British Consulate, which might bring comfort to some. It is run by an Italian family in a quiet and efficient manner. The rooms vary in style because of the nature of the old house, but everywhere there is a pleasant and comfortable atmosphere. The food is unremarkable but good. The real delight is to eat or take a drink in the garden on a hot day. A Venetian experience.' (*Brian Taylor;* also *Jan Morris, Mark Boxer*)

Open: all year.
Rooms: 26—most with bath or shower.
Garden/restaurant overlooking the water.
Terms: bed: 6,500 L. (breakfast extra); full board: 16,500 L.

Hotel Do Pozzi   *Telephone:* (041) 707855
Calle Larga 22 Marzo 2373, 30124

'A small hotel, modern, clean and comfortable, a few minutes' walk from St Mark's Square, very central for sightseeing. The *Do Pozzi* is at the end of a tiny alleyway. Inside it's warm and welcoming, though there is little in the way of public rooms. The lounge is tiny; so is the breakfast room; guests sometimes have to share tables, so actually have to talk to one another. Rebuilt in 1972, corridors and walls are lined with modern paintings; bedrooms are bright and comfortable, though single ones are on the small side. You may be wakened early by shopkeepers pulling up shutters and gossiping. Ring the bell if you're back late at night; you may get one of the staff out of bed, but they're always friendly. For meals other than breakfast, they have an arrangement with the Ristorante di Raffaele round the corner, with tables in the open overlooking a canal.' (*Susan Grossman*)

Open: all year.
Rooms: 22 double, 13 single—all with bath or shower, and telephone. Small sitting room with TV; air-conditioning. Pretty courtyard with flowers and seating.
Terms: B & B: 18,500 L.; half board: 19,600 L.; full board: 24,000 L.

La Fenice et des Artistes   *Telephone:* (041) 32333
Campiello de la Fenice 1936, 30124

'Almost equidistant from the Piazza San Marco and the Accademia—
both within easy walking distance—the hotel is tucked away in a courtyard near the Teatro Fenice (occasionally one hears a soprano rehearsing
an aria, but who could call that a disturbance?). It consists of two buildings with a plant-filled courtyard between, where one can enjoy a
delicious breakfast or refreshing evening drink. The service is friendly
and efficient, the rooms extremely comfortable, and there is a large,
pleasant sitting room which overlooks a narrow canal. No restaurant,
but it is surrounded by plenty of good ones both grand and simple. Not
cheap, but extremely good value and we are already planning our next
visit there.' (*Maggie Noach*)

Open: all year.
Rooms: 64 double—most with bath or shower; air-conditioning.
Lift; sitting room. No restaurant, but breakfast, etc., in courtyard.
Terms: B & B: 10,750–15,000 L.

Casa Frollo   *Telephone:* (041) 22723/703930
Giudecca 50, 30123

'If you want to stay in the *Casa Frollo* it's best to telephone rather than
to write, as Signora Flora (a latter-day younger and benign Marlene
Dietrich) who runs it, is not fond of corresponding, but has the universal
Italian enthusiasm for the telephone. Once having persuaded her to
accept you, you are in for a treat if what you like is an unspoiled 16th-
century palazzo bang on the waterfront of the island of the Giudecca,
with uninterrupted views across the water to St Mark's and the Doge's
Palace, with a garden behind overlooked by a statue of Mercury and
overseen by a gardener and his dog straight out of a Carpaccio painting.
Renaissance rooms with Renaissance furniture, and an endlessly divert-
ing drama played out in the main reception room, with a cast of assorted
relatives and guests dominated by the constantly telephoning figure of
the Signora, making and unmaking labyrinthine booking arrangements.
You won't find it a treat if you expect large numbers of bathrooms,
prompt breakfast attention, and *haute cuisine* at dinner. But the solid
tables have snowy linen, and the coffee (from the visible kitchen) is
good; and one can step out on to the balcony to take in that fabulous
morning view. Prices vary considerably according to whether you have
a front room overlooking the water, or the quieter back ones overlooking
the garden. Highly recommended to connoisseurs of atmosphere and
eccentricity.' (*Rosemary Davidson; also H.R.*)

Open: 1 April–31 October.
Rooms: 17 double, 9 single—3 with bath or shower.
Main reception room, dining room with balcony looking across the
water to 'mainland' Venice. Large garden with trees and flowers.
Terms: bed, from 5,000 L. (breakfast extra).

Gritti Palace *Telephone:* (041) 26044
Campo Santa Maria del Giglio 2467, 30124 *Telex:* 41125 Gritti

'Beautifully situated on the Grand Canal, the *Gritti* was once the home of Doge Andrea Gritti. It has none of the gaudy trappings of many grand hotels, but offers quiet understated elegance, immaculate service, and extremely good food. Previous guests are unfailingly remembered; the service is remarkably unobtrusive. For much of the year dining is by candlelight on the lovely terrace overlooking the Grand Canal. The company launch will take you (free of charge) to the Lido for swimming or lunch. Few hotels manage to combine such efficiency with friendliness, but the *Gritti* does.' (*Anthony Hayes*)

Open: all year.
Rooms: 74 double, some suites, some apartments with kitchenette, 17 single—all with bath and shower, telephone, radio and TV.
Several salons, bar/lounge; terrace for meals and refreshments on the Grand Canal; air-conditioning. During summer months gourmet cooking schools are held, with internationally famous chefs.
Terms: B & B: 29,000–39,000 L.

Pensione Seguso *Telephone:* (041) 22340
Zattere ai Gesuati 779, 30123

'I have been going to this pensione for thirty years. On the Zattere, it is five minutes' walk from the Accademia landing stage facing the Canal of the Giudecca, and with a charming (and clean) canal by its side, which some windows overlook. There is always something going on: liners and big ships pass one's windows; and one can sit in a sort of semi-private little piazza. The food is excellent and so is the service (one of the maids has been there for over thirty years). The furniture is deliciously old-fashioned and Venetian; the dining room has old embroidered silk wall covering. The sitting room is nothing special, but useful if it rains.' (*Sheridan Russell*)

Open: all year.
Rooms: 36—all with bath or shower.
Lift; sitting room, charming dining-room; semi-private piazza for sitting out; air-conditioning.
Terms: B & B: 8,650 L.; meals: 6,000 L.; full board: 20,000–22,000 L.

VERONA, 37100

Colombo D'Oro *Telephone:* (045) 21510
via Cattaneo 10

'Delightful spacious hotel (no package tours) with a large and well-disposed staff. No sign of cost effectiveness anywhere. Three large elegantly furnished sitting rooms, including the hall, and really splendid bedrooms with good lighting. Only two minutes from the centre of town, but in a quiet side street. No restaurant, but delicious breakfasts as late as you want.' (*Mary Cunynghame*)

Open: all year.
Rooms: 55—40 with bath, 9 with shower, most with air-conditioning. and with telephone.
Three salons, bar.
Terms: B & B: 11,300-16,000 L.

VICENZA, 36100

Hotel Basilica   *Telephone:* (0444) 21204
Piazza delle Erbe 9

'A real find. The hotel is in a marvellous situation in the centre of the town opposite Palladio's Basilica. Very Italian atmosphere among both staff and guests; excellent cooking and good house wine. The hotel is run by the proprietor himself who is a distinct "character".' (*Guy and Wendy Payen-Payn*)

Open: all year, except August.
Rooms: 21—with bath or shower.
Ristorante da Carlo (part of the hotel) serves all meals.
Terms: B & B: 4,700 L.; meals: 4,500-7,000 L.

VICO EQUENSE, 80069 Napoli

Le Axidie Hotel   *Telephone:* (081) 8798180
Marina di Equa

'Vico Equense is in the Gulf of Naples, on the southern shore. With Pompeii, Herculaneum, Paestum and Vesuvius all near by, there is plenty of sightseeing. It is not far from Sorrento, but utterly different. It is a small town, almost a village, on a cliff-top about 300 feet above the sea. It has quite good shops, but really centres on one Square full of traffic, cafés, and general Italian noise with never a dull moment. Far below the town and right on the sea level is a small fishing village, Marina di Equa; when you think you have come to a full stop, there is the *Axidie*. (As every schoolboy knows, the Axidie were the three sirens who bewitched Ulysses; the sirens' rock—according to legend—is a few yards from the hotel.)

'The *Axidie* has been in existence for about eighteen years. It was built by its present owner, who also owns the surrounding land, including a small farm and vineyard. The bathing from the private beach is absolutely safe, with a "pier" and ladder for cautious bathers. The sea is always quite remarkably clean, and the temperature is blissful. There is always an attendant on duty. The hotel is small and quiet; the food is excellent, and the chef is always ready to provide any special dish. It is designed for summer sunshine, with outdoor restaurant and outdoor sitting in the evening. The indoor rooms are adequate but not particularly impressive—but rain is a rarity. All the bedrooms are floored with exquisite Salerno tiles, and most have balconies overlooking the sea.

'My wife and I started going to the *Axidie* in the summer of 1965 and we have been back every year. Perhaps the most remarkable quality of the hotel is the fact that there has been virtually no change in the key members of the staff since its original opening, and the service is unbelievably good. There is NO NIGHTLIFE, NO TELEVISION, NO DISCO AND NO COACHES! But there is plenty of conversation and laughter, the latter provided liberally by the owner, Fernando Savarese, a fantastic character in his own right, supported by his very beautiful and talented wife, remembered by many as the Prima Ballerina, Violetta Elvin.' (*Colonel C. F. H. Gough*)

Open: April–October.
Rooms: 28 double, 2 single—16 with bath or shower, all with telephone. Baby-sitting arranged if required.
Two salons; 4 acres of gardens with tennis courts, swimming pool and private beach.
Terms (excluding tax):   bed: 8,250–12,150 L.; meals: breakfast, 1,500 L.; lunch, 7,000 L.; dinner, 7,000 L.; half board: (minimum 3 days): 13,000–18,400 L.; full board (minimum 3 days): 16,500–22,000 L.

Prices quoted, unless otherwise specified, are for bed and breakfast for a person sharing a double room with bath or shower in the high season. We have also given half and full board prices per person in high season when available.

Madeira

FUNCHAL

Hotel Miramar   *Telephone:* Funchal 21141/2
Estrada Monumental

Madeira is a delightful island for relaxing all year round, and particularly in winter when the weather is mild. There's little for enthusiastic sightseers to see, but the island is scenically lovely, with exotic vegetation; even tea clings to the slopes, mountains and forests. Bathing is strictly off rock. Funchal itself is the hub of the island, as busy with businessmen as visitors, a small town and a port, full of colour and character. Women in national dress sell lilies and orchids outside the white Cathedral, and in springtime the town is smothered in flowers. *Reid's Hotel* (see below) and a few other large hotels stand slightly aloof to the west, a short walk from the town in splendid positions on the cliffs overlooking the sea. Not everyone wants (or can afford) the grandeur of *Reid's*, and the *Miramar* is an altogether satisfactory alternative. Originally a private '*quinta*', it is now British managed and much patronised by English visitors. It has the atmosphere of a small holiday hotel and is set back across the road from the sea (with no access) about a fifteen-minute walk or bus ride from the town. It has an attractive garden where in summer, meals ('adequate but with little variety') are served under a thatched roof. There is no pool, but the Country Club close by has a pool, along with tennis, squash and other clubbish facilities. There is a large comfortable lounge, a bar and discotheque, in an adjoining building. The staff are friendly, though few speak much English; and the rates—the same throughout the year—offer extremely good value. (*Cecil Blatch*)

Open: all year.
Rooms: 32 double, 10 single—18 with bath or shower, 4 with telephone.
Lounge, bar and discotheque in adjoining building; swimming pool and other sporting facilities in Country Club near by.
Terms: B & B: 100–152 esc.; half board: 390–525 esc.; full board: 560–715 esc.

Reid's Hotel

Telephone: Funchal 23001
Telex: 72139 Reids P.

'*Reid's* is a Grand Hotel in the old tradition—very large with opulent public rooms. The bedrooms are spacious, well furnished and comfortable, and many have secluded balconies overlooking the ocean. The swimming-pool complex, at garden level, is one of the finest to be found at any hotel. A lift takes you down to sea level, where there is a rocky pool, and facilities for water-skiing. The gardens are world-famous, of course, and for the elderly or infirm they have the advantage of being served by lifts so that you may stroll down from a higher level and find a lift without having to retrace your steps uphill. The gardens are so large that even when the hotel is full it is possible to find a secluded corner where you may read undisturbed by fellow guests. This also applies to the hotel. It has so many spacious lounges that it is quite easy to be alone for the entire morning if you wish. Lunchtime snacks and drinks are served by the pools, with luncheon in the Garden Restaurant overlooking the sea during much of the year. The Grill Room, at the top of the hotel, commands superb views over Funchal and the harbour, and offers a very good *à la carte* menu for dinner by candlelight. The food on both the *table d'hôte* and *à la carte* menus is good—extremely good by Portuguese standards—and on both menus a wide choice is offered. The service in the Grill is immaculate, and although the other restaurants do not quite come up to this standard, the service is more than adequate. The housekeeping is exceptionally good, with towels changed two or three times daily. The hall porter is helpful, and the hotel has a very efficient representative to meet you at the airport or steamer quay.

'It is not an easy hotel to fault. There is a house rule which prevents coffee being served in the Garden Restaurant after 2 p.m. which I found annoying. After this time it must be served in the lounge—but many people like their coffee in the lounge. Perhaps too many meals are cooked at the table in the Grill. The waiters cope magnificently, but this does tend to slow the service—again, however, it is something which people seem to like now. One wonders if the increasing number of package tours which the hotel now accepts will not result in a lowering of standards before long. This seems inevitable, but at the moment it has not done so.' (*Anthony Hayes*)

Open: all year.
Rooms: 140 double, 28 single—all with bath, telephone, radio, air-conditioning.

Six main rooms, including a separate TV room, billiard room, card room. Ladies hairdresser; boutique; 10 acres of lovely semi-tropical gardens (with lifts to various levels), 2 heated swimming pools, children's playground, tennis courts. Access to sea, with sun terrace at sea level. Dancing to orchestra in the cocktail bar.

Terms: B & B: 527–742 esc.; lunch/dinner: 250 esc.; half board: from 837 esc.; full board: from 1,027 esc.

If you consider any entry inadequate or misleading, please let us know <u>now</u>.

The Ta' Cenc, Gozo

Malta

GOZO

The Ta' Cenc
Sannat

Telephone: Gozo 76819
Telex: 479 Refinz MW

'A small Mediterranean island, a friendly English-speaking population, prices that are roughly 20 per cent less than at home—these features alone would recommend Gozo, three miles off Malta. The fact that it is well off the packaged tourist map, and has just one first-class hotel is an extra bonus. The *Ta' Cenc*, beautifully sited on a high promontory, is built in the local honey-coloured limestone on a low-profile principle: it's all one storey and cunningly terraced to blend into the hillside. The rooms are individually designed bungalows, each with a private patio for breakfast or sun-worship, ranged round a central pool, with plenty of space between for oleanders, fig trees, cacti and the like. The pool itself offers a breath-taking view of the sea and Malta beyond, and many residents are content to brown and browse there all day. But for the more adventurous, there is lots to see on Gozo—on foot, by bus or by cheap rented car. There's plenty of good rock bathing all round the island, but only one first-class sandy beach, six miles from the hotel —lovely golden sands, but not much shade.

'The food at the *Ta' Cenc*, apart from poor breakfast coffee, has been consistently excellent and enterprising. It's not *haute cuisine*, but alpha-standard Italian cooking: a different home-made pasta at every meal, and always, among the choice of entrées, a local fresh-caught fish. The greedy will take the full pension: you won't get food as good anywhere else on Gozo, or indeed, some say, on Malta either. For the one-good-meal-a-day group, there are fridges in the rooms for keeping fresh your mid-day snacks. The service is friendly and efficient without bullshit. There is a spacious lounge for sitting about in the evenings, and a modest disco, but don't expect any flashy nightlife. For the retiring, there is TV in the bedrooms, with an English channel.' (*H.R.*)

Open: 25 March–15 November.
Rooms: 48 double—all with bath, telephone, TV, radio, and fridge.
Lounge, bar, wine cellar; billiards and table tennis room; conference facilities; tennis courts, swimming pool; sand and rock beach 2 kms away, with boating.
Terms: half board: £M 8.50; full board: £M 10.00; meals: £M 4.00.

All prices include tax and service unless otherwise specified.

Hotel El Minzah,
Tangier

Morocco

CHAOUEN, Nr Tangier

Hotel Parador   *Telephone:* Chaouen 190

'About two hours' drive east of Tangier, through green, wooded hills,
is the small ancient town of Chaouen, buildings of all shapes and sizes
with rusty-red rooftops, piled and jumbled up the hillside, spiked here
and there with the slim towers of minarets. It is utterly charming—a
place full of trees and flowers, streams pitching down from the mountains, pools where local women do their washing; small, intimate blue-
washed souks—markets where you can buy fruits and spices and local
crafts. An ancient palace stands in beautiful flower gardens where you
can wander. The streets are incredibly narrow and often incredibly
steep, sometimes short flights of worn crumbly stone steps.

'To put a hotel in such a place was a blessed thought, and the *Hotel
Parador*—State-run inn—could not possibly be better sited. Here, surrounded by modern comforts, you have old Morocco on the doorstep;
and what's more, from the spacious sun-terrace, there are amazing,
dreamlike views over the town and surrounding countryside. There is
an excellent indoor restaurant and bar, but many prefer to eat out on the
shaded terrace, now flanked by a sizable swimming pool. Bedrooms are
very much in Moroccan style—low divans with hand-woven covers,
rugs on tiled floors—simple but most comfortable. All have either bath
or shower. A friend who went out there for a meal, sat spellbound on the
terrace and said he could spend the rest of his life doing just that. Anyone preferring a more active visit would need a car—there is little public
transport, although there are day and overnight excursions from
Tangier. It's a place not to be missed.' (*Richard Lucas*)

Open: all year.
Rooms: 37 double, 5 with bath, the rest with shower.
Restaurant, bar/lounge; large outdoor terrace; swimming pool.
Terms: B & B: from 22 dms; meals: from 25 dms.

MARRAKESH

Hotel de la Mamounia   *Telephone:* Marrakesh 22381; 23241/42

'If you want a spacious refuge from the insistent touts and ubiquitous street urchins of the Berber market, the Saadi tombs, and Allah knows what else of Marrakesh, you can just stay within the high garden walls —part of them in fact the magnificently rectangular old city wall—of the *Mamounia*, in its own inimitable way surely one of the world's truly great hotels. You don't have to occupy the Churchill Suite—but unless you want to be blasted out of bed by the morning prayers (at 4.15 a.m.) from the minaret of the Koutoubia, avoid the East wing. Specify the upper floors of the south front and you have the orange groves, the tangerine and olive trees, the fountains and the pool below your balcony, and the white icing-sugar horizon of the Atlas Mountains in front, only occasionally, it would seem, wreathed in morning clouds. You can wander in the gardens picking up your own tangerines, play tennis, and in the middle two or three hours of the day even in December—and for five or six hours in February—tan yourself under the Nelson column palms by the (slightly heated) pool.

'The hotel was built in the 1920s, and there is a charming informality and lack of polish about it. Corridors are padded with rush matting, the public rooms are somewhat cavernous and lined with showcases full of over-priced kaftans and hideous oriental trinkets, the garden is a little unkempt and the friendly staff sometimes a little fatalistic—but the separate bathrooms, lavatories, bedrooms and balconies are spotless and there is nothing amateurish about the way the hotel is run for total relaxation or even perhaps convalescence. There is a "nightclub" in a cellar, a small Moroccan restaurant (for which one should book in advance) and very reasonable French cuisine. Unfortunately French wines are prohibitively priced everywhere, and it is not easy to develop enthusiasm for the standardised Moroccan wines. If you want a stronger cocktail, or a change of menu, you can always wander down the road to the *Hotel Es Saadi*, which is newer and more nondescript, but has a barman who will, on one "White Lady", send you back reeling to *la Mamounia* as "home".' (*Uwe Kitzinger*)
(Major renovations have been carried out during the last six months of 1977.)

Open: all year.
Rooms: 150 double, 30 single, some suites—all with bath/shower,
            telephone, radio, colour TV, mini-bar; most with balconies.
Large lounge, several restaurants including a Moroccan Room, cellar nightclub, conference rooms, beauty shop. Extensive grounds full of palms, fruit trees and exotic flowers and shrubs; swimming pool (heated

in winter), tennis courts, handicraft shop.
Terms: B & B: 198 dms; meals: 50 dms.

TANGIER

Hotel El Minzah   *Telephone:* Tangier 35885/39744
85 rue de la Liberté   *Telex:* 33031

'Does a great deal to stop you feeling that Tangier is just a North African Southend. It is an old-world hotel with wood panelled rooms, simple, elegant and comfortable. There's a nice bar where someone plays the piano most evenings, a tiled courtyard complete with fountain and flowers where you can sit and drink, a medium-sized swimming pool, and you can choose between local and international cuisine in the dining room. You are within five minutes' walk of the Casbah in one direction, and the main town centre in the other. It's easy to miss the entrance, which is not very grand, but inside is a hotel of real character and distinction.' (*Robert Cassen*)

Open: all year.
Rooms: 100 double, 6 suites—all with bath/shower, telephone, radio and TV; air-conditioning in rooms facing the street.
Two salons, TV room, restaurants and coffee shop, bar, conference rooms; patio, beautiful courtyard/garden full of palms and flowering shrubs, swimming pool, tennis, mini-golf—all with views over the Straits of Gibraltar.
Terms: B & B: from 70 dms; meals: 35 dms; half board: from 100 dms; full board: from 130 dms.

Sterling and dollar equivalents of foreign currencies at the date of going to press will be found under Exchange Rates on p. 243.

*Grand Hotel
Krasnapolsky,
Amsterdam*

Netherlands

AMSTERDAM

Grand Hotel Krasnapolsky *Telephone:* (020) 263163
Dam 9 *Telex:* 12262

'Very handy for central shopping, walking by some of the prettier canals, or visiting the red light district, and it is not too far from the railway station. Its most memorable feature is the dining room, like some gigantic greenhouse, surrounded with enormous potted plants, and many hanging from the ceiling; and excellent food, as well. What is really nice about the hotel is that it is modern without being clinical, and the staff are friendly and helpful without being intrusive—the kind of place that really doesn't seem to exist any more!' (*Robert Cassen*)

Open: all year.
Rooms: 257 double, 30 single, some suites—most with bath or shower, telephone and radio; TV on request; baby-sitting service.
Lounge, lift, TV room, conference facilities; air-conditioning.
Terms: B & B: 85 glds; lunch: from 16 glds; dinner: from 25 glds.

BLOEMENDAAL, Nr Haarlem, Noord-Holland

Hoteliepenhove *Telephone:* (023) 258301
Hartenlustlaan 4

'There are some occasions when one wants to be outside a big city, to be very quiet, and to stay in a hotel that is totally unpretentious yet has a cosy atmosphere and is right off the main stream. This is such. The small town is 4 kilometres from Haarlem, and about twice that distance from the North Sea beaches. It is a typical, neat, well-organised Dutch small town. There is a charming village-green-like area with duck pond and ducks, and the hotel sits across the quiet street from it. The owner and his staff speak excellent English and are kind and helpful. It has a justified reputation for good and varied fare and so is popular for weddings and other celebratory parties. These, although sequestered, can interfere with the normally smooth-running of the dining room (also popular) and with early-to-bed sleepers on the lower floors if and when singing starts. The bedrooms are not large, but are practical and, of course, spotlessly clean. Some rooms have no bathroom, and some singles have a perfectly adequate shower stall. These will give piping-hot shower baths, but the fine adjustments needed can cause, for the ham-handed, severe and understandable yelps of pain. Nothing fancy; a good, practical, friendly, quiet small hotel with good food. It's the sort of place which has regulars.' (*Frank Falkner*)

Open: all year.
Rooms: 40 double, 16 single—27 with bath or shower, all with telephone, some with TV.
Lift; lounge, TV room, hall; quiet garden; lake in front of the hotel. Sea, with safe sandy beaches and boating, 3 kilometres. Nearest railway station: 500 metres (4 trains an hour to Haarlem, Amsterdam and The Hague).
Terms: B & B: 47.50 glds; meals: 25 glds; full board: 56-65 glds.

DELFT, Zuid-Holland

De Oude Delft   *Telephone:* (015) 125661
Oude Delft 134

'Not so much a hotel—more like staying as a guest in a pleasant middle-class house. Bedrooms are furnished in excellent taste, with good modern or traditional Dutch furniture, usually masses of lighting fittings and lamps everywhere; fully central-heated. Real, pleasing watercolours on the walls, and a small but powerful radio concealed on top of the wardrobe which was capable of receiving anything broadcast anywhere, presumably to allow the traveller to feel at home if he wished. Adjoining, but not *en suite*, a positively palatial shower-room, complete with electric massage-reducing machine ... and weighing machine, of course.

'Unique features: during the daytime, two rooms on the first floor are rented by what we would call a solicitor, and you often passed clients on the stairs. The smallest loo I have *ever* seen (it said in the bedroom "*de klein toiletten*"). When the door closed, your knees touched it, and your elbows were tightly clamped to your sides, making the usual actions difficult if not impossible. To be fair, there were two others. Breakfast only was normally served, although a notice said that any other meal or service (*sic*) could be provided on request. Rumoured that visiting BBC personalities, seeking peace and quiet, occasionally stay here. One minor drawback: it is practically next door to the Oude Kerke, which has the largest clock bell in Delft. I don't know if they switch it off at night, but at 7 a.m. it made itself felt rather than heard. Otherwise, it is perfectly situated on a quiet canal in the old part of the town, but only about two minutes' walk from the Grosse Markt, the centre of life in Delft. Nowhere to park a car unless you get in early on the canal side, and no sitting room. Probably better for one or two nights than a long stay, but what a haven for the weary traveller.' (*A. W. Pemberton*)

Open: all year.
Rooms: 9.
Terms: B & B: 27 glds. No restaurant.

Length of entries is not an indication of comparative merit, but of the relative attractiveness of the contribution.

A bedroom in the Pousada de Rainha Santa Isabel

Portugal

ESTREMOZ, Evora, Alto Alentejo

Pousada de Rainha Santa Isabel   *Telephone:* Estremoz 22618

'Estremoz is a rather dull town on the road from Lisbon to Badajoz. It has a market square, a barracks, a bull ring, interesting local pottery, and many marble quarries. The castle has now been turned into a medium-sized hotel run by the State. Generally, the Portuguese *pousadas* are modest, but this one has gone in for grandeur—unavoidably, because the building is on a grand scale. The bedrooms have high ceilings, four-poster beds, heavy antique furniture, and many dark paintings showing gloomy bishops or the unlikely miracles of Queen Saint Isabel. However, if one wants to savour something of life in a palace without paying ruinous prices, this *pousada* is a place to try. The food was good, but did not merit the palaver with which it was served; the service was efficient but impersonal. But it is the ideal place for a one-night-stand—a modest degree of luxe, anonymity and medieval sound-proofing.' (*Dugal Campbell*)

Open: all year.
Rooms: 23 double—with bath or shower, some suites.
Terms: B & B: 230–315 esc.; meals: from 150 esc.; suites (per person, bed only): 425–650 esc.

Sterling and dollar equivalents of foreign currencies at the date of going to press will be found under Exchange Rates on p. 243.

Pousada de Santa Maria   *Telephone :* Marvão 93201/2

'Marvão lies about 6 kilometres north and about 500 metres above the road from Abrantes and the valley of the Tagus into Spain. The village, of tiny white houses and narrow cobbled streets, is entirely inside the walls of a castle whose keep sits above the village. It is possible to walk round the ramparts in about half an hour, looking within at the roofs, gardens, chicken runs, kitchens and television sets, or without over the Sierra de Torrico in Spain, and the valleys below in Portugal. In every direction there are fine landscapes of hill and rock and, on other hills, ruins of castles which do not have the company of a small village. A car would be essential to explore the region.

'The *Pousada*, like everything else in Marvão, is tiny. There are perhaps nine or ten rooms, the building is of stone with tile floors, the public rooms are well furnished, the beds comfortable and you could see to read, and the hot water dependable. As befits, the staff is small (when we were there, meals tended to be later than the advertised times) but amiable; the food was plain but good. No lunches are served, but it would be possible to buy picnic food in the village. There is absolutely no nightlife or entertainment to be had, but the view from the bar is fine, and the local wine excellent. The price was very reasonable. If you favour quiet, remoteness, walking, reading, then Marvão will do very well; children might get bored, and there are no other great sights within 50 kilometres or so. The Portuguese know their State hotels are good and use them—so make reservations.' (*Dugal Campbell*)

Open :   all year.
Rooms :   9 double—most with bath.
Bar.
Terms :   B & B: 205–55 esc.; dinner: 130–60 esc.

If you can endorse any entry in this book, please do so <u>now</u>. We need a quick feedback on all our entries to help prepare our next edition.

Hotel Mijas,
Mijas, Málaga

Spain (including the Balearics and the Canaries)

BAÑALBUFAR, Mallorca

Mar I Vent
José Antonio 49

Telephone: (971) 610025

'This family-run hotel is set in the tiny fishing and agricultural village of Bañalbufar on the ruggedly picturesque west coast of the island with a glorious view along the cliffs and out to sea. It has accommodation for only thirty-six people in rooms some of which are old-world Moorish style with antique furniture and open fireplaces. The brother and sister who run the hotel trained for six years in Swiss hostelry and can offer excellent food of any type, but specialise in providing the delicious dishes of their own village: roast suckling pig, colourful paellas, the fabulous fish zarzuela, and a large variety of vegetable dishes. There is a swimming pool on the sun terrace and also good bathing in the tiny cove reached by winding pathways through the famous terraced tomato fields where some of the 500 villagers still work with wooden tools and load the produce into ancient carts pulled by mules. The scenery is the best of a magnificent coast, and there are only two other small hotels in the village, which is not plagued by the noises and crowds normally associated with the island. Most of the numerous walks are hilly, so beware, the aged and infirm. Rule out dances, nightclubs, and the usual tourist traps and accept three local bars where the fisherfolk and farm-workers drink ... and rejoice in rock-bottom prices.' (*Bert Horsfall*)

'Unlike George Sand, I loved winter in Mallorca and particularly the tiny village of Bañalbufar, surrounded by mountains and good walking country. It's only a short walk away from the cause of George Sand's troubles—the monastery at Valldemosa, where she and Chopin spent a winter (today still remembered locally by a luxury block of flats called Chopin Heights). When I stayed at the *Mar i Vent*, the only other people there were an elderly English couple who were settled comfortably in deep armchairs in front of the log fire, in slippers, and reading Iris Murdoch from the collection in the bookcase. We joined them for drinks before dinner and then proceeded to the dining room where they were given their usual table (they'd been coming there for years) overlooking the sea. The homely Spanish lady of the house emerged from the kitchen, hot from the stove, bearing a huge bowl of chicken soup which she left on the table for us to finish. The meal was simple and home-cooked and there was plenty of it. After dinner some relatives came in to discuss costumes for the Festival of San Antonio which was taking place the next week, and is celebrated with decorated carts, bonfires and processions. The bedroom, downstairs from the main part of the building (as it's built into the cliffside) was small and cosy. It had net curtains opening on to a terrace and fine views of the sea, and a bathroom *en suite* with a large, old-fashioned bath. The owners couldn't have been more charming, and when to my dismay I discovered that I'd left my passport at the hotel I'd stayed in the night before (some fifty miles away), the owner offered to send the village taxi to get it first thing in the morning so that I'd have it back before breakfast. I did—and I wonder how many other hotels in the world would have done the same?' (*Susan Grossman*)

Open: all year, except 15 December–15 January.
Rooms: 15—some with bath/shower.
Salon; outdoor swimming pool.
Terms: B & B: 235–85 pts; meals: 275–375 pts; full board: 645–770 pts.

BURGOS

Landa Palace Hotel   *Telephone:* (947) 206343/4

The *Landa Palace*, 3½ kilometres outside Burgos on the Madrid road, belongs to the category of the exclusive de luxe in contrast to some of the more capacious palaces on the expensive hotel circuit. But it is certainly as grand as any maharajah could wish. The main hall is an impressive tower, reconstructed from some country castle. Above it is the King of Spain's permanent suite, with gold fittings in the bathroom, Isabel II's bed, sumptuously comfortable sofas, and walls hung with English prints. Bedrooms are large with plenty of cupboard space, and the bathrooms, too, are equally spacious: two people can easily change in a hurry as there are two wash-basins, a bath with a shower, and another shower separately—all, needless to say, in marble. The public rooms, hallways, etc., are full of green plants and with some unusual furnishings: collections of beds and cribs from many places, wall clocks of various kinds, box irons, pestles and mortars, a collection of teapots. Below vaulted arches is a large indoor swimming pool flanked by a profusion of plants and with a spiral staircase leading back to the hotel. Bathers can swim out at one end to the outdoor pool surrounded by lawns. Food and service are impeccable and the staff seem extremely proud of their hotel and take an almost personal satisfaction in the fact that you have chosen to stay there. (*Helen Baker*)

Open: all year.
Rooms: 35 double, 4 single—all with bath, telephone and air-conditioning.
Salons, separate TV room, bars, nightclub, indoor swimming pool, air-conditioned restaurant; garden with swimming pool.
Terms: B & B: 1,425 pts; meals: 750 pts; full board: 2,650–3,400 pts.

CASTRO URDIALES, Santander

Hotel Miramar   *Telephone:* (944) 860200

One of the oldest and most agreeable fishing ports along the northern coast of Spain, Castro Urdiales encompasses a good deal of European history: it was founded by the Romans and attacked by the Vikings; the Black Prince was nominal lord for a short period in the 14th century; there's a ruined College of the Knights Templar; Cesare Borgia sheltered here, and so forth. At one end of the town is the bustling little harbour on a peninsula dominated by the fine Gothic church of Santa Maria, and with two excellent fish restaurants. A mile along the promenade in the opposite direction, the bay sweeps round and the *Miramar*, well placed right on the fine, sandy beach, stands on its own. It's a two-storeyed modern building with its ground-floor rooms opening straight on to the beach. It's a simple family-type hotel, offering good plain Basque cooking. Many of the rooms have large balconies overlooking the sea. The public rooms are limited, but there is a lively bar patronised by the locals. A car is essential if you want to explore the surrounding country, with a varied coastline and spectacular mountains behind. (*Hugh Wyatt*)

Open: all year.
Rooms: 32 double, 2 single—all with bath or shower and telephone.
Lift; salon, bar; large terrace with direct access to the sandy beach.
Terms: B & B: 400 pts; meals: 350 pts; full board: 925 pts.

COMILLAS, Santander

Casal del Castro   *Telephone:* Comillas 89

'Small unspoilt seaside resorts are hard to find along the north coast of Spain, particularly the eastern half. Comillas, thirty-five miles from Santander, and ten miles from the showplace village of Santillana del Mar and the awesome Altamira Caves (almost worth a visit to the region for these alone) is a rare exception. One reason is that it's not just a resort, but the home of a pontifical university. The priests and nuns mostly stay behind their impressive Gothic walls, but their presence in the town may account for the absence of the huge and hideous hotel developments that desecrate so much of the Costas. It's essentially a family resort, and a domestic one—not many Brits in evidence—a kind of Spanish Totland Bay. Comillas's beach is all that a beach should be: wide, long and blessed with top-quality sand. There's safe kids' bathing at one end by the little harbour and gusty, exciting breakers at the other; and it's so big that there's plenty of breathing space for everyone, even in August.

'The *Casal del Castro* is five minutes from the bustling, scruffy, cheerful plaza up a steepish hill. Half of it is old, noble and castellated, as its name implies; the other half, the wing with the bedrooms, is unobjectionably modern. The furnishing is simple and elegant, with the north rooms getting the sea view and the south ones enjoying a vista of hills. It's a splendidly quiet hotel, except at times for plangent wails from a near-by abattoir. The food is generous and distinctly superior for this part of Spain.' (*H.R.*)

Open: all year.
Rooms: 44—all with bath/shower and telephone.
Salon, bar, lift; tennis court in grounds.
Terms: B & B: 500 pts; meals: 400 pts; full board: 1,200 pts.

EL GROVE, Pontevedra

Hostal El Besugo *Telephone:* (986) 730211
González Besada 84

'We had a horror of going to Spain—vision of egg-and-chips and tea-like-mother-makes, etc. We were advised to go to Galicia in the north-west, and ended up having the holiday of a lifetime. For the kids' sake, we elected to spend a week in a fishing village, and because I got the wrong bus, ended up in the small (8,000-ish) town of El Grove. We were lucky enough to strike the "pension" *El Besugo* which, in 1975, cost us £10 a day for my wife and myself and the two children, full pension. The accommodation (one room with 3 beds—the boys doubled up) was pretty basic. There was hot water when the sun was at its highest, the water tank being on the roof. The meals were absolutely outstanding, the accent being on seafood. Lunch, from 2–4 p.m., was four courses: a fish soup crammed with shellfish, steamed cod and mashed potatoes, a pork chop or mouth-watering stew of marinated mutton or rabbit, fresh fruit and coffee. Dinner, from 8–11 p.m., was a simplish meal: a fish-base soup (really outstanding), fried fish or chicken and chips, crème caramel and coffee. Each of our fourteen meals were different, and without exception excellent. The restaurant was packed, mainly with Spanish holidaymakers; the service was of the "hash-slinging" variety.

'El Grove is a truly delightful town, crammed with bars, restaurants, only a few small "*hostales*", and a cinema which in August tended to show family films of the Mary Poppins variety. The adjacent Atlantic beaches were magnificent, and the little island of La Toja is about twenty minutes' walk from our *hostal*. No one speaks English, but everyone is helpful and communicative.' (*John Duerden*)

Open: 1 June–30 September.
Rooms: 36—some with bath or shower.
Bar.
Terms: B & B: 150 pts; meals: 130 pts; full board: 400 pts.

FUENTERRABIA, Guipúzcoa

Parador El Emperador *Telephone:* Fuenterrabia 642140

'Much of Fuenterrabia dates from the 15th century. It is a small Basque village of steep narrow streets and ancient mansions with immense stone shields above doorways, perched high above the border river with France, the Bidasoa. During the 17th-century wars with France, the *Parador*, then a near-impregnable fortress, was triumphantly held against the French, and the final victory attributed to Nuestra Señora de Guadelupe; an annual celebration is still held on 8 September each year. Apart from history, of which the place positively reeks, it is a perfect spy-hole into France: down below winds the river, the French Basque coast, and the great border mountains. To stay in the *Parador* is still to have a feeling of embattlement, though you don't have to fight for anything: the service is good and willing. Much of the original structure has survived, but reconstruction has been pointedly faithful, even to leaving trees and greenery sprouting from walls. You live in a maze of great Gothic arches, old stone stairways, heavily beamed ceilings, polished floors, slabbed stone courtyards. There is nothing spartan about the bedrooms: they are the essence of comfort with all modern requirements. The food, as is customary in these State-run inns, is largely based on the produce of the area, so you get an excellent selection of imaginative fish dishes.' (*Diana Petry*)

Open: all year.
Rooms: 16—all with bath and telephone.
Terms: B & B: 450 pts; meals: 400 pts; full board: 1,150 pts.

GOMERA, Canary Islands

Parador Colombino Conde de la Gomera
Telephone: Gomera 871100

'Anyone who loves the climate of the Canaries but finds the three well-known islands becoming almost too popular, might like to try Gomera. Famous as the point of departure for Columbus on his epic voyages to the West Indies, the island is still not on the tourist map. There are no golden beaches and there is no airport. A comfortable, thrice-daily ferry, however, connects the capital, San Sebastián, with Tenerife. On a hill overlooking the small capital is one of the most attractive paradors that Spain can boast, with spectacular views of the harbour, the surrounding mountains, and the beautiful 12,000-foot peak of Tenerife's Mount Teide across the straits.

'The *Parador Colombino Conde de la Gomera* is modern but tactfully built in traditional style with cool patios. It is surrounded by a well-groomed, spacious garden on several levels with many secluded corners, and there is a fish pond and large swimming pool. Nowadays, promoters tend to design hotels so that the greatest number of beds can be crammed into the smallest possible space. This *Parador* has only twenty bedrooms, all large. Though standards are 4-star, prices are only 3-star. The Spanish Government regulates rates according to a set code, and the hotel has no air-conditioning except in the restaurant. Some Paradors can be a little austere with the service too coldly correct. Staff at the *Conde de la Gomera* are warm-hearted as well as efficient, and the food more than good—it is interesting. The high standard of the hotel is largely due to the Manager who supervises everything meticulously and still finds time to be friendly and helpful to his guests. Take a Spanish dictionary. No one has much English.' (*Anne Bolt*)

Open: all year.
Rooms: 20—all with bath and balcony or private terrace overlooking gardens and sea.
Bar, restaurant with air-conditioning; gardens with swimming pool; beach, with fishing and sailing near by.
Terms: B & B: 575–705 pts; lunch or dinner: 470 pts.

MIJAS, Nr Fuengirola, Málaga

Hotel Mijas   *Telephone:* (952) 463940
Urbanización Tamisa

'Does anyone want to go to the Costa del Sol any more? The tourist towers offer formidable deterrents, but the new vulgarity of the southern coast of Spain cannot entirely destroy its old beauty, and even vulgarity has a gaudy charm if it can be visited only when the appetite strikes. The *Hotel Mijas*, a few miles north and up from Fuengirola, provides a perfect eyrie from which to survey the man-made Mammon-mad Malagueñan coastline and from which, if the fever comes, to mount sorties into its bric-à-brackish depths.

'The advantage of Mijas lies in its height and in the efforts at conservation made (at last, at last) by the Spanish authorities. There are many tourist shops, but they are esconced in old and charming buildings, so too are the restaurants. The *Hotel Mijas* is away from the town centre and built in the traditional Andalusian style, though it is not itself old. The materials have been chosen with care and taste; the bar and public rooms are handsome with comfortable upholstery, the terraces pretty with cane chairs and broad umbrellas. The bedrooms are not luxurious, but nor are they expensive (save by package standards, perhaps) and each has a private bath and small terrace. There is a swimming pool (for those who do not care to go down to the sea) and there is a tennis court with a resident professional. For those with fancier tennis ambitions, Lew Hoad's tennis ranch is only a mile or so away; Hoad runs an efficient and friendly place, where even those with no backhand (and not much forehand) can find company and, maybe, remedy. The *Mijas* restaurant is not particularly good, but it is clean and reliable. A car is desirable, for getting to the coast, and for expeditions into the remarkably unspoilt hinterland between Coín and Ronda. An excellent place for a party of friends, not *too* worried about money, to lord it without too much sense of guilt.' (*Frederic and Beetle Raphael*)

Open: all year.
Rooms: 106—all with bath, telephone, radio and private balcony. Three salons, 3 bars, disco, conference rooms, hairdressing facilities, boutique, games and reading rooms, sauna, barbecue; garden with swimming pool and tennis courts; 8 kilometres from the sea (bus) with sandy beach and safe bathing.
Terms: B & B: 550 pts; meals: 440 pts; full board: 1,237–1,300 pts.

MOJÁCAR, Almería

El Moresco
Telephone: Mojácar 106

'You may think it unlikely that there could be a hotel worth recommending on the Costa Blanca—but it isn't all brashness and Benidorm. In fact Mojácar is quiet and deserted even in August. It's at the southern end of the Costa Blanca and its nearest big town is Almería to the south or, slightly further, Cartagena to the north. Mojácar is a tiny hillside village about 1½ miles from the sea, almost Moorish in appearance. The *El Moresco* blends in well with the glinting white façade of the town and has wonderful views of the almost deserted plains below, the sea, and the distant mountains. There's a free hotel bus down to the sea if you don't fancy the walk, and the beach used by the hotel has been cleared of pebbles and seaweed and there's a bar, sun-beds and umbrellas. There is little else apart from occasional villas. In the hotel, there's a pool—though its somewhat cramped seating arrangements on the concrete surround make it a bit crowded when the hotel is full. Bedrooms are exceptionally large, light and cool, and decorated in typical Spanish style with white stucco walls, ceramic tiles, and dark, carved wooden furniture. They each have a balcony and splendid views. The whole hotel has an elegant atmosphere without being uncomfortable, and is of the type seldom found on this part of the coast. There's an underground disco, you can eat outside on the terrace, and the ornately tiled bar serves its own special cocktails. The village has narrow streets and tiny shops, some run by English people who own villas in the surrounding area.' (*Susan Grossman*)

Open: all year.
Rooms: 147—all with bath or shower.

Lift; salon, bar, nightclub, shops, skittle alley, hairdressing salon, conference facilities. Rooftop swimming pool.
Terms: B & B: from 450 pts; meals: 414 pts; full board: 1,255–1,530 pts.

MURCIA

Hotel Reina Victoria
Plaza Martínez Tornel 1

Telephone: (968) 212269

Murcia is a bustling provincial capital, on one of the main routes from the north to the Costa del Sol. It is surrounded by farms and orchards and the whole area is known as 'the fruit basket'. The city itself is mostly modern, with chrome and glass skyscrapers and good cheap(ish) shops. But the *Reina Victoria*, slap in the middle of the city, is in the old Spanish-Moorish style, and possesses a serenity and charm which is in contrast to the bustle and clatter outside. It isn't just broad halls, high ceilings and old wood that gives it so much atmosphere. It is also the efficient but old-world staff who look as if they had grown old with the hotel which was founded in 1897. The rooms are large and comfortable, with highly-polished wooden floors, 'some of them warped to a point which makes one feel that last glass of the excellent bodega wine was maybe too much.' The restaurant is much patronised by the locals as well as the residents. (*Bert Horsfall*)

Open: all year.
Rooms: 75—some with bath or shower, all with telephone.
Lift, salon, bar; air-conditioned restaurant; hairdressing salon; shops.
Terms: B & B: 400 pts; meals: 340 pts; full board: 900 pts.

Rincón de Pepe
Plaza Apostoles 34

Telephone: (968) 212239

'A small and charming hotel that is as discreet as its clientele of visiting businessmen. It's on the edge of the old medieval centre of the town within a few minutes' walk of the impressive Cathedral with its Renaissance and Baroque exterior. Rooms at the back are quiet (apart from the church bells), and if you get a room at the top as I did, there's a splendid vista of belfries and rooftops. Bedrooms are modern and comfortable and my bathroom looked brand-new with maroon tiles and fitments. Downstairs the public rooms are elegantly furnished and suitably shaded from the glare of the light outside. There's no restaurant and you eat breakfast in the same small smoky bar that clinched last night's business deals (though thankfully the lighting is subdued enough not to aggravate the obvious hangovers).' (*Susan Grossman*)

Warning: prices quoted are 1977 prices.

Open: all year.
Rooms: 122 double—all with bath or shower and telephone, some air-conditioned.
Lift, bar, conference facilities.
Terms: B & B: 600 pts. No restaurant.

ORIENT, Mallorca

Hotel de Muntanya   No telephone
Carretera Bunola-Alaro

'In the mountains away from the sea, and so remote, the village has no telephone, no telegraph, and the school is an all-ages one-room affair set in a flower garden directly opposite the only hotel. This has sixteen double rooms, a large dining room which, on fiestas and Sundays, is the mecca for people from the towns who rave about country-style eating. Tourists are still a rare sight for the 160 inhabitants and local farmers. It is ideal for an away-from-it-all holiday if what you are looking for is clean mountain air, clear skies and glorious countryside. Most nights the village goes to bed after dinner, unless some of the local characters join the hotel guests over jugs of tangy wine after they have eaten the superb dishes of *Tumbet*, a tasty but meatless vegetable pot-pourri, or mutton rice *brut*, or delicious stews. Apart from the village dishes, which are the speciality of the hotel and its big attraction, there is a vast *à la carte*. There is no swimming and anyone wanting transport must hire a car in Palma before taking up residence. Paradise for those who want peace, quiet, and a lazy holiday in beautiful natural surroundings.' (*Bert Horsfall*)

Open: all year.
Rooms: 16—some with bath or shower.
Garden.
Terms: B & B: 210 pts; meals: 160 pts; full board: 455-65 pts.

PALMA, Mallorca

The Racquet Club   *Telephone:* (971) 280050

'I was in Mallorca at the best possible time—winter—when the almond blossom is out on the trees and the island's undoubted beauty isn't smothered by thousands of tourists. *The Racquet Club* isn't in Palma itself, but in Son Vida, 6 kilometres away or ten minutes by bus. It's in quiet peaceful countryside away from the suburbs of the town among hills and trees. It was once the tennis club of the formal and castle-like Son Vida hotel, and stands in its grounds, now converted into a hotel in its own right, though specialising—as its name implies—in sports.
  'Almost like an English country hotel, it's small and charming, with a log fire and deep armchairs. Though the furniture is modern, it's

covered in bright and tasteful fabrics that looked as if they had been bought in Heal's. The bedrooms were also brightly decorated with matching wallpapers and curtains, and carpets and bedspreads blending in or complementing the colours. They were warm too, which was a good thing as on some mornings there was a slight frost in the air. However, this didn't deter some of the more hardy guests from a quick dip in the Olympic-size outdoor pool, even if it was meant to be heated. There are a lot of sports activities: floodlit tennis courts, sauna, riding, and there's also a cinema and disco. The food wasn't superb and I suspected packet orange juice for breakfast, but there are some very good restaurants in Palma itself, and you can always eat in the stately Son Vida, with its Palm Court orchestra to serenade you. I found few hotels in Mallorca as intimate and relaxing as this one.' (*Susan Grossman*)

Open: all year.
Rooms: 51—all with bath and telephone, some air-conditioned.
Salons, bars, disco, sauna; garden with heated Olympic-sized swimming pool and tennis courts; golf and riding near by.
Terms: B & B: 680 pts; meals: 450 pts; full board: 1,315–1,510 pts.

SAN MIGUEL, Ibiza

Hotel Hacienda   *Telephone:* (971) 333046

'My wife and I spent three weeks at the *Hacienda* in May 1974, four weeks in May/June 1975, and we have been there three times this year (1976). So much for its power of attraction. The *Hacienda*, given 4 stars by the Spanish authorities, provides the opposite of what is popularly imagined as a holiday on Ibiza. Situated 600 feet above the sea on the rocky north-west coast of the island, it is far enough from any of the over-populated tourist centres. It is also the Ibizencan dream of a Belgian/Polish architect called Lipzig. A small architectural masterpiece, strictly true to style, discreetly elegant, yet friendly and welcoming. It was opened in 1971 and since then appears sporadically in some of the more exclusive travel prospectuses, sometimes described as "for individualists", whatever that may mean.

'The *Hacienda* is situated on the edge of a sparsely-populated urbanisation called Na Xamena, under Belgian management. The nearest village, San Miguel, is a two-hour walk away through wild, unspoilt country. Guests who hanker for the flesh-pots of Ibiza Town or San Antonio need a car or a scooter—but taxis are cheap on the island anyway. Access to the sea from the hotel is strictly for experienced mountaineers—a precarious path which zig-zags down the almost vertical cliff. Some attempt it with success, others prefer to remain by the extremely well-appointed swimming pool. In any case, for salt-water fans there is a perfect little lonely beach only ten minutes away—a short drive from the hotel and an equally short trip on a speed-boat from Puerto San Miguel.

'Guests at the *Hacienda* tend to be of mixed nationalities: Belgian, Spanish, French, British, German, Swiss, Dutch, and occasional

Luxemburgers. Thus the conversation at the bar and other places where people meet, tends to turn into a kind of international pidgin, very amusing and refreshing. As far as sociability is concerned, the *Hacienda* easily accommodates to all types. Those who wish to keep themselves to themselves can do so without exciting comment, those who are sociably inclined can be so without disturbing others. Casualness is all, and that is the nice thing about it. The food is consistently good (half-pension is enough for normal stomachs), the service prompt and efficient. The first impression is breathtaking, as if one were looking at a film set. Pure *Kitsch*, in fact. But soon one comes to understand that the scenery is "real", and that's when the holiday begins.' (*Kenneth Warner*)

Open: 1 April–30 September.
Rooms: 48 double, 4 single—all with bath, telephone, radio, air-conditioning, fridge, and all with terrace and a sea view.
Sitting rooms and TV room, indoor heated swimming pool, hairdressing facilities; garden surrounded by pine woods, with 2 swimming pools, tennis court; 2 kilometres from the sea (daily mini-bus service).
Terms: B & B: 1,200 pts; meals: 600 pts; half board: 1,900 pts; full board: 2,300 pts.

SANTO DOMINGO DE LA CALZADA, Logroño

Parador de Santo Domingo de la Calzada   *Telephone:* (941) 340300
Plaza del Santo 3

'Once an early medieval hospice built by Santo Domingo (St Dominic) to alleviate the sufferings of poor pilgrims journeying along the hazardous road to Burgos (69 kilometres away), and Santiago de Compostela, the *Parador* stands solidly on the village square facing across to the original church where the Saint's tomb lies. A highly original feature in the church is a cage on one of the walls containing a live cock and hen, commemorating the legend of a wretched pilgrim who was hanged for a theft he did not commit. His parents were told by the authorities that in spite of a vision they had received to the contrary, their son was as dead as the chickens on the table prepared for eating, at which the birds promptly sprang to life and, miraculously, so did the young man. It remains to be said that the caged birds in the church are replaced as they reach retiring age, and all are de-voiced so that there shall be no crowing at services.

'The *Parador*, which is the converted Hospice, still retains the splendour of medieval times. The great hall, now the visitors' lounge, is punctuated with heavy stone arches and niches with statuary; above, stained glass gleams in the ceiling. Huge wrought-iron candelabra, suspended from chains, are supplemented by modern table lamps softly illuminating groups of comfortable chairs and tables for guests. Bedrooms, in the style of the locality, have all the proper concessions to modern requirements. The food is part-local part-international, with a range of fine, full-bodied wines from the near-by Rioja vineyards. Watch you don't slip on the flagged floors which are industriously polished to a mirror-like shine.' (*Diana Petry;* also *Bert Horsfall*)

Open: all year.
Rooms: 27—all with bath, telephone and fridge.
Hall-cum-lounge.
Terms: B & B: 400 pts; meals: 360 pts; full board: 1,100 pts.

TOLEDO

Parador del Conde de Orgaz   *Telephone:* (925) 221850
Cerro del Emperador

Toledo is only fifty miles from Madrid, and is a favourite excursion from
the capital, by train, coach or car. Despite its popularity with coach
parties, and the omnipresence of souvenir shops selling tawdry Toledo
metalware, it remains a fascinating and beautiful city, full of narrow,
winding streets and crammed with historic buildings and churches. If
you are travelling to the south from the Basque ferry ports, it makes an
ideal place for a journey break.

The *Conde de Orgaz* is one of the Paradors run by the Spanish State
Tourist organisation, and is one of their showpieces. The first impression, and it's a powerful one, is of 16th-century Spain at its most
baronial: coats of arms, shields and antique weapons forged from
Toledo steel abound in halls and corridors, hung with banners and por-
traits of grave-faced bearded grandees. In fact, it's all a big cheat, though
carried out with panache. The hotel was built in 1968, and the rooms,
although furnished in the old style, with aged wood, wrought iron and
velvet, have every modern amenity including, in the bedrooms, a well-
disguised fridge stacked with drinks and cocktail snacks. It's a de luxe
hotel with all the trimmings—and even a 'dogeria' where clients can
leave their pets. The restaurant's menu is extensive and famous for its
quality, and even Madrileños consider it worth the journey. Advance
booking essential in the season. (*Bert Horsfall*)

Open: all year.
Rooms: 22—all with bath, telephone, radio and fridge.
Lift, salon, bar, disco, air-conditioning throughout.
Terms: B & B: 500 pts; meals: 450 pts; full board: 1,300 pts.

Details of amenities vary according to the information—or lack of
it—supplied by hotels in response to our questionnaires. The fact
that lounges or bars or gardens are not mentioned must not be taken
to mean that a hotel lacks them.

Ombergs Turisthotell, Ödeshög

Sweden

ÖDESHÖG, Östergötland

Ombergs Turisthotell
Alvastra 59900

Telephone: (0144) 33002

'This hotel is beautifully situated on a slight rise, overlooking rolling countryside and the lake of Vättern. It is about 1 kilometre off the main E4 road between Stockholm and Helsingborg, and approximately midway between these two towns. It is a genuine example of the Swedish "Late Victorian" period architecture. Mainly of wood, beautifully preserved, with the main structure painted a dark Venetian red so common in rural Sweden. Window frames and balconies, looking like an English seaside "private hotel" of the early 1900s, were painted a dazzling white, and the entrance, up a sweeping gravel drive, had a flight of stone steps to the double-doored porch. The whole place is furnished exactly in period, from the antimacassars on the plush settees, to the painted whitewood Swedish furniture and the typical-of-the-period heavy handed oil-paintings of local and national scenes. A huge open fireplace surrounded by what appeared to be dozens of wicker basket chairs, stood in the centre of the main hallway, dining room to the left, sitting rooms to the right, in a series of three, each more delightfully period than the last.

'We were made very welcome, though really just a couple of casuals; we noticed that about ten places were laid for evening meal besides ours. A gong sounded for dinner; as we entered the dining room we were preceded by a number of *very* elderly men and women, who immediately sorted themselves out into an obviously strictly maintained "pecking order" and filed to help themselves, Swedish style, from the laid-out meal. We had our place—at the tail of the queue—and there was exactly enough food left for us and two more weary travellers who had just arrived. Each mealtime the same performance was repeated, with perfect decorum and courtesy, the gentlemen bowing stiffly to the ladies, who rewarded them with a gracious smile. They were all apparently contemporary with the building, and one had the feeling they'd lived there ever since. The bedrooms were beautifully furnished in the same manner, down to the brass bedsteads and the patchwork quilts. Concessions to modernity were the usual fitted basins and excellent bathrooms. As a hotel: food good, traditional Swedish, well cooked, service excellent. Also very good walking, fishing, swimming and boating facilities within a kilometre or so. We are certain none of this was a deliberate tourist attraction—it was the way of life. We felt as though we had stepped back in time seventy years.' (*A. W. Pemberton*)

Open: all year.
Rooms: 17 double, 10 single—1 with bath, 3 with shower, some with radio.
Three salons (1 with TV); large garden.
Terms: bed: 50 kr (breakfast extra); full board: 80 kr.

Most hotels have reduced rates out of season and for children. For details, you will need to write to the hotel direct.

Chalet du Bon Accueil, Château d'Oex

Switzerland

CHÂTEAU D'OEX, 1837 Vaud

Chalet du Bon Accueil

Telephone: Château d'Oex 46320
Telex: 36418 Chato CH.

Château d'Oex is a wide and sunny Alpine village on the French side of the Bernese Oberland, about 3,000 feet above Montreux. It has a long tradition of catering for British visitors, which perhaps explains why it is a bit cheaper than some of the other holiday resorts in the vicinity. It has an all-round season: the usual winter sports and, in summer, golf, tennis, riding, swimming—and of course wonderful walking. The *Chalet du Bon Accueil* is a traditional Swiss chalet built in 1756. It stands in its own grounds on a hillside overlooking the village, which is about ten minutes' walk away (but the hotel lays on transport whenever required), and all the rooms have magnificent views. The hotel is almost entirely furnished with 17th- and 18th-century local Swiss furniture, but the central heating, the lighting, the double-glazing in the winter, are all of the 20th century. A feature of the hotel is its cellar bar, excavated by the present proprietor from what was originally a cattle byre. It has recently been enlarged so that dancing can take place without interrupting the conversation of the drinking fraternity.

The hotel is a very personal affair, run almost on house-party lines by the English owners, Curtis and Sally Wilmot-Allistone, who have had the place for more than two decades; they are assisted by a bilingual staff of young British girls. The chef, Louis, has been in charge of the kitchens for the past twenty-one years. It is the sort of friendly relaxing hospitable house that attracts exceptional devotion from its customers: 'One feels at home straight away.' 'My family and I have stayed at the

Chalet for the past three years, and have just booked for 1977.' 'Over the past few years, my wife and I have travelled extensively through Central Europe; without reservation, this is our choice for *The Good Hotel Guide*.' 'We have been going there for the past twenty-three years, and have always had *really* happy and comfortable holidays with excellent food. We return at every opportunity.' To receive five such letters in as many posts suggests an element of collusion, but only an outstanding hotel will attract loyalty and enthusiasm as eloquent as this. (*Air Vice-Marshal A. C. Davies, Jean Proctor, Malcolm Hey, C. Lewis, F. C. Margetts*)

Open: all year.
Rooms: 14 double, 3 single—8 with bath, all with baby-listening service.

Three salons (1 with TV), cellar-bar, disco; 4 sun terraces; 9 acres of meadows and forest with mountain stream; children's play park. All winter sports. In spring-summer: tennis, riding, swimming, fishing, golf, climbing, hang-gliding and gliding.

Terms: full board (high season: 20/6-10/9; 15/12-10/1; 1/2-10/3): 60-80 S. frs.

STÄFA AM ZÜRICHSEE, 8712

Gasthof zur Sonne   *Telephone:* (01) 9261110
Seestrasse 37

'Stäfa's Roman name dates from the days when Switzerland was called Helvetia. The little town lies in the heart of Switzerland's Gold Coast, facing south, overlooking the lake, and when the weather is clear, with a splendid view of the Grisons Alps and those round Engelberg.

'Switzerland's Gold Coast is not greatly frequented by tourists; it is fairly dear, though not as astronomical as Geneva or the huge hotels of Zürich itself. It gets its name because it is the home of Zürich's famous Gnomes, the rich bankers who live along the lake's north shore. The main road and autobahn leading from Zürich to the Engadine is on the south side, but it is easy to cross to the north at Zürich, or coming west, by crossing the causeway over the lake that leads to Rapperswil (Town of Roses). The *Gasthof Sonne* adjoins the main street looking over the square and the steamer landing stage (an attractive way of reaching it). It has a Swiss Inn atmosphere, very friendly, very Swiss (none of your fondus parties laid on for tourists, though they have them sometimes). Sepp Meyer, the young owner, was born in Stäfa, and trained as a chef in Zürich's Bahnhof buffet, and Kussnacht's Hermitage. He started the kitchen in Le Couperon de Rozel, Jersey, back in 1958. You dine on a balcony overlooking the lake and the speciality of the house is lake fish, for Sepp's father is one of the twelve fishermen licensed to take fish in the Zürich canton. The *Gasthof Sonne* was awarded the Golden Fish plaque (only twenty-seven or so in the country) some years back. There are several private dining rooms, a banqueting room as well as the main bar restaurant, and a large choice of menu besides the fish. Modest bedrooms; rather ordinary, Swiss, country town style. Friendly, efficient service. The place is always busy with local patronage: best to book in advance.' (*George Behrend*)

Open: all year.
Rooms: 6 double, 3 single—4 with bath or shower.
Bar/restaurant, several other private dining and banqueting rooms; safe bathing, sailing, fishing and water-skiing on the lake.
Terms: B & B: 26 S. frs.

TEGNA, 6652 Ticino Svizzera

Casa Barbatè   *Telephone:* (093) 811430

'Tegna is a small unspoilt village in the Centovalli area of the Ticino, near Locarno at the north-east end of Lake Maggiore. It is an excellent centre for walking in lake, valley and mountain scenery, and with a car the scope extends to remote Alpine villages and the Italian border. The hotel, which is just off the main street of the village, is a modern one-storey building of character set in a pretty garden. It is light and spacious, and everything in it carries the stamp of the owner, Madame Jenny. The decor is restful and imaginative. The lounge has books, record-player, pictures, flowers, and the atmosphere of a private house. All the bedrooms have bathrooms and are furnished as bed-sitting rooms. Most open on to their own section of the garden, so one sun-bathes in peace and seclusion. The small railway from Locarno to Domodossola passes the north side of the house, but I slept on that side and hardly heard the trains. Because there are no steps, the hotel can take guests in wheelchairs. The cooking is consistently excellent, and the service efficient and friendly.

'Madame Jenny speaks English, French, German and Italian, and most of the girls who help her run the hotel seem able to cope with two or three languages. I did not meet any English visitors either time I stayed. Swiss, German and Italians were there and people came back year after year. Madame Jenny likes to introduce newcomers to other guests, and often joins everyone in the lounge in the evening when talk is general. One would miss a lot by opting out of this informal, friendly atmosphere. She is interested in helping each guest to have the holiday he or she wants—lending local maps to walkers, telling one where to look for gentians, recommending a concert in Locarno, advising on local wines. She enjoys the company of artists, writers and musicians, and the hotel attracts people with similar interests. It is a place which suits people wanting to relax in lovely surroundings rather than those with a taste for crowds and mass entertainment, or people wanting anonymity in an impersonal atmosphere. Altogether, most unusual and delightful.' (*Miss H. M. Dillon*)

Open: mid-March to end of October.
Rooms: 10 double, 4 single—all with bath and telephone, kitchenette, and private terrace.

Large salon (no TV); terrace garden with swimming pool. Lake bathing, 15 minutes by car; river bathing, 5 minutes. Good centre for mountain excursions and country walks. Golf and tennis in Ascona. Skiing above Locarno, ½-hour by car.
Terms: B & B: 43-50 S. frs; half board: 63-70 S. frs.

THUN, 3600 Bernese Oberland

Hotel Beau-Rivage   *Telephone:* (033) 222236

'The small town of Thun is the gateway to the Bernese Oberland, at the western end of Lake Thun. It is a popular nightstop for motorists on their way to Interlaken, Gstaad, Wengen, etc., but is also an excellent centre for exploring the Bernese Alpine region, with first-rate public transport. It is far less crowded than Interlaken, at the other end of the lake, less touristy, more genuinely Swiss, and also offers a better view of the High Alps. What lifts the *Beau-Rivage* above all others in Thun is its marvellous position. It is an imposing old building which overlooks the river Aare as it leaves the lake. There is no road for cars on either side of the Aare, so the rooms facing south (the majority—but it is worth specifying the south side when booking: rooms facing north are noisy and without an outlook) have a spectacular view across the river and the Alps beyond. No traffic noise, only the sound of rushing water from a near-by weir. Being large and roomy, the hotel offers that solid comfort so often absent in new hotels. The bedrooms are airy, with plenty of space to move around. Furnishings are not luxurious, but adequate. Downstairs, there is a large lounge with easy chairs, more English than Swiss, which leads out on to a garden terrace with tables and chairs facing the river and mountains. Until May, the hotel is run as a *"Garni"* —i.e. no main meals provided, but there are plenty of good restaurants in the town, a few minutes' walk away. Prices are very reasonable for what is offered. The proprietors, Mr and Mrs J. Wüthrich, both speak excellent English.' (*Richard Pinner*)

Open: March–October.
Rooms: 25 double, 8 single—15 with bath or shower, all with telephone; some rooms have views of lake and Alps.
Lift; salon, breakfast room, games room; roof garden and sun terrace; indoor swimming pool.
Terms: B & B: 30-50 S. frs; meals: 16-20 S. frs; half board: 55-85 S. frs.

WILDERSWIL, Nr Interlaken, 3812 Bernese Oberland

Hotel Bären   *Telephone:* (036) 223521

'This sympathetic traditional Swiss hotel in a small village halfway between Interlaken (2 miles, frequent buses) and Lauterbrunnen, has been in the hands of the Swiss family Zurschmeide since it opened some time in the 18th century. But though the building is old, the accommodation is contemporary in the best sense—no neon lighting, no piped music, no shoddy modern furniture, but full of charm and character. The service is friendly and efficient, and the food is as good as one would expect from a well-run hotel of this kind, whose present manager, still a Zurschmeide of course, was trained at the Mayfair. The management show that they care about the welfare of their guests, and are particularly helpful to those who are new to the district.' (*Malcolm V. Campbell*)

Open: all year, except November.
Rooms: 5 triple, 35 double, 20 single—8 with bath or shower.
Residents' salon (with TV), bar/restaurant, games room; large terrace with view of the Jungfrau. Small garden. Safe bathing, rowing, sailing, water skiing on the lake, 2 miles. In winter, skiing (with ski-lift and ski school), tobogganing, and skating.
Terms: half board: 74–84 S. frs; full board: 82–92 S. frs.

ZERMATT, 3920 Valais

Hotel Metropol   *Telephone:* (028) 673231

Some people like to be in the thick of things at Zermatt, on or close to the winding main street and within easy ski-carrying distance of the Gornergrat or the Schwarzsee cable car. Others prefer to be well away from the crowd. The *Metropol*, an unpretentious, medium-sized family hotel, is a compromise: you can be in any part of the town within a few minutes, but you are out of the hurly-burly. You won't even hear the church clock at midnight. Not because it's so distant, but because the *Metropol* is on the banks of the fast-flowing Vispa and the sound of falling water smothers most human and mechanical noises. No main meals are served. The dining room, alongside the spacious lounge on the ground floor, chiefly serves the generous *Metropol* breakfasts, though snacks as well as drinks are available in the evenings. The bedrooms are on the four upper floors, and the ones to go for are the dozen on the south side, each with a private bathroom, and a roomy balcony facing the Matterhorn. The hotel is run by the Taugwalder family, who speak good English. 'A comfortable, homely hotel, quiet (except for the water), and not for people who need "life" and entertainment. It is near to perfect for those who want to be physically active during the day (walking, climbing, skiing) and then have a restful evening. I have often felt that I should like to take this hotel around with me on my travels; in none other have I felt so relaxed, so much at home.' (*Richard Pinner*)

Open: 20 November–1 May and 1 June–15 October.
Rooms: 20 double, 4 single—20 with bath or shower, all with radio and telephone, some with balconies.
Salon; bar; small garden.
Terms: summer: B & B, 34–45 S. frs; winter: B & B: 40–55 S. frs.

El Menzel, Djerba

Tunisia

DJERBA

El Menzel

Telephone: (05) 57070
Telex: 40830

The island of Djerba, joined to the mainland by a causeway (though there are also car and passenger ferries from the little port of Ajim), is reputed to be Homer's Land of the Lotus Eaters. Its area is 246 square miles—a bit less than twice that of the Isle of Wight and, like the latter, there are things to see if you feel like some cultural exertions: a museum or two, some Roman remains, a Spanish fort and an early synagogue. Less cultural but fun, you can pour over the amazing collection of goods in the markets: embroideries, sheepskins, beads, brass and copperware, pots and birdcages—thin, painted ironwork, delicate as lace, all sizes from matchbox to dog kennel, and with as many uses. But most visitors are content to indulge their lotus-eating proclivities and just relax.

Djerba itself has plenty of modern hotels, but the beaches are still less crowded than in other resorty parts of the country. The *El Menzel* is one of the three luxury hotels, but by no means the largest; and is unusual in that it is constructed of single-unit bungalows set round a central quad in groups of eight, and dotted round the hotel grounds.

'Each dwelling has its own little garden, brimming over with flowers and shrubs, which not only look beautiful but also fill the air with a glorious scent. Inside, there's a well-equipped bathroom, an enormous bedroom and a completely private solarium. Everything is whitewashed —floors, walls, stairs and ceilings, and look as though they are re-whitewashed every morning. The service was absolutely splendid—all the staff seemed to go out of their way to make sure that the guests were comfortable and enjoying themselves. I am the kind of person who enjoys a quiet holiday, and for me the *El Menzel* offered all that I needed —and more. If sitting by the beach became boring, there was always the pool. In the evenings, the hotel always had some kind of entertainment for those who wanted it. It's a hotel I look forward to returning to often.' (*K. P. Laughton*)

Open: all year.
Rooms: 140 double—all with bath and private solarium.
Air-conditioned throughout; nightclub, hairdressing salon, boutique, nursery, swimming pool. The hotel faces the beach.
Terms: B & B: 6.500 dnrs.

SFAX

Les Oliviers   *Telephone:* Sfax 0420188
Ave Habib Thameur

'South from Tunis the olive groves run on, the trees wider spaced for moisture as one nears the Sahara; on through El Djem with its great Roman Colosseum, and on to Sfax, 200 miles south on the Gulf of Gabes. The centre of the Tunisian olive oil industry, Tunisia's second city, Phoenician in origin and rich in Roman fragments gathered in its municipal museum—but definitely not on the tourist industry map. Perhaps it is too proud to subdue itself to the tourist industry. Certainly the Sfaxians are the most successful Tunisians at business and commerce. So the main hotel is not grand, but it is named after the town's traditional source of trade: *Les Oliviers*. A former French colonial hotel —and there are few such in Tunisia—which has been transposed into the approximate present. Anyone with a nostalgia for the old hotels which have survived from the British Raj—especially those in the medium-sized Indian cities would be interested to try the French version.

'Largish rooms, with tall windows and the usual French profusion of window frames, shutters and jalousies folding inwards or outwards. Wide corridors and a broad staircase. A dark bar on one side of the entrance and a light, airy dining room on the other. The food is well and slowly served. *Crevette* dishes are excellent, so are the *mechouia* and *chakchouka*—two varieties of Tunisian salad—and standard French meat dishes. An old-fashioned French bourgeois restaurant with an admixture of Tunisian food. Breakfast *à la chambre*, *café* or *thé complet*, brought without delay upon telephoned request. The service has a degree of polite impersonality perhaps learned from the French. Recently a swimming pool has been built at the back, with plenty of space for sunbathing, and a bar. Somewhat overlooked by old apartment blocks, it is true, but in the centre of a busy commercial city, not particularly devoted to tourists, this is an amenity. Perhaps the wedding season is the time to avoid. During this period, which seems to stretch from late August into September—though it must surely shift with

Ramadan—the wedding parties seem to drive round the city, especially round the square where *Les Oliviers* stands, all night, hooting continuously in celebration. The answer is to book later or earlier in the year—or, as we did, transfer, after a sleepless night, into one of the rooms which contains an ancient air-conditioner. Then, with windows and shutters tightly shut, one may sleep under blankets with only the regular internal noise of the antique machine, occasionally interspersed with mechanical gulps and groans.

'What else? A truly splendid walled city, a joy to see from afar, and the medina inside a pleasure for those who enjoy wandering in ancient streets and bazaars almost untouched by modernity; and where the shopkeepers are untainted by the desire to treat every European as prey. And a number of small restaurants in the new city, not far from *Les Oliviers*, which recall those little establishments in France twenty or thirty years ago, with a simple menu and waiters in long white aprons. And with prices to match and wine at half the European prices. The restaurant at *Les Oliviers* is one of the best in the town. Coffee can be had endlessly at pavement cafés. One does not, perhaps, go looking for the colonial past in the post-colonial world—that might be an insult to the inhabitants. But it is a bonus if one comes upon it unexpectedly. There are whispers of it in Sfax, and much else beside: an elegant and ancient city, proud and friendly people, though the Sahara and beaches are some miles off.' (*John Spencer*)

Open: all year.
Rooms: 50 double—30 with bath, 20 with shower, some with air-conditioning.
Lounges, bars; swimming pool.
Terms: B & B: 5.200 dnrs; full board: from 7 dnrs.

Prices quoted, unless otherwise specified, are for bed and breakfast for a person sharing a double room with bath or shower in the high season. We have also given half and full board prices per person in high season when available.

Hotel Imbat, Kusadasi

Turkey

ISTANBUL

Pera Palace Hotel *Telephone:* Istanbul 452230
Mesrutiyet Cad.

'One of the grand hotels of Europe, built in the 1890s to accommodate passengers on the Orient Express. Ornate in traditional Turkish style; marble and gilt with well-worn carpets complete the air of faded elegance; an immediate impression is one of spaciousness. The hotel lacks many modern facilities: packaged nightlife, discos, cabaret, belly dancers and the like, are totally absent. Yet it is impossible to walk through the public rooms without feeling a whiff of intrigue and conspiracy coming down from a bygone age. Once the venue of great State occasions, you are now more likely to mix with businessmen and holiday-makers. New international hotels have opened up the hill at Taksim Square, yet the *Pera Palace* is very central to all you want to see. And here must still be many people who would forgo thick pile carpets for a hotel offering the traditional Turkish atmosphere.' (*David Kenny*)

Open: all year.
Rooms: 84 double, 32 single—94 with bath, others with shower, all
            with telephone and baby-listening service.
Lift; large lounge; 2 private meeting rooms; bar.
Terms: B & B: 350 TL.; full board: 740 TL.

Hotel Imbat

Telephone: Kusadasi 85475480
Telex: 59119

'The *Imbat* is situated 3 miles outside the charming old fishing village of Kusadasi on a cliff overlooking a crystal-clear sea, with colours ranging from deep Quink blue to light turquoise. It has its own private beach well-equipped with sunshades and deck chairs. The bathing and snorkelling are excellent. The restaurant is of a very modern style and separate from the guest rooms. Many of the latter are built in charming Arab style, all with private bathrooms which really worked, and supplied with the thickest and most luxurious Turkish towels. Most rooms have a superb view of the sea. The service in the restaurant was as variable as the food, which I found generally as indifferent as in all other Turkish restaurants, but the staff were always very friendly. Public and private rooms showed high standards of cleanliness. Alcoholic drinks were extortionately expensive at the hotel, with the exception of local Raki. There are beautiful gardens with a fine swimming pool plus its own bar. The nightlife was somewhat disappointing, but the Caravanserai, in Kusadasi, was well worth visiting for a superb meal and unlimited wine. The cuisine here was French and produced by the Club Mediterranée. Interesting shops provided a special attraction for the ladies.

'Kusadasi is a very good centre from which to explore Ephesus, some 12 miles to the north, and Priene Miletus and Didymus somewhat further to the south. Pamukkale and Aphrodisias are within reasonable distances for a day trip. Having one's own car would be ideal, but taxis are easily available and not too expensive if shared between five or six passengers. Coach trips to some of the places mentioned can be arranged through the hotel.' (*Dr L. J. Morgan*)

Open: April–1 November.
Rooms: 138 double, 2 single—all with bath and telephone.
Lobby bar, snack bar, beach bar, terrace bar, disco/nightclub. Large grounds with swimming pool. The hotel adjoins a sand and rock beach with safe bathing and boating.
Terms: B & B (not acceptable 1 July–30 September): 202.50 TL. half board: 277.50 TL.; full board: 352.50 TL.

Hotel Report forms will be found on pp. 257–67.

Yugoslavia

BLED, Slovenia

Grand Hotel Toplice

Telephone: Bled 77222
Telex: 34-588 yu toplice

'This area of Slovenia, just across the border from Austria, is a paradise for fishermen, hunters, painters and wine connoisseurs; the Riesling here is fabulous. The *Toplice* (meaning "spa"), though expensive, is in the best traditions of 19th-century Hapsburg Vienna, with a modernised Yugoslav accent.' (*R. H. Owen*)

Open: all year.
Rooms: 121—all with bath, some with telephone.
Lift; swimming pool; own bathing beach on Lake Bled.
Terms (excluding tax): B & B: 175-213 dnrs; full board: 272-325 dnrs.

DUBROVNIK

Hotel Dubravka

Telephone: Dubrovnik 26293

The *Dubravka* lacks many of the qualities which, elsewhere in this Guide, we regard as essential criteria for inclusion: it's old-fashioned, somewhat scruffy, has no very comfortable public rooms, and is quite spectacularly noisy from 5 a.m. onwards. But it has a unique advantage over any other hotel in Dubrovnik, being the only one in the dramatically beautiful old city. There are no cars allowed in the old town, and extra-mural parking in the high season can be a long and tiresome business; and then you have to find a porter with a cart to lug your baggage a good half mile from the city gates. But the rewards, for those who like to be at the centre of things, are considerable. To wake up to a dress circle seat at a colourful market in the old cathedral square adjoining the hotel is one such delight; to be at hand for the teeming *korzo* in the Placa is another; to inherit the quiet of the city late at night, when the daytime trippers have left the stage, is a third. Many people will feel the sacrifice of a few mundane creature comforts well worth it for the sake of such an exceptional location. (*H.R.*)

Open: all year.
Rooms: 22—10 with bath or shower, some with telephone.
Terms (excluding tax):   126 dnrs. No restaurant.

The Villa Dubrovnik   *Telephone:* Dubrovnik 23466

This smallish hotel is not in the old town, but only twenty minutes' stroll away—or five minutes by the hotel's own motor boat. Perched on a cliff on the south side of Dubrovnik, it has lovely views of the old town and harbour and also looks over to the Island of Lokrum opposite. The hotel is terraced into the cliff on at least five different levels with lifts to all floors, except to the bathing rocks. Pine trees, flowers and blue awnings give a Riviera flavour. The bar and dining room both have superb views, and you eat outdoors in fine weather. The service is excellent and the food good by Yugoslav standards. Most bedrooms face the front with small balconies, and are well furnished. There are high standards of cleanliness. The hotel has its own 'concrete' beach with rock bathing in unpolluted water; there are plenty of chairs and beach umbrellas and a bar service. There is no nightlife on the spot, but the boat goes into Dubrovnik in the evening and it is easy to get a taxi back. Not recommended for the elderly or infirm as there are steps up from the hotel entrance to the road above. (*Mrs Peploe*)

Open: all year.
Rooms: 56—all with bath/shower, telephone and air-conditioning. Lift; own bathing beach.
Terms (excluding tax):   bed: 236-90 dnrs; full board: 302-81 dnrs.

SVETI STEFAN

(1) Hotel Milocer   *Telephone (both):* Sveti Stefan 82233
(2) Hotel Sveti Stefan

The area round the old walled city of Budva, in the southern part of Yugoslavia, is full of rewarding excursions. The bay of Kotor is strikingly beautiful, and behind the city of Kotor lie the twenty-five hairpin bends to the former capital of the kingdom of Montenegro, Cetinje, in its mountain fastness—rich in museums and soaked in the awe-inspiring history of its fearless people. There is no shortage of hotels along the coast, most indistinguishably commonplace. But there are exceptions.

About six miles south from Budva is a complex of three hotels, *Sveti Stefan* itself, the *Milocer*, and the *Maestral*. Residents of any one can take advantage of the facilities of the other two, but they are sufficiently far apart, and so totally different in character, that they might well be unconnected. The *Maestral* is the biggest and most modern of the three, also the most conventional. It has a casino and plenty of dancing or cabaret at night. Clearly block bookings are an important part of its economy. The public rooms resemble airport lounges. *Chacun à son goût.*

The *Milocer*, half a mile down a private road, is in contrast a sedate establishment and cheaper than either of its neighbours. Built as a summer palace by Alexander I for his wife, though unfinished at the time of his assassination in Marseilles in 1934, it still retains an air of modest regal opulence. The central block with rather inadequate public rooms (you need to go to one of the other hotels if you want any night-life) has an exceptionally handsome vine-shaded terrace where meals are served. The food is well above Yugoslav par, with generous helpings, plenty of choice, and at every meal at least one regional speciality. Most of the bedrooms are in separate annexes set discreetly in the grounds a few minutes' walk from the hotel proper: no sea view, but marvellously quiet, except for the rustle of crickets and the ear-splitting roar of frequent night-time thunderstorms. Furnishings are simple but adequate. One of the attractions of the hotel is its two beaches—well-kept, never too crowded and offering an opportunity for matiness if you feel so inclined. There are first-rate tennis courts—something of a rarity in this country. Another major attraction is its exceptionally fine and well maintained gardens, both formal and informal, stretching a good half-mile on either side of the central block, and overlooking the sea; and like a jewel in its midst, the island of Sveti Stefan, joined to the mainland by a long causeway, with an extensive but rather bleak sand and shingle beach on either side.

Partisans of the *Milocer* complain that the *Sveti Stefan* is over-precious. It is certainly the most luxurious and most unusual of the three hotels—also the most expensive, with bar prices considerably in excess of the others. But here is how one enthusiast for *Sveti Stefan* describes its pleasures:

'*Sveti Stefan* cuts a beautiful figure on the posters; in reality it is even more beautiful. The end of the war found the island inhabited by only a few fisher families. War orphans were billeted there for a while. Then the families were moved out and houses built for them on the mainland from which they can gaze across at their old homes—which has now undergone beauty treatment. Someone had the ambitious idea of restoring the houses and converting the whole island into one big hotel, the individual cottages serving as separate suites. The result is the most sumptuous holiday resort in Yugoslavia, with its own wonderful views up and down the coast to Budva and beyond, and its own private beach.

The walls of the cottages are thick, the rooms dim and cool; outside, the sea and sky blaze. And flowers and flowering shrubs, cacti and trees, blaze between the houses and along the little alleys. On the highest point of the island is a little church. The whole thing stands or falls, of course, by the restaurant, where one sits on a wide terrace as if on the prow of a ship. Happily, the cooking is wonderful. The service is stylish and friendly. Heaven knows, I have grumbled enough about Yugoslav hotels, but for *Sveti Stefan* there is only praise. Even the underwater scenery is good here, and the snug bar is unpassable as well as unsurpassable.' (*Brian Aldiss* on Sveti Stefan; *H.R.* on Milocer)

(1) MILOCER
Open: all year.
Rooms: 42—22 with bath/shower.
Bar, terrace, formal gardens; 2 private beaches; tennis courts.
Terms (excluding tax):   B & B: 381–412 dnrs; full board: 458–88 dnrs.
(2) SVETI STEFAN
Open: all year.
Rooms: 117—all with bath and telephone.
Several lounges, bars, casino, nightclub; outdoor swimming pool; private beaches.
Terms (excluding tax):   B & B: from 458 dnrs; half board: from 535 dnrs.

Important reminder: terms printed must be regarded as a rough guide only as to the size of the bill to be expected at the end of your stay. For latest tariffs, check when booking.

Tourist Offices

National Tourist Offices will supply general information and literature on request. Among the booklets and leaflets available (many of them free) are accommodation lists, regional pamphlets, catalogues of the main sights and events, and details of sporting, travel and other facilities. Ask for the area which particularly interests you. Within each country there are Information Offices in main towns and resorts, able to supply more detailed local information, maps, itineraries, etc., and sometimes to assist visitors to find accommodation.

GREAT BRITAIN   London: The British Tourist Authority, Queen's House, 64 St James's St, London SW1.

     New York: 680 Fifth Avenue, New York, NY 10019.

ENGLAND   London: *Correspondence:*
English Tourist Board,
4 Grosvenor Gardens, London SW1.
Personal callers:
(1) London Tourist Board,
26 Grosvenor Gardens,
London SW1.
(2) London Tourist Board, Victoria Station, London SW1
(adjacent to Platform 15).

WALES   Wales Tourist Board,
Welcome House, High Street,
Llanduff, Cardiff.

SCOTLAND   Scotland: *Correspondence:*
Scottish Tourist Board
23 Ravelston Terrace, Edinburgh.
Personal callers:
Scottish Tourist Board,
5 Waverley Bridge, Edinburgh.

     London: 137 Knightsbridge, London SW1.

CHANNEL ISLANDS   Alderney: Recreation and Tourist Committee, States Office, New Street, Alderney.

	Guernsey:	States of Guernsey Tourist Committee, PO Box 23, St Peter Port, Guernsey.
	Herm:	Herm Island Administrative Office, Herm Island, via Guernsey.
	Jersey:	States of Jersey Tourism Office, Weighbridge, St Helier, Jersey.
	Sark:	Tourist Information Officer, Sark.
IRELAND	London:	Irish Tourist Board, 150 New Bond Street, London W1.
	Dublin:	Baggot Street Bridge, Dublin 2.
	New York:	590 Fifth Avenue, New York, NY 10036.
AUSTRIA	London:	Austrian National Tourist Office, 30 St George Street, London W1.
	New York:	545 Fifth Avenue, New York, NY 10017.
DENMARK	London:	Danish Tourist Board, Sceptre House, 169/73 Regent Street, London W1.
	New York:	75 Rockefeller Plaza, New York, NY 10019
FRANCE	London:	French Government Tourist Office, 178 Piccadilly, London W1.
	New York:	610 Fifth Avenue, New York, NY 10020.
GERMANY	London:	German National Tourist Office, 61 Conduit Street, London W1.
	New York:	630 Fifth Avenue, New York, NY 10020.
ISRAEL	London:	Israel Government Tourist Office, 59 St James's Street, London SW1.
	New York:	488 Madison Avenue, New York, NY 10022.
ITALY	London:	Italian State Tourist Office, 201 Regent Street, London W1.
	New York:	630 Fifth Avenue, New York, NY 10020.
MALTA	London:	Malta Government Tourist Office, Malta House, 24 Haymarket, London SW1.
	New York:	Malta Consulate, 249 East 35th Street, New York, NY 10016.

| MOROCCO | London: | Moroccan National Tourist Office, 174 Regent Street, London W1. |
| | New York: | 597 Fifth Avenue, New York, NY 10017. |

| NETHERLANDS | London: | Dutch National Tourist Office, 143 New Bond Street, London W1. |
| | New York: | 576 Fifth Avenue, New York, NY 10036. |

| PORTUGAL (and MADEIRA) | London: | Portuguese National Tourist Office, 1–5 New Bond Street, London W1. |
| | New York: | 548 Fifth Avenue, New York, NY 10036. |

| SPAIN (and BALEARICS and CANARY ISLANDS) | London: | Spanish National Tourist Office, 70 Jermyn Street, London SW1. |
| | New York: | 589 Fifth Avenue, New York, NY 10017. |

| SWEDEN | London: | Swedish National Tourist Office, 3 Cork Street, London W1. |
| | New York: | 75 Rockefeller Plaza, New York, NY 10019. |

| SWITZERLAND | London: | Swiss National Tourist Office, Swiss Centre, 1 New Coventry St, London W1. |
| | New York: | Swiss Centre, 608 Fifth Avenue, New York, NY 10020. |

| TUNISIA | London: | Tunisian Tourist Centre, 7a Stafford Street, London W1. |
| | New York: | 630 Fifth Avenue (Room 863), New York, NY 10020. |

| TURKEY | London: | Turkish Tourism Information Office, 49 Conduit Street, London W1. |
| | New York: | 821 United Nations Plaza, New York, NY 10017. |

| YUGOSLAVIA | London: | Yugoslav National Tourist Office, 143 Regent Street, London W1. |
| | New York: | 509 Madison Avenue, New York, NY 10022. |

Exchange Rates

These are correct at time of printing but check with bank or newspapers for up-to-date dollar equivalents.

	$1 U.S.
Austria (Schillings)	15.99
Denmark (kroner)	6.04
France (francs)	4.77
Great Britain (pounds)	1.95
Germany (Deutschmarks)	2.22
Holland (guilders)	2.39
Israel (Israeli pounds)	13.01
Italy (lire)	864.50
Malta (Maltese pounds)	0.40
Morocco (dirhams)	4.47
Portugal and Madeira (escudos)	40.11
Spain, including Balearics and Canaries (pesetas)	83.33
Sweden (kroner)	4.75
Switzerland (Swiss francs)	2.20
Tunisia (dinars)	0.45
Turkey (Turkish lira)	21.14
Yugoslavia (dinars)	20.19

Maps

Rathmullan

ULSTER

Riverstown

Dublin

IRELAND

Oughterard

Ballyvaughan

Lahinch

Shanagarry

Ballylickey

N

0   30
miles

SWEDEN

Ödeshög

0   200
    miles

N

DENMARK

Vejle
Bramminge   Jyllinge
Ribe   Odense
          Faldsled

Hamburg

WEST
GERMANY

Linz am Rhein
Bamberg   Bayreuth

Baden-Baden   Wildbad im
Freudenstadt   Schwarzwald

FRANCE
          Hinterzarten   Munich   Salzburg   Vienna

                         AUSTRIA

Stäfa am Zürichsee   Pörtschach am
Château d'Oex   Thun   Wörther See
          SWITZERLAND
Zermatt   Wilderswil   Tegna

ITALY

NETHERLANDS

Bloemendaal

Amsterdam

Delft

Ardres

Port Racine

Trelly

Tancarville

Perros-Guirec

Paris

Champillon

Quimper

Barbizon

Strasbourg

Fontainebleau

Flagy

Clery-St-André

Avallon

Mouthier-Haute-Pierre

Noirmoutier

Savigny-les-Beaune

Chassey-le-Camp

Givry

Airvault

F R A N C E

Mirabel-aux-Baronnies

Aubenas

Saint-Jean-Cap-Ferrat

Gréolières-les-Neiges

Les Eyzies-de-Tayac

Meyronne

Cap d'Antibes

Beynac-et-Cazenac

Siorac-en-Périgord

Mercuès

Conques

Théoule

Grimaud

Nîmes

Lauris

Les Baux-de-Provence

Marseillan

Arles

St Paul-de-Vence

Le Castellet

Bandol

La Croix-Valmer

Ramatuelle

Villefranche-de-Rouergue

CORSICA

Algajola

Monticello

C O R S I C A

N

0   200

miles

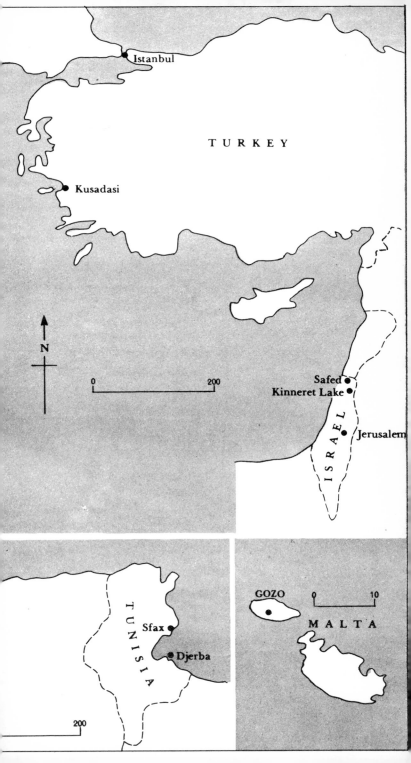

TURKEY

Istanbul

Kusadasi

Safed
Kinneret Lake
I S R A E L
Jerusalem

N

0 ———— 200

TUNISIA

Sfax
Djerba

200

GOZO
0 ———— 10

M A L T A

Hotel Reports

The report forms on the next ten pages may be used to endorse or black-ball an existing entry or to nominate a hotel that you feel deserves inclusion in next year's guide. Either way, there is no need to restrict yourself to the space available. All nominations (each on a separate piece of paper, please) should include your name and address, the name and locale of the hotel, when you stayed there and for how long. Please only nominate hotels you have visited in the past eighteen months unless you are sure from friends that standards have not fallen off since your stay. And please be as specific as possible, and critical where appropriate, about the character of the building, the public rooms, the sleeping accommodation, the meals, the service, the nightlife, the grounds. We should be glad if you would give some impression of the location and country around as well as of the hotel itself, particularly in less familiar regions.

You should not feel embarrassed about writing at length. More than anything else, we want the guide to convey the special flavour of its hotels; so the more time and trouble you can take in providing those small details which will help to make a description come alive, the more valuable to others will be the final published result.

There is no need to bother with prices or with routine information about number of rooms and facilities. We can obtain such details direct from the hotels selected. What we are anxious to get from readers is information which is not accessible elsewhere.

Name of Hotel ....

Address ....

....

Date of most recent visit .... Duration of visit ....

☐ New Recommendation   ☐ Comment on existing entry

Report:

Signed ....

Name and address ....

....

TO: The Editor, *Europe's Wonderful Little Hotels and Inns*,
   61 Clarendon Road, London W11, England

Name of Hotel ....

Address ....

....

Date of most recent visit .... Duration of visit ....

☐ New Recommendation   ☐ Comment on existing entry

Report:

Signed ....

Name and address ....

....

NOTE: Unless we are asked not to, we shall assume that we may publish your name if you are recommending a new hotel or supporting an existing entry.

TO: The Editor, *Europe's Wonderful Little Hotels and Inns,*
   61 Clarendon Road, London W11, England

Name of Hotel ....

Address ....

....

Date of most recent visit .... Duration of visit ....

☐ New Recommendation   ☐ Comment on existing entry

Report:

Signed ....

Name and address ....

....

NOTE: Unless we are asked not to, we shall assume that we may publish your name if you are recommending a new hotel or supporting an existing entry.

TO: The Editor, *Europe's Wonderful Little Hotels and Inns,*
  61 Clarendon Road, London W11, England

Name of Hotel ....

Address ....

....

Date of most recent visit .... Duration of visit ....

☐ New Recommendation   ☐ Comment on existing entry

Report:

Signed ....

Name and address ....

....

NOTE: Unless we are asked not to, we shall assume that we may publish
your name if you are recommending a new hotel or supporting an
existing entry.

TO: The Editor, *Europe's Wonderful Little Hotels and Inns,*
61 Clarendon Road, London W11, England

Name of Hotel ....

Address ....

....

Date of most recent visit .... Duration of visit ....

☐ New Recommendation   ☐ Comment on existing entry

Report:

Signed ....

Name and address ....

....

NOTE: Unless we are asked not to, we shall assume that we may publish
your name if you are recommending a new hotel or supporting an
existing entry.

TO: The Editor, *Europe's Wonderful Little Hotels and Inns*,
61 Clarendon Road, London W11, England

Name of Hotel ....

Address ....

....

Date of most recent visit .... Duration of visit ....

☐ New Recommendation   ☐ Comment on existing entry

Report:

Signed ....

Name and address ....

....

NOTE: Unless we are asked not to, we shall assume that we may publish
your name if you are recommending a new hotel or supporting an
existing entry.

TO: The Editor, *Europe's Wonderful Little Hotels and Inns*,
61 Clarendon Road, London W11, England

Name of Hotel ....

Address ....

....

Date of most recent visit .... Duration of visit ....

☐ New Recommendation   ☐ Comment on existing entry

Report:

Signed ....

Name and address ....

....

NOTE: Unless we are asked not to, we shall assume that we may publish
your name if you are recommending a new hotel or supporting an
existing entry.

TO: The Editor, *Europe's Wonderful Little Hotels and Inns,*
61 Clarendon Road, London W11, England

Name of Hotel ....

Address ....

....

Date of most recent visit .... Duration of visit ....

☐ New Recommendation   ☐ Comment on existing entry

Report:

Signed ....

Name and address ....

....

NOTE: Unless we are asked not to, we shall assume that we may publish your name if you are recommending a new hotel or supporting an existing entry.

TO: The Editor, *Europe's Wonderful Little Hotels and Inns,*
61 Clarendon Road, London W11, England

Name of Hotel ....

Address ....

....

Date of most recent visit .... Duration of visit ....

☐ New Recommendation   ☐ Comment on existing entry

Report:

Signed ....

Name and address ....

....

NOTE: Unless we are asked not to, we shall assume that we may publish
your name if you are recommending a new hotel or supporting an
existing entry.

Notes

Notes

Notes